Lecture Notes in Artificial Intelligence 12280

Subseries of Lecture Notes in Computer Science

More information about this subseries at http://www.springer.com/series/1244

Hiroshi Uehara · Takayasu Yamaguchi ·
Quan Bai (Eds.)

Knowledge Management and Acquisition for Intelligent Systems

17th Pacific Rim Knowledge Acquisition Workshop, PKAW 2020
Yokohama, Japan, January 7–8, 2021
Proceedings

 Springer

Editors
Hiroshi Uehara
Akita Prefectural University
Akita, Japan

Takayasu Yamaguchi
Akita Prefectural University
Akita, Japan

Quan Bai 🅾
University of Tasmania
Sandy Bay, TAS, Australia

ISSN 0302-9743   ISSN 1611-3349   (electronic)
Lecture Notes in Artificial Intelligence
ISBN 978-3-030-69885-0   ISBN 978-3-030-69886-7   (eBook)
https://doi.org/10.1007/978-3-030-69886-7

LNCS Sublibrary: SL7 – Artificial Intelligence

This Springer imprint is published by the registered company Springer Nature Switzerland AG
The registered company address is: Gewerbestrasse 11, 6330 Cham, Switzerland

Preface

This volume contains the papers presented at the Principle and Practice of Data and Knowledge Acquisition Workshop 2020 (PKAW 2020), held in conjunction with the International Joint Conference on Artificial Intelligence - Pacific Rim International Conference on Artificial Intelligence (IJCAI-PRICAI), from January 7–8, 2021, in Yokohama, Japan.

Over the past two decades, PKAW has provided researchers with opportunities to present ideas and have intensive discussions on their work related to knowledge acquisition, which is one of the core fields of artificial intelligence (AI). Over the years, PKAW has dealt with a wide variety of topics, in accordance with the progress in AI research.

In recent years, AI has been unprecedently in the spotlight owing to its remarkable success in several industries, and presently, research on AI is entering into an important stage in terms of how it will contribute to the forthcoming AI society. Among the numerous AI-related workshops that are conducted throughout the world, PKAW primarily focuses on the multidisciplinary approach of human-driven and data-driven knowledge acquisition, which is the key concept that has remained unchanged since the workshop was first established. In general, the recent approach of AI sheds light on a data-driven approach that requires an enormous volume of data. Even in the ongoing era of "big data", quite a few cases of data analysis come across scarcity of data because of the cost, privacy issues, and the sporadic nature of its occurrence. We believe that human-driven approaches, such as modeling the implicit knowledge of human experts, might be effective in such cases. Thus, a multidisciplinary approach is the much-needed breakthrough for efficient integration of AI-based advanced research for the upcoming AI society. This is the direction that PKAW takes.

The year of PKAW 2020 has gone through exceptionally difficult circumstances due to the global coronavirus pandemic. Despite this situation, we received 28 submissions, and finally accepted 10 regular papers and 5 short papers. All papers were peer reviewed by three independent reviewers. These papers demonstrate advanced research on AI and allied fields.

These successes would not have been attained without the support of the people involved in this workshop. The workshop co-chairs would like to thank all the people who supported PKAW2020, including the PKAW Program Committee members and sub-reviewers who contributed their precious time towards reviewing the submitted papers, the IJCAI-PRICAI Organizing Committee, who dealt appropriately with our requests and all of the administrative and local matters. We thank Springer for publishing the proceedings in the Lecture Notes in Artificial Intelligence (LNAI) series.

Further, we would like to extend a special thanks to all the authors who submitted their papers, presenters, and attendees.

January 2021

Hiroshi Uehara
Quan Bai
Takayasu Yamaguchi
PKAW 2020 Program Chairs

Organization

Program Chairs

Quan Bai   University of Tasmania, Australia
Hiroshi Uehara   Akita Prefectural University, Japan
Takayasu Yamaguchi   Akita Prefectural University, Japan

Program Committee

Takahira Yamaguchi   Akita Prefectural University, Japan
Matthew Kuo   Auckland University of Technology, New Zealand
Shuxiang Xu   University of Tasmania, Australia
Yi Yang   Deakin University, Australia
Xiongcai Cai   University of New South Wales, Australia
Weihua Li   Auckland University of Technology, New Zealand
Zi-Ke Zhang   Zhejiang University, China
Fenghui Ren   University of Wollongong, Australia
Xiang Zhao   National University of Defense Technology, China
Jihang Zhang   University of Wollongong, Australia
Toshiro Minami   Kyushu Institute of Information Sciences
                             and Kyushu University Library, Japan
Dayong Ye   University of Technology Sydney, Australia
Kazumi Saito   University of Shizuoka, Japan
Toshihiro Kamishima   National Institute of Advanced Industrial Science
                             and Technology (AIST), Japan
Akihiro Inokuchi   Kwansei Gakuin University, Japan
Hayato Ohwada   Tokyo University of Science, Japan
Lei Niu   Central China Normal University, China
Ulrich Reimer   Eastern Switzerland University of Applied Sciences,
                             Switzerland
Tetsuya Yoshida   Nara Women's University, Japan
Tomonobu Ozaki   Nihon University, Japan
Hye-Young Paik   The University of New South Wales, Australia
Qing Liu   Data61, CSIRO, Australia

Honorary Chairs

Paul Compton   University of New South Wales, Australia
Hiroshi Motoda   Osaka University, Japan

Advisory Committee

Maria Lee   Shih Chien University, Taiwan
Kenichi Yoshida   University of Tsukuba, Japan
Byeong-Ho Kang   University of Tasmania, Australia
Deborah Richards   Macquarie University, Australia

Publicity Chairs

Soyeon Han   University of Sydney, Australia
Son Tran   University of Tasmania, Australia
Weiwei Yuan   Nanjing University of Aeronautics and Astronautics,
                                  China

Webmaster

Shiqing Wu   University of Tasmania, Australia

Contents

Accelerating the Backpropagation Algorithm by Using NMF-Based Method on Deep Neural Networks

Suhyeon Baek[1]($\boxtimes$), Akira Imakura[1]🆔, Tetsuya Sakurai[1], and Ichiro Kataoka[2]

[1] University of Tsukuba, Tennodai 1-1-1, Tsukuba, Ibaraki 305-8573, Japan
s1920699@u.tsukuba.ac.jp, {imakura,sakurai}@cs.tsukuba.ac.jp
[2] Hitachi, Ltd., Research & Development Group, Horiguchi 832-2, Hitachinaka,
Ibaraki 312-0034, Japan
Ichiro.kataoka.vf@hitachi.com

Abstract. Backpropagation (BP) is the most widely used algorithm for the training of deep neural networks (DNN) and is also considered a de facto standard algorithm. However, the BP algorithm often requires a lot of computation time, which remains a major challenge. Thus, to reduce the time complexity of the BP algorithm, several methods have been proposed so far, but few do not apply to the BP algorithm. In the meantime, a new DNN algorithm based on nonnegative matrix factorization (NMF) has been proposed, and the algorithm has different convergence characteristics from the BP algorithm. We found that the NMF-based method could lead to rapid performance improvement in DNNs training, and we developed a technique to accelerate the training time of the BP algorithm. In this paper, we propose a novel training method for accelerating the BP algorithm by using an NMF-based algorithm. Furthermore, we present a technique to boost the efficiency of our proposed method by concurrently training DNNs with the BP and NMF-based algorithms. The experimental results indicate that our method significantly improves the training time of the BP algorithm.

Keywords: Deep neural networks · High performance · Nonlinear semi-nonnegative matrix factorization · Backpropagation

1 Introduction

In recent years, with the advent of high computing power, deep neural networks (DNN) techniques have achieved many successes in various fields, such as image and speech recognition. As a means of training DNN models, Rumelhart [11] proposed the backpropagation (BP) algorithm, which has since become the most widely used method.

The present study is supported in part by JST/ACT-I (No. JPMJPR16U6), NEDO and JSPS/Grants-in-Aid for Scientific Research (Nos. 17K12690, 18H03250, 19KK0255).

© Springer Nature Switzerland AG 2021
H. Uehara et al. (Eds.): PKAW 2020, LNAI 12280, pp. 1–13, 2021.
https://doi.org/10.1007/978-3-030-69886-7_1

However, the BP algorithm often requires a lot of computation time to converge, and this remains a huge challenge. To address this problem, a range of methods have been studied to accelerate the training of DNN models. For example, the graphic processing unit (GPU) computing can be used in this regard. Otair and Salameh [10] proposed a new algorithm optical backpropagation (OBP), an improved variant of the BP algorithm. Norhamreeza [2] proposed a new modified back propagation learning algorithm by introducing adaptive gain together with adaptive momentum and adaptive learning rate into the weight-updating process.

On the other hand, Sakurai [12] recently proposed a novel algorithm for training DNN models, which is based on nonnegative matrix factorization (NMF). The NMF-based method has different characteristics compared to the BP algorithm, for example, it has a larger batch size than the BP and thus shows higher parallel performance [7]. Moreover, Arai [3] has broadened its applicability by improving the method by considering bias and regularization parameters even on the NMF-based method. However, most of the approaches for accelerating the time of DNN models are based on the BP algorithm, while few are not. Perhaps because there are few algorithms other than the BP to train DNN models.

In this paper, we propose a novel method to improve the computation time of the BP algorithm by using the NMF-based algorithm and a strategy, which improves the method using concurrent training. We show the validity of the proposed method through comparison experiments with the conventional BP algorithm on multiple datasets. The experimental results indicate that the proposed method significantly improves the computation time of the BP algorithm.

This paper is organized as follows. In Sect. 2, we review the training of DNNs, especially focusing on the comparison between BP and NMF-based algorithms. In Sect. 3, we propose a novel method to accelerate the BP algorithm. In Sect. 4, we show the preliminary experimental results and the performance evaluation results of our proposed method. Section 5 presents our conclusions.

2   Training of DNN

In this section, we briefly review the training algorithms of DNNs.

Notations

- n_{in} denotes size of input layer, and n_{out} output layer.
- n_i denotes size of units for $i = 0, 1, ..., d$ (note that $n_0 = n_{\text{in}}, n_d = n_{\text{out}}$).
- m denotes size of training data.
- $X \in \mathbb{R}^{n_{\text{in}} \times m}$ and $Y \in \mathbb{R}^{n_{\text{out}} \times m}$ denote input and target data.
- $W_i \in \mathbb{R}^{n_i \times n_{i-1}}$ and $\boldsymbol{b}_i \in \mathbb{R}^{n_i}$ denote weight matrices and bias vector of the i-th layer respectively for $i = 0, 1, ..., d$.
- θ denotes vector of parameters of all weight matrices and biases.
- Z_i denotes the activation of i-th layer for $i = 0, 1, ..., d$.
- $\mathbf{1}$ denotes a vector of all elements is 1.
- $\widehat{A} \in \mathbb{R}^{(n+1) \times m}$ denotes vertical concatenation of a matrix $A \in \mathbb{R}^{n \times m}$ and $\mathbf{1}_m \in \mathbb{R}^m$.

- $f(\cdot)$ denotes elementwise activation function.
- $L(\cdot,\cdot), h(\cdot)$ denotes loss and regularization function, respectively.
- $\|\cdot\|_F$ denotes the Frobenius norm.

In this study, we focus on fully connected neural networks. With a loss function L and regularization function h, the objective function can be written as:

$$L(Y, Z_d) + h(\theta), \tag{1}$$

where

$$\begin{aligned} Z_0 &= X, \\ Z_i &= f(W_i Z_{i-1} + b_i \mathbf{1}^\top) \ (i = 1, 2, ..., d-1), \\ Z_d &= W_d Z_{d-1} + b_d \mathbf{1}^\top. \end{aligned} \tag{2}$$

Since Z_d is a function of X and θ, that $L(Y, Z_d)$ is a function of Y, X, θ. Then, the objective function presented in (1) can be rewritten as $E(Y, X, \theta)$ and the optimization problem of the DNNs is expressed in the following manner:

$$\underset{\theta}{\text{minimize}} \quad E(Y, X, \theta). \tag{3}$$

The main purpose of the training the DNNs is to solve this optimization problem. In this paper, activation function $f(\cdot)$ is set as ReLU [9], i.e., $f(U) = max(U, O)$, Loss function $L(U, V)$ is set as mean squared error norm, i.e., $f(U, V) = \|U - V\|_F^2$, Regularization term $h(\cdot)$ is defined as $h(\theta) = \lambda \|\theta\|_F^2$ with some constant λ.

2.1 Backpropagation

In this subsection, we introduce the BP algorithm. The BP algorithm is the most widely used method for training DNNs and is based on stochastic gradient descent. The name of this algorithm stems from the procedures of computing the gradient but usually refers to the overall process in training DNNs as well as the steps of computing the gradient. The training process is described as follows. First, initialize the weight matrices and bias vectors for each layer. Then compute the gradient of objective function and update over the number of iterations as suggested below:

$$\theta \leftarrow \theta - \alpha \frac{\partial E(Y, X, \theta)}{\partial \theta}. \tag{4}$$

In a practical implementation of the BP algorithm, several techniques are employed such as the batch technique, which employs the splitting data and the technique of adjusting the learning rate by the gradient. The pseudocode of the BP algorithm is presented in Algorithm 1.

Algorithm 1. Backpropagation

Input: Input and target data X, Y, mini-batch size s

Output: Weight matrices and bias vectors $\widetilde{W}_i = [W_i, b_i]$ for $i = 1, ..., d$

1   Set initial guess $\widetilde{W}_1^{(0,0)}, \widetilde{W}_2^{(0,0)}, ..., \widetilde{W}_d^{(0,0)}$ for $k = 0, 1, ..., \text{iter}_{\max}$ **do**

2   $\quad$ **for** $l = 0, 1, ..., m/s - 1$ **do**

3   $\quad\quad$ Set the index of mini-batch $J_l^{(k)}$ and $X_l = X(:, J_l^{(k)}), Y_l = Y(:, J_l^{(k)})$

$\quad\quad$ compute gradient of weight matrices and biases $\frac{\partial E}{\partial \widetilde{W}_i^{(k,l)}}$ for $i = 1, ..., d$

4   $\quad\quad$ Update $W_i^{(k,l+1)} = W_i^{(k,l)} - \alpha_k \frac{\partial E}{\partial \widetilde{W}_i^{(k,l)}}$

5   $\quad$ **end**

6   $\quad$ Update $W_i^{(k+1,0)} = W_i^{(k,m/s)}$ for $i = 1, ..., d$

7   **end**

2.2   NMF-Based Algorithm

In this subsection, we introduce the NMF-based algorithm. The NMF-based algorithm employes alternating optimization algorithm for computing weight matrices and biases by using semi-NMF and the nonlinear semi-NMF. This algorithm can be outlined as follows. First, for the output layer, solve (approximately) the semi-NMF optimization:

$$\underset{\widetilde{W}_d, Z_{d-1} \geq 0}{\text{minimize}} \left\| Y - \widetilde{W}_d \widehat{Z}_{d-1} \right\|_F^2 + \lambda_{\widetilde{W}} \left\| \widetilde{W}_d \right\|_F^2 + \lambda_Z \left\| Z_{d-1} \right\|_F^2 . \tag{5}$$

Next, for the hidden layer, solve (approximately) the nonlinear semi-NMF optimization for $i = d - 1, d - 2, ..., 2$:

$$\underset{\widetilde{W}_i, Z_{i-1} \geq 0}{\text{minimize}} \left\| Z_i - f(\widetilde{W}_i \widehat{Z}_{i-1}) \right\|_F^2 + \lambda_{\widetilde{W}} \left\| \widetilde{W}_i \right\|_F^2 + \lambda_Z \left\| Z_{i-1} \right\|_F^2 . \tag{6}$$

Finally, for the input layer, solve (approximately) the following nonlinear optimization problem of:

$$\underset{\widetilde{W}_1}{\text{minimize}} \left\| \widehat{Z}_1 - f(\widetilde{W}_1 \widehat{X}) \right\|_F^2 + \lambda_{\widetilde{W}} \left\| \widetilde{W}_1 \right\|_F^2 . \tag{7}$$

Similar to the BP, in a practical implementation of the NMF-based algorithm, several techniques are employed such as batch technique and low-rank approximation. The pseudocode of the NMF-based algorithm is presented in Algorithm 2.

Algorithm 2. NMF-based algorithm

Input: Input and target data X, Y, mini-batch size s
Output: Weight matrices and bias vectors $\widetilde{W}_i = [W_i, b_i]$ for $i = 1, ..., d$

1   Set initial guess $\widetilde{W}_1^{(0,0)}, \widetilde{W}_2^{(0,0)}, ..., \widetilde{W}_d^{(0,0)}$
2   Compute a low-rank approximation $X \approx U \Sigma V^\top$
3   **for** $k = 0, 1, ..., \text{iter}_{\max}$ **do**
4   $\quad$ **for** $l = 0, 1, ..., m/s - 1$ **do**
5   $\quad\quad$ Set the index of mini-batch $J_l^{(k)}$ and $X_l = U\Sigma V(J_l^{(k)}, :)^\top, Y_l = Y(:, J_l^{(k)})$
6   $\quad\quad$ Set $Z_l^{(k,l)} = f(\widetilde{W}_i^{(k,l)} \widehat{Z}_{i-1}^{(k,l)})$ for $i = 0, 1, ..., d - 1$ where $Z_0^{(k,l)} = X_l$
7   $\quad\quad$ solve approximately (5) with initial guesses $\widetilde{W}_d^{(k,l)}, Z_{d-1}^{(k,l)}$ and get $\widetilde{W}_d^{(k,l+1)}, Z_{d-1}^{(k,l+1)}$
8   $\quad\quad$ **for** $i = d - 1, d - 2, ..., 2$ **do**
9   $\quad\quad\quad$ solve approximately (6) with initial guesses $\widetilde{W}_i^{(k,l)}, Z_{i-1}^{(k,l)}$ and get $\widetilde{W}_i^{(k,l+1)}, Z_{i-1}^{(k,l+1)}$
10 $\quad\quad$ **end**
11 $\quad\quad$ solve approaximately (7) with initial guess $\widetilde{W}_1^{(k,l)}$ and get $\widetilde{W}_1^{(k,l+1)}$
12 $\quad$ **end**
13 $\quad$ Update $\widetilde{W}_i^{(k+1,0)} = \widetilde{W}_i^{(k,m/s)}$ for $i = 1, ..., d$
14 **end**

---

3   Proposed Method

In this section, we propose a novel method to improve the computation time of BP using NMF-based algorithm.

Before explaining the proposed method, we will talk about the motivation for the method. We found that the method of switching algorithms from BP to NMF-based algorithm leads to radical performance improvements in training DNNs, even by just one epoch of the NMF-based algorithm. We tried to take advantage of such radical improvements and devised a new method. Detailed explanations and experimental results of the method will be covered in the next section.

The pseudocode of the proposed method is presented in Algorithm 3. In general, when using the BP algorithm, checking of stopping criterion is performed on the parameters of a DNN model at a given interval. Here, the key idea for our method is to check the stopping criterion after training the DNN model with the NMF-based algorithm. At this time, training by the NMF-based algorithm is to be done just one epoch. Note that when the stopping criterion is satisfied, the NMF(θ), which is the result of training by the NMF-based algorithm, is returned. On the other hand, when the stopping criterion is not satisfied, the BP training continues with the original value θ.

Algorithm 3. Proposed Method

Input: Input and target data X, Y, interval of checking the stopping criterion p
Output: All parameters of Weight matrices and bias vectors θ
`// BP(`θ`) and NMF(`θ`) denote the results of the after 1-epoch`
`   training by the BP and NMF-based algorithm respectively, when`
`   the initial value is `θ

1   Set initial guesses $\theta^{(0)}$ and $\theta = \theta^{(0)}$
2   **for** $k = 0, 1, ..., \text{iter}_{max}$ **do**
3     $\theta^{(k+1)} = \text{BP}(\theta^{(k)})$;   `// BP training`
4   **if** $\theta^{(k+1)}$ satisfy the stopping criterion **then**
5       $\theta = \theta^{(k+1)}$
6   exit
7   **else**
8   **if** $k \equiv 0 \pmod{p}$;   `// Acceleration by the NMF-based algorithm`
9   **then**
10   **if** $\text{NMF}(\theta^{(k+1)})$ satisfy the stopping criterion **then**
11           $\theta = \text{NMF}(\theta^{(k+1)})$ exit
12   **end**
13   **end**
14   **end**
15 **end**

Although, this method incurs a time loss due to the additional computation with the NMF-based algorithm, the gain by the additional computation fully compensate for the time loss. This is because the switching method from BP to NMF-based algorithm not only results in rapid performance improvements, but also requires a very short time. This is related to the preliminary test results mentioned earlier.

Here, we introduce a concurrent training technique for our proposed method. In the proposed method, the BP and NMF-based algorithms are alternately applied sequentially. However, the time loss caused by the NMF-based algorithm can be completely eliminated by concurrently training with the two algorithms because the BP and NMF-based algorithms can be applied independently. To be specific, for the same initial value θ, one processor trains with BP, while the other processor trains with NMF-based algorithm in concurrently. After the certain epochs of training progresses, the stopping criterion is checked with the result by the NMF-based algorithm, and if it is not satisfied and therefore training needs to be continued, the training result by BP is used as the initial value for NMF-based algorithm. This methods can save considerable time by allowing BP to train without delay.

4   Experimental Results

In this section, we show experimental results on the proposed method discussed in the previous sections. For the experiments, the evaluation data are all from UCI repository [5], and we employed two regression datasets (airfoil self-noise, concrete) and two classification datasets (letter recognition, image segmentation). To measure the accuracy performance for the regression problems, we used Relative Residual Norm (RRN), which is given by $\|Y - Z\|_F^2 / \|Y\|_F^2$ for the target data Y and predicted data Z. For the classification problems, we used error rate (%).

For each dataset, the training and test data were randomly selected to be around 70% and 30% of the dataset, respectively. We applied minimax normalization to input data to ensure that all values are between 0 and 1. For the initial guess, we used a stacked denoising autoencoder [4] with randomly sampled data. The performance evaluations were carried out on Intel(R) Xeon(R) CPU E5-1650 v4 (3.60 GHz). The BP algorithm was implemented using Tensorflow [1] and used the ADAM optimizer [8] to adjust the learning rate, and its initial value and momentum were set as the default values of the Tensorflow. The proposed method was implemented in Numpy, the core library for scientific computing in Python [13].

4.1   Preliminary Experiments on the BP and the NMF-Based Algorithm

In this subsection, we introduce the results of the experiment on convergent characteristics of the switch method that served as a motive for the proposed method. We have found that for some datasets, the BP and NMF-based algorithms showed noticeable differences in convergence characteristics (See Fig. 1). While the BP algorithm gradually improves the accuracy performance as the epoch progresses, the NMF-based algorithm produces a radical performance improvement. However, the NMF-based algorithm would stay in a local minimum and stop further performance improvement.

Meanwhile, we tried to find the high performance training algorithm by combining the BP and NMF-based algorithm. We assumed that high performance could be achieved by starting the training with from the BP algorithm and then switching to the NMF-based algorithm as illustrated in Fig. 2(a) (hence, it is called a switch method). We experimented on the switch method and observed remarkable results.

This experimental results revealed a noticeable phenomenon and we took note of this phenomenon from three perspectives. First, at the epoch when the training process switched to the NMF-based algorithm has a radical accuracy improvement. Second, such improvement could be fully achieved by just one epoch by the NMF-based algorithm. Third, the accuracy achieved by the switch method is superior than that of the NMF-based algorithm.

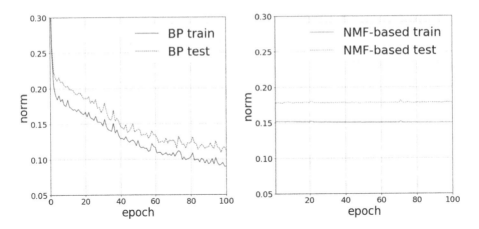

Fig. 1. Convergence history of the BP and the NMF-based algorithm.

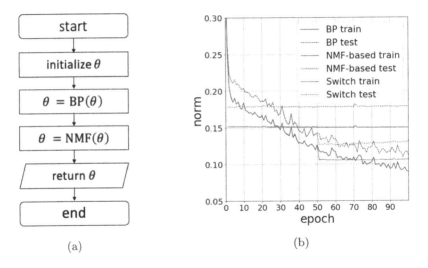

(a)   (b)

Fig. 2. (a) Schematic diagram of the switch method. (b) Comparison of convergence history of the BP and the NMF-based algorithm and the switch method. The switching to the NMF-based algorithm took place at the 50th epoch.

4.2   Performance Evaluation

In this subsection, we conduct a comparison experiment with the conventional BP algorithm to evaluate the effectiveness of our proposed method. We represented the results on two dataset: airfoil self-noise and letter recognition. Figures 3 and 4 show the experimental results on the BP and the proposed method for $p = 1, 4, 16$ and 64. These results indicate that the proposed method significantly improves the computation time of the BP algorithm.

To discuss the results of the experiment, the proposed method for $p = 1$ shows a slower convergence speed than the BP algorithm. This is because

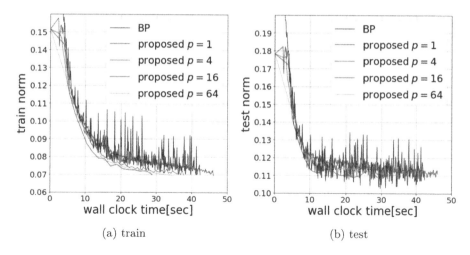

(a) train   (b) test

Fig. 3. Comparison of convergence history on a regression dataset (airfoil self-noise) of the BP and the proposed method. We set the stopping criterion below 0.07 of train norm.

computations by the NMF-based algorithm are so frequent that they take a lot of time. However, by setting a wide p interval for the NMF-based computation, this time loss can be reduced, and in this case for $p = 4, 16$ and 64 the proposed method achieves a superior training time than the BP algorithm.

Meanwhile, we can see from Fig. 4 that if p is 64, it takes more time to reach stopping condition than if p is 16. This is because, if the interval is too large, it causes the checking of the stopping criterion to be too sparse, missing the proper stopping time. In other words, we will be able to get the maximum effect by taking a balanced p to ensure that the NMF computations are not too time consuming, but at the right time to identify the stopping criterion. In addition, while the BP algorithm shows an unstable convergence history, our proposed method shows a stable one, which means that our proposed method is more robust than the BP algorithm and hence has better accuracy performance than the BP algorithm [6].

We conducted additional experiments on concurrent training with the two algorithms in our proposed method. Figure 5 illustrates the convergence history of the BP algorithm and the sequential and the concurrent use of the two algorithms (BP and NMF-based algorithm) in the proposed method. Even though, the proposed method performs better than the BP algorithm when the two algorithms are sequentially used in training, it can be improved further by concurrently training. Figure 6 shows the elapsed time per each epoch for them. To avoid confusion, only the training with the BP algorithm was considered as an epoch. The time delay by the NMF-based algorithm is constantly occurring for the sequential training approach presented in Algorithm 3. However, it can be seen that this time delay was offset by the concurrent training technique. Even with concurrent training, the time delay by overhead is inevitable. But this shows that training time taken by the NMF-based algorithm can be significantly attenuated.

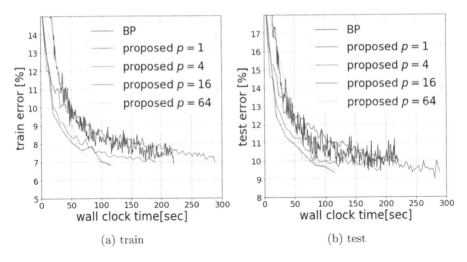

Fig. 4. Comparison of convergence history on a classification dataset (letter recognition) of the BP and the proposed methods. We set the stopping criterion below 7% of train error.

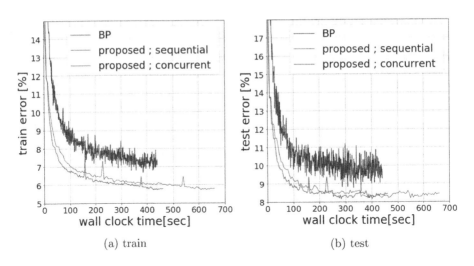

Fig. 5. The convergence history of the BP algorithm and the sequenitial and the concurrent use of our proposed method.

Finally, we evaluated our proposed method on all the datasets mentioned above. For comparison, the values were measured at the point of reaching the arbitrarily defined stopping conditions for each dataset. In the experiment, the comparison targets are the conventional BP and the improved BP by our proposed

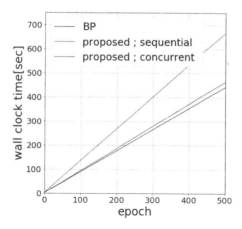

Fig. 6. The elapsed time of the BP algorithm and the sequenitial and the concurrent use of our proposed method as the BP-epoch progresses. The time delay by the NMF-based algorithm is significantly offset by the concurrent training technique

Table 1. Parameter settings for the performance evaluation.

Method	Airfoil self-noise		Concrete		Letter recognition		Image segmentation	
	BP	NMF	BP	NMF	BP	NMF	BP	NMF
Hidden layer	100	100	300	300	500	500	300	300
Stopping tolerance on the train	0.07	0.07	0.08	0.08	7%	7%	2%	2%
Number of samples for the autoencoder	500	–	500	–	1000	–	500	–
Batch size	10	1052(full)	10	721(full)	50	14000(full)	10	2100(full)
Regularization parameter	5×10^{-3}	5×10^{-3}	1×10^{-3}	1×10^{-2}	1×10^{-3}	1×10^{-3}	1×10^{-2}	1×10^{-2}

method for $p = 1, 4, 16$, and 64. The number of epochs, elapsed time, and test accuracy were used as measurements. The parameter settings for the experiment are shown in Table 1. Note that unlike the BP, the NMF-based algorithm has two regularization parameters $\lambda_{\widetilde{W}}, \lambda_Z$ and we unified them into one by $\lambda = \lambda_{\widetilde{W}} = \lambda_Z$. All experiments were run 10 times and the results at 95% confidence interval are presented in Table 2. The results show that our proposed method allows the BP algorithm to compute in less number of epochs, in less time, and better test accuracy.

Table 2. Performance evaluation of the BP and the proposed methods.

		Airfoil self-noise	Concrete	Letter recognition	Image segmentation
Elapsed BP epochs	Conventional BP	385.2 ± 75.0	418.6 ± 19.9	261.2 ± 37.9	110.9 ± 6.5
	Proposed $p = 1$	$\mathbf{271.0 \pm 48.1}$	$\mathbf{297.5 \pm 17.9}$	$\mathbf{91.7 \pm 9.9}$	$\mathbf{15.2 \pm 7.5}$
	Proposed $p = 4$	311.6 ± 48.7	313.2 ± 24.9	98.4 ± 10.7	25.2 ± 12.9
	Proposed $p = 16$	310.4 ± 46.2	329.6 ± 25.4	140.8 ± 16.9	46.4 ± 12.6
	Proposed $p = 64$	345.6 ± 23.6	364.8 ± 30.9	169 ± 24.1	76.8 ± 19.3
Elapsed Time (sec)	Conventional BP	43.5 ± 8.1	31.9 ± 2.0	229.7 ± 32.3	26.1 ± 1.6
	Proposed $p = 1$	$\mathbf{32.2 \pm 5.4}$	43.7 ± 3.7	261.4 ± 29.0	$\mathbf{8.2 \pm 3.3}$
	Proposed $p = 4$	35.7 ± 5.4	30.4 ± 2.3	160.8 ± 36.8	8.8 ± 3.4
	Proposed $p = 16$	35.4 ± 4.9	$\mathbf{27.8 \pm 1.8}$	$\mathbf{141.9 \pm 16.7}$	12.8 ± 2.9
	Proposed $p = 64$	39.2 ± 2.3	28.8 ± 2.5	157.0 ± 21.7	18.9 ± 4.5
Test norm or error (%)	Conventional BP	0.109 ± 0.002	0.167 ± 0.002	9.905 ± 0.323	3.190 ± 0.395
	Proposed $p = 1$	0.110 ± 0.001	$\mathbf{0.153 \pm 0.002}$	9.567 ± 0.151	2.952 ± 0.575
	Proposed $p = 4$	0.109 ± 0.001	0.157 ± 0.001	9.370 ± 0.155	2.762 ± 0.575
	Proposed $p = 16$	0.109 ± 0.002	0.158 ± 0.004	$\mathbf{9.217 \pm 0.153}$	2.571 ± 0.400
	Proposed $p = 64$	0.109 ± 0.001	0.163 ± 0.002	9.250 ± 0.105	$\mathbf{2.143 \pm 0.401}$

5   Conclusion

In this paper, we proposed a novel training method to improve the computation time of the BP algorithm by using an NMF-based algorithm. We also proposed the concurrent use of the two algorithms for training, which improves the performance achieved when the two algorithms are sequentially used, as in the earlier technique used in our method.

The experimental results show that our method significantly reduces the computation time of the BP algorithm. Moreover, our proposed method also improves the BP algorithm in terms of performance, as it makes the BP algorithm more robust.

The proposed method employs an algorithmic switching approach that has been rarely used. We believe our method would have a significant impact on training DNNs not only because of its effectiveness and novelty, but also because of its smooth compatibility with the BP algorithm.

As future work, we propose the implementation of the proposed method on super computer system. We also consider the application of the proposed method on deep learning technologies, for example, the surrogate model.

References

1. Abadi, M., et al.: Tensorflow: a system for large-scale machine learning. In: 12th {USENIX} Symposium on Operating Systems Design and Implementation ({OSDI} 2016), pp. 265–283 (2016)
2. Abdul Hamid, N., Mohd Nawi, N., Ghazali, R., Mohd Salleh, M.N.: Accelerating learning performance of back propagation algorithm by using adaptive gain together with adaptive momentum and adaptive learning rate on classification problems. In: Kim, T., Adeli, H., Robles, R.J., Balitanas, M. (eds.) UCMA 2011. CCIS, vol. 151, pp. 559–570. Springer, Heidelberg (2011). https://doi.org/10.1007/978-3-642-20998-7_62

3. Arai, R., Imakura, A., Sakurai, T.: An improvement of the nonlinear semi-NMF based method by considering bias vectors and regularization for deep neural networks. Int. J. Mach. Learn. Comput. **8**, 191–197 (2018). https://doi.org/10.18178/ijmlc.2018.8.3.686
4. Bengio, Y., Lamblin, P., Popovici, P., Larochelle, H.: Greedy layer-wise training of deep networks. In: Advances in Neural Information Processing Systems, vol. 19. MIT Press, Cambridge (2007)
5. Dua, D., Graff, C.: UCI machine learning repository (2017). http://archive.ics.uci.edu/ml
6. Huber, P., Wiley, J., InterScience, W.: Robust Statistics. Wiley, New York (1981)
7. Imakura, A., Inoue, Y., Sakurai, T., Futamura, Y.: Parallel implementation of the nonlinear semi-NMF based alternating optimization method for deep neural networks. Neural Process. Lett. **47**, 1–13 (2017). https://doi.org/10.1007/s11063-017-9642-2
8. Kingma, D.P., Ba, J.: Adam: a method for stochastic optimization (2014). http://arxiv.org/abs/1412.6980, cite arxiv:1412.6980 Comment: Published as a conference paper at the 3rd International Conference for Learning Representations, San Diego (2015)
9. Nair, V., Hinton, G.E.: Rectified linear units improve restricted Boltzmann machines. In: Fürnkranz, J., Joachims, T. (eds.) Proceedings of the 27th International Conference on Machine Learning (ICML 2010), pp. 807–814 (2010)
10. Otair, M., Walid, A.S.: Speeding up back-propagation neural networks. In: Proceedings of the 2005 Informing Science and IT Education Joint Conference, vol. 1 (0002)
11. Rumelhart, D.E., Hinton, G.E., Williams, R.J.: Learning Representations by Back-propagating Errors. Nature **323**(6088), 533–536 (1986). https://doi.org/10.1038/323533a0. http://www.nature.com/articles/323533a0
12. Sakurai, T., Imakura, A., Inoue, Y., Futamura, Y.: Alternating optimization method based on nonnegative matrix factorizations for deep neural networks. In: Hirose, A., Ozawa, S., Doya, K., Ikeda, K., Lee, M., Liu, D. (eds.) ICONIP 2016. LNCS, vol. 9950, pp. 354–362. Springer, Cham (2016). https://doi.org/10.1007/978-3-319-46681-1_43
13. van der Walt, S., Colbert, S.C., Varoquaux, G.: The numpy array: a structure for efficient numerical computation. Comput. Sci. Eng. **13**(2), 22–30 (2011). http://dblp.uni-trier.de/db/journals/cse/cse13.html#WaltCV11

Collaborative Data Analysis: Non-model Sharing-Type Machine Learning for Distributed Data

Akira Imakura$^{(\boxtimes)}$ (ID), Xiucai Ye(ID), and Tetsuya Sakurai

University of Tsukuba, 1-1-1 Tennodai, Tsukuba, Ibaraki 305-8573, Japan
{imakura,yexiucai,sakurai}@cs.tsukuba.ac.jp

Abstract. This paper proposes a novel non-model sharing-type collaborative learning method for distributed data analysis, in which data are partitioned in both samples and features. Analyzing these types of distributed data are essential tasks in many applications, e.g., medical data analysis and manufacturing data analysis due to privacy and confidentiality concerns. By centralizing the *intermediate representations* which are individually constructed in each party, the proposed method achieves collaborative analysis without revealing the individual data, while the learning models remain distributed over local parties. Numerical experiments indicate that the proposed method achieves higher recognition performance for artificial and real-world problems than individual analysis.

Keywords: Collaborative data analysis · Distributed data · Classification · Dimensionality reduction

1 Introduction

Distributed data analysis is concerned with the computation of models from data that are distributed among multiple parties. Sharing data for model computation may be difficult due to the privacy and confidentiality requirement. Thus, how to analyze the distributed data without revealing the individual data is challenging and has recently attracted much research attentions [3,12,13,17,18,22,30].

Cryptographic computation (i.e., secure multiparty computation) is one of the most well-known methods for distributed data analysis considering privacy-preserving [5,9,15]. Cryptographic methods can compute a function over distributed data while retaining the privacy of the data. By applying fully homomorphic encryption [8], it is known that one can compute any given function; however, it is impractical for large datasets due to huge computational cost even with the latest implementations [4].

The present study is supported in part by JST/ACT-I (No. JPMJPR16U6), NEDO and JSPS/Grants-in-Aid for Scientific Research (Nos. 17K12690, 18H03250, 19KK0255).

H. Uehara et al. (Eds.): PKAW 2020, LNAI 12280, pp. 14–29, 2021.
https://doi.org/10.1007/978-3-030-69886-7_2

Another type of privacy-preserving methods is differential privacy, in which the usage of randomization protects the privacy of the original datasets [1,6, 16]. Differential privacy computation is cost-efficient compared to cryptographic computation; however, it may lead to low-prediction accuracy due to the noise added for protecting privacy.

Recently, federated learning has also been actively studied for distributed data analysis [17,18,22,30], in which a learning model is centralized while the original datasets remain distributed in local parties. Google has first proposed the concept of federated learning in [17,18], which is typically used for Android phone model updates [22]. There are several efforts for improving federated learning; see e.g., [30] and reference therein. However, for federated learning, we need to care a privacy of the original dataset due to the shared functional model [29].

In this paper, we propose a novel non-model sharing-type collaborative learning method, named *collaborative data analysis*, for distributed data. Instead of sharing the individual data and models, the proposed method share *intermediate representations* generated in local parties from individual data. The usage of intermediate representations is an effective technique for distributed data analysis, which has much lower computational cost compared to cryptographic computation and differential privacy. Methods using intermediate representations have been proposed and demonstrated for supervised learning [12,13] and feature selection [31] for distributed data. The performance comparison between collaborative data analysis and federated learning has been studied in [3]. However, these methods only consider the distributed data that are partitioned based on samples, which cannot be applied to the case that data are partitioned based on features.

To meet a wide range of application needs, this paper considers a case that data are partitioned based on both samples and features. A motivating example could be found in distributed medical data analysis of employees in multiple companies. Data samples are distributed in multiple institutions, e.g., the employees distributed in different companies. Moreover, the medical records (i.e., features) of the samples in each institution are distributed in multiple parties, e.g., the records of diagnostic information about different diseases are distributed in different hospitals. Due to the limited number of samples and features, the data in one party maybe lack some useful information for data analysis. Centralizing data from multiple parties for collaborative analysis can help to learn more useful information and obtain high-quality predictive results. However, due to privacy and confidentiality concerns, it is difficult to share individual medical data from multiple parties. The proposed collaborative data analysis would overcome these difficulties.

The contributions of the proposed method are summarized as follows.

– Collaborative data analysis via intermediate representations without revealing individual data and sharing model is proposed for distributed data analysis, in which data are partitioned based on both samples and features.

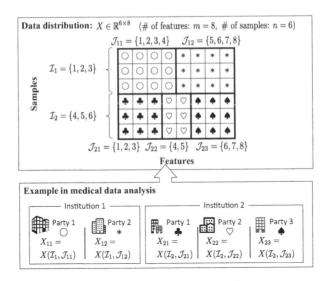

Fig. 1. A simple example of data distribution with $c = 2, d_1 = 2, d_2 = 3$ for $X \in \mathbb{R}^{6 \times 8}$.

- Numerical experiments on both artificial and real-world data show that the proposed method achieves higher recognition performance than that of individual analysis and competitive to that of centralized analysis.

In this paper, we use MATLAB colon notation to refer to ranges of matrix elements.

2   Distributed Data

Let m and n denote the numbers of features and training data samples. In addition, let $X = [\boldsymbol{x}_1, \boldsymbol{x}_2, \ldots, \boldsymbol{x}_n]^{\mathrm{T}} \in \mathbb{R}^{n \times m}$ be the training dataset. The dataset X is partitioned based on both samples and features as follows. For a sample (horizontal) partitioning, let $\mathcal{I}_1, \mathcal{I}_2, \ldots, \mathcal{I}_c$ be mutually exclusive and collectively exhaustive sample index sets:

$$\mathcal{I}_i \cap \mathcal{I}_{i'} = \emptyset \quad (i \neq i'), \quad \mathcal{I}_1 \cup \mathcal{I}_2 \cup \cdots \cup \mathcal{I}_c = \{1, 2, \ldots, n\},$$

where c is the number of partitions based on samples, $|\mathcal{I}_i| = n_i$ is the number of samples in the institution i and $\sum_{i=1}^{c} n_i = n$. Additionally, for a feature (vertical) partitioning, let $\mathcal{J}_{i1}, \mathcal{J}_{i2}, \ldots, \mathcal{J}_{id_i}$ be mutually exclusive and collectively exhaustive feature index sets for the i-th sample set:

$$\mathcal{J}_{ij} \cap \mathcal{J}_{ij'} = \emptyset \quad (j \neq j'), \quad \mathcal{J}_{i1} \cup \mathcal{J}_{i2} \cup \cdots \cup \mathcal{J}_{id_i} = \{1, 2, \ldots, m\},$$

where d_i is the number of partitions based on samples in the institution i, $|\mathcal{J}_{ij}| = m_{ij}$ is the number of features in the party j for the institution i and $\sum_{j=1}^{d_i} m_{ij} = m$.

Then, the dataset X is partitioned into $d = \sum_{i=1}^{c} d_i$ parties and each (i, j)-th party has only the sub-dataset,

$$X_{ij} = X(\mathcal{I}_i, \mathcal{J}_{ij}) \in \mathbb{R}^{n_i \times m_{ij}}. \tag{1}$$

Figure 1 illustrates a simple example of data distribution with $c = 2, d_1 = 2, d_2 = 3$ for $X \in \mathbb{R}^{6 \times 8}$. In this example, the dataset $X \in \mathbb{R}^{6 \times 8}$ is distributed into $d = d_1 + d_2 = 5$ parties denoted by $\circ, *, \clubsuit, \heartsuit$ and $\spadesuit$. $X(\mathcal{I}_1, :)$ and $X(\mathcal{I}_2, :)$ are the datasets of samples distributed in institutions 1 and 2, respectively. $X_{11} = X(\mathcal{I}_1, \mathcal{J}_{11})$ and $X_{12} = X(\mathcal{I}_1, \mathcal{J}_{12})$ are the datasets partitioned based on features and distributed in parties 1 and 2, respectively, for institution 1. Considering an example of distributed medical data analysis of employees of companies, $X(\mathcal{I}_1, :)$ and $X(\mathcal{I}_2, :)$ are the datasets of employees in companies 1 and 2, respectively. X_{11} and X_{12} are the medical records of different diseases distributed in hospitals 1 and 2, respectively, for the employees in companies 1. For supervised learning, we additionally let $Y_i \in \mathbb{R}^{n_i \times \ell}$ $(i = 1, 2, \ldots, c)$ be the ground truth for the training data. Let $X^{\text{test}} \in \mathbb{R}^{s \times m}$ be a test dataset. Herein, we assume that the test dataset X^{test} is distributed in feature

$$X_{i'j}^{\text{test}} = X^{\text{test}}(:, \mathcal{J}_{i'j}) \quad (j = 1, 2, \ldots, d_{i'}),$$

where $i' \in \{1, 2, \ldots, c\}$.

Individual analysis using only the dataset in a local party may not have high-quality prediction results due to lack of feature information or insufficient number of samples, e.g., X_{11} in Fig. 1 are limited to the partial features in party 1 in institution 1. If we can centralize the datasets from multiple parties and analyze them as one dataset, i.e., centralized analysis, then we can achieve a high-quality prediction. However, it is difficult to share the individual data for centralization due to privacy and confidentiality concerns.

3   Collaborative Data Analysis

This section proposes a novel non-model sharing-type collaborative learning method for distributed data analysis by utilizing intermediate representations. Compared with the existing methods, the proposed method does not use privacy-preserving computations or share the model. Additionally, the proposed method is applicable for distributed data that are portioned based on both samples and features.

3.1   Basic Concept

Instead of centralizing the original dataset X_{ij}, we consider centralizing an intermediate representation, which is individually generated in each party. Here, we allow each party to select a function for the intermediate representation individually. We cannot analyze the intermediate representations as one dataset because of the usage of the independent functions. To address this issue, we transform the individual intermediate representations to an incorporable form called *collaboration representations*. Then, we analyze the collaboration representations as one dataset.

The fundamental strategy of the proposed collaborative data analysis method is shown below.

1. **Construction of intermediate representations**
   Each party individually constructs the intermediate representation and centralizes them.
2. **Construction of collaboration representations**
   The collaboration representations are constructed from the centralized intermediate representations.
3. **Analysis of collaboration representations**
   The collaboration representations are analyzed as one dataset.

3.2   Derivation of the Proposed Method

Outline. In the proposed method, each party constructs the intermediate representation,

$$\widetilde{X}_{ij} = f_{ij}(X_{ij}) \in \mathbb{R}^{n_i \times \widetilde{m}_{ij}},$$

where f_{ij} denotes a linear or nonlinear row-wise mapping function. Then the resulting intermediate representations $\widetilde{X}_{ij}$ are centralized. A typical setting for f_{ij} is a dimensionality reduction with $\widetilde{m}_{ij} < m_{ij}$. By achieving collaborative analysis while the original dataset X_{ij} and the mapping function f_{ij} remain distributed in each party, the proposed method can avoid the issue of centralized analysis. Since each mapping function f_{ij} is generated in each party from X_{ij}, the mapping function f_{ij} and the dimensionality $\widetilde{m}_{ij}$ of $\widetilde{X}_{ij}$ depend on i and j.

Since the dataset X is distributed as (1), for each i, the following sub-dataset

$$X_i = X(\mathcal{I}_i, :) \in \mathbb{R}^{n_i \times m}$$

denotes the dataset for the partial samples in $\mathcal{I}_i$ and

$$\widetilde{X}_i = [\widetilde{X}_{i1}, \widetilde{X}_{i2}, \dots, \widetilde{X}_{id_i}] \in \mathbb{R}^{n_i \times \widetilde{m}_i}$$

where $\widetilde{m}_i = \sum_{j=1}^{d_i} \widetilde{m}_{ij}$ can be regarded as the corresponding intermediate representation, i.e., there is f_i such that

$$\widetilde{X}_i = f_i(X_i).$$

We cannot analyze intermediate representations as one dataset, since f_{ij} depends on the party (i, j). To overcome this difficulty, we transform the intermediate representations $\widetilde{X}_i$ to an incorporable collaboration representation:

$$\widehat{X}_i = g_i(\widetilde{X}_i) \in \mathbb{R}^{n_i \times \widehat{m}}$$

with a row-wise mapping function g_i preserving the relationships of the original dataset. Here, we typically set $\hat{m} = \min_i \tilde{m}_i$.

To construct the mapping function g_i for incorporable collaboration representations without using the original dataset X and functions f_{ij}, we introduce an *anchor dataset* $X^{\mathrm{anc}} \in \mathbb{R}^{r \times m}$ with $r \geq \tilde{m}_i$, which is a shareable data consisting of public data or dummy data randomly constructed. Sharing the anchor data X^{anc} and applying each mapping function f_{ij} to the subset of the anchor data:

$$X_{ij}^{\mathrm{anc}} = X^{\mathrm{anc}}(:, \mathcal{J}_{ij}) \in \mathbb{R}^{r \times m_{ij}},$$

we have the (i,j)-th intermediate representation of the anchor dataset:

$$\tilde{X}_{ij}^{\mathrm{anc}} = f_{ij}(X_{ij}^{\mathrm{anc}}) \in \mathbb{R}^{r \times \tilde{m}_{ij}}.$$

We then centralize $\tilde{X}_{ij}^{\mathrm{anc}}$. Here, we set

$$\tilde{X}_i^{\mathrm{anc}} = [\tilde{X}_{i1}^{\mathrm{anc}}, \tilde{X}_{i2}^{\mathrm{anc}}, \ldots, \tilde{X}_{id_i}^{\mathrm{anc}}] \in \mathbb{R}^{r \times \tilde{m}_i}$$

and construct g_i satisfying

$$\hat{X}_i^{\mathrm{anc}} \approx \hat{X}_{i'}^{\mathrm{anc}} \quad (i \neq i'), \quad \hat{X}_i^{\mathrm{anc}} = g_i(\tilde{X}_i^{\mathrm{anc}}) \in \mathbb{R}^{r \times \hat{m}}$$

in some sense. By preserving the relationships of the original dataset, we can analyze the obtained data $\hat{X}_i$ $(i = 1, 2, \ldots, c)$ as one dataset as follows:

$$\hat{X} = \begin{bmatrix} \hat{X}_1 \\ \hat{X}_2 \\ \vdots \\ \hat{X}_c \end{bmatrix} \in \mathbb{R}^{n \times \hat{m}}.$$

Note that the function g_i does not aim to approximate the inverse of f_i. Typically, the dimensionality $\hat{m}$ of the collaboration representation $\hat{X}$ is smaller than the dimensionality m of the original data X, i.e., $\hat{m} \leq \tilde{m}_i < m$.

For Constructing f_{ij}. In this paper, we assume that the function f_{ij} is a linear or nonlinear mapping function.

Examples of the mapping function include unsupervised dimensionality reductions, such as principal component analysis (PCA) [23], locality preserving projections (LPP) [10], t-distributed stochastic neighbor embedding (t-SNE) [21] and supervised dimensionality reductions, such as Fisher discriminant analysis (FDA) [7], local FDA (LFDA) [27], locality adaptive discriminant analysis (LADA) [20], complex moment-based supervised eigenmap (CMSE) [11].

Additionally, one can also consider a partial structure of deep neural networks, e.g., used in transfer learning or auto encoder.

For Constructing g_i. The function g_i can be constructed through the following two steps:

- We set a target matrix $Z \in \mathbb{R}^{r \times \widehat{m}}$ for achieving $Z \approx \widehat{X}_i^{\mathrm{anc}}$ $(i = 1, 2, \ldots, c)$.
- We compute g_i for each i such that $Z \approx g_i(\widetilde{X}_i^{\mathrm{anc}})$.

For setting Z, the simplest idea is $Z = \widetilde{X}_1^{\mathrm{anc}}$. Herein, we introduce another practical algorithm based on the assumption that g_i is a linear map. If g_i is a linear map, we have $G_i \in \mathbb{R}^{\widetilde{m}_i \times \widehat{m}}$ such that

$$\widehat{X}_i = g_i(\widetilde{X}_i) = \widetilde{X}_i G_i, \quad \widehat{X}_i^{\mathrm{anc}} = g_i(\widetilde{X}_i^{\mathrm{anc}}) = \widetilde{X}_i^{\mathrm{anc}} G_i.$$

Then, we set the target matrix Z via the following minimal perturbation problem:

$$\min_{E_i, G_i' (i=1,2,\ldots,c), Z \neq O} \sum_{i=1}^{c} \|E_i\|_{\mathrm{F}}^2 \quad \text{s.t.} \quad (\widetilde{X}_i^{\mathrm{anc}} + E_i) G_i' = Z \tag{2}$$

that can be solved by applying a singular value decomposition (SVD)-based algorithm for total least squares problems [14]. Let

$$[\widetilde{X}_1^{\mathrm{anc}}, \widetilde{X}_2^{\mathrm{anc}}, \ldots, \widetilde{X}_c^{\mathrm{anc}}] = [U_1, U_2] \begin{bmatrix} \Sigma_1 & \\ & \Sigma_2 \end{bmatrix} \begin{bmatrix} V_1^{\mathrm{T}} \\ V_2^{\mathrm{T}} \end{bmatrix} \approx U_1 \Sigma_1 V_1^{\mathrm{T}} \tag{3}$$

be a low-rank approximation based on SVD of the matrix combining $\widetilde{X}_i^{\mathrm{anc}}$, where $\Sigma_1 \in \mathbb{R}^{\widehat{m} \times \widehat{m}}$ denotes a diagonal matrix whose diagonal entries are larger parts of singular values, U_1 and V_1 are column orthogonal matrices whose columns are the corresponding left and right singular vectors. Then, the target matrix Z (solution of (2)) can be obtained as $Z = U_1 C$, where $C \in \mathbb{R}^{\widehat{m} \times \widehat{m}}$ is a nonsingular matrix, e.g., $C = \Sigma_1$. For the details for solving (2), we refer to [14].

The matrix G_i is then computed by solving the following linear least squares problem:

$$G_i = \arg \min_{G \in \mathbb{R}^{\widetilde{m}_i \times \widehat{m}}} \|Z - \widetilde{X}_i^{\mathrm{anc}} G\|_{\mathrm{F}}^2 = (\widetilde{X}_i^{\mathrm{anc}})^\dagger U_1 C.$$

Here, we can also use the ridge regression [25] or lasso [28] for reducing the risk of over-fitting.

For the case of a nonlinear map g_i, we may apply some machine learning techniques to construct it. For example, we can use some dimensionality reduction method to set Z in step 1 and some machine learning or deep learning algorithm for step 2. In the future, we will investigate practical algorithms of a nonlinear map g_i.

Pseudo Code of the Proposed Method. Algorithm 1 summarises the algorithm of the proposed method for supervised learning. Here, we set $C = I$.

The recognition performance of the proposed method depends on the anchor data X^{anc}. A random matrix is a simple way to set X^{anc}. The usage of statistics may improve recognition performance. The authors intend to investigate practical techniques to construct a suitable anchor data in the future.

Algorithm 1. Collaborative data analysis

Input: $X_{ij} \in \mathbb{R}^{n_i \times m_{ij}}, Y_i \in \mathbb{R}^{n_i \times \ell}, X_{i'j}^{\text{test}} \in \mathbb{R}^{s \times m_{i'j}}$ $(i' \in \{1, 2, \ldots, c\})$ individually.
Output: $Y^{\text{test}} \in \mathbb{R}^{s \times \ell}$

{Phase 0. Preparation}
1: Centralize $X^{\text{anc}} \in \mathbb{R}^{r \times m}$ and set $X_{ij}^{\text{anc}} = X^{\text{anc}}(:, \mathcal{J}_{ij})$

{Phase 1. Construction of intermediate representations}
2: Construct $\widetilde{X}_{ij} = f_{ij}(X_{ij})$ and $\widetilde{X}_{ij}^{\text{anc}} = f_{ij}(X_{ij}^{\text{anc}})$ for each (i, j) individually
3: Centralize $\widetilde{X}_{ij}, \widetilde{X}_{ij}^{\text{anc}}, Y_i$ for all i and j
4: Set $\widetilde{X}_i, \widetilde{X}_i^{\text{anc}}$ for all i

{Phase 2. Construction of collaboration representations}
5: Compute left singular vectors U_1 by SVD (3)
6: Compute $G_i = (\widetilde{X}_i^{\text{anc}})^\dagger U_1$
7: Compute $\widehat{X}_i = \widetilde{X}_i G_i$
8: Set $\widehat{X} = [\widehat{X}_1^{\text{T}}, \widehat{X}_2^{\text{T}}, \ldots, \widehat{X}_c^{\text{T}}]^{\text{T}}$ and $Y = [Y_1^{\text{T}}, Y_2^{\text{T}}, \ldots, Y_c^{\text{T}}]^{\text{T}}$

{Phase 3. Analysis of collaboration representations}
9: Construct a model h by applying a machine learning or deep learning algorithm using $\widehat{X}$ as training date and Y as the ground truth, i.e., $Y \approx h(\widehat{X})$.
10: Centralize $\widetilde{X}_{i'j}^{\text{test}} = f_{i'j}(X_{i'j}^{\text{test}})$ and set $\widetilde{X}_{i'}^{\text{test}}$
11: Predict test data X^{test} using a model h and obtain $Y^{\text{test}} = h(\widetilde{X}_{i'}^{\text{test}} G_{i'})$.

3.3 Practical Operation Strategy Regarding Privacy and Confidentiality Concerns

Here, we introduce the following practical operation strategy:

- The proposed method is operated as demonstrated in Fig. 2 and Table 1 with two roles: *user* and *analyst*. A certain number of users have the training and test datasets individually. An analyst centralizes the intermediate representations and analyzes them via the collaborative representations.
- Each user sets a mapping function f_{ij} satisfying the following requirements:
  • A useful information of the private data X_{ij} can be obtained only if anyone has both the corresponding intermediate representation $\widetilde{X}_{ij}$ and the mapping function f_{ij} or its approximation.
  • The mapping function f_{ij} can be approximated only if anyone has both the input and output of f_{ij}.

Then, we simply discuss the privacy of the private dataset X_{ij} in the proposed method. Here, we assume that the users do not trust each other and want to protect their training dataset X_{ij} against honest-but-curious users and analyst. That is, users and analyst will strictly follow the strategy, but they try to infer as much information as possible. We also assume that the analyst does not collude with any users.

Based on the above operation strategy, since each map function f_{ij} is operated only to X_{ij} and X_{ij}^{anc} and X_{ij} is private, both X_{ij}^{anc} and $\widetilde{X}_{ij}^{\text{anc}}$ are required

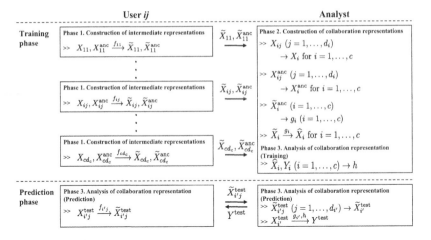

Fig. 2. A practical operation strategy: algorithm flow.

to obtain an approximation of f_{ij}. However, each user does not possess the intermediate representations $\widetilde{X}_{ij}^{\mathrm{anc}}$ of other users, and analyst does not possess the original anchor data X^{anc}. Note that all users share the anchor data, but the analyst does not know the actual anchor data used in the algorithm. Therefore, no one can approximate f_{ij}. Thus, all users and analyst cannot obtain a useful information of the private dataset X_{ij} of other users, even if users are malicious and collude together to attack a particular user.

In our future studies, the authors will further analyze more details of the privacy of the proposed method.

Table 1. A practical operation strategy: role and data in training phase.

Role		Data
user (i,j)	:	$X_{ij}, \widetilde{X}_{ij}, Y_i, X^{\mathrm{anc}}, \widetilde{X}_{ij}^{\mathrm{anc}}, f_{ij}$
analyst	:	$\widetilde{X}_{ij}, Y_i, \widetilde{X}_{ij}^{\mathrm{anc}}, g_i$ (for all i,j), h

Data		Role
X_{ij}, f_{ij}	:	user (i,j)
$\widetilde{X}_{ij}, \widetilde{X}_{ij}^{\mathrm{anc}}$	:	user (i,j) and analyst
X^{anc}	:	all users
g_i, h	:	analyst

4   Numerical Experiments

This section evaluates the recognition performance of the proposed collaborative data analysis method (Algorithm 1) and compares it with that of centralized and individual analyses for classification problems. It is noteworthy that centralized analysis is just ideal since one cannot share the original datasets X_{ij} in our target situation. The proposed collaborative data analysis aim to achieve a recognition performance higher than that of individual analysis.

We used a kernel version of ridge regression (K-RR) [25] with a Gaussian kernel for data analysis. We set the regularization parameter for K-RR to $\lambda = 0.01$. In the proposed method, each intermediate representation is designed from X_{ij} using LPP [10] that is an unsupervised dimensionality reduction method. Since the mapping functions of LPP depend on the dataset, f_{ij} depends on i and j. The anchor data X^{anc} is constructed as a random matrix and $r = 2,000$.

We utilized the ground truth Y as a binary matrix whose (i, j) entry is 1 if the training data x_i is in class j and otherwise 0. This type of ground truth Y is applied for various classification algorithms, including ridge regression and deep neural networks [2].

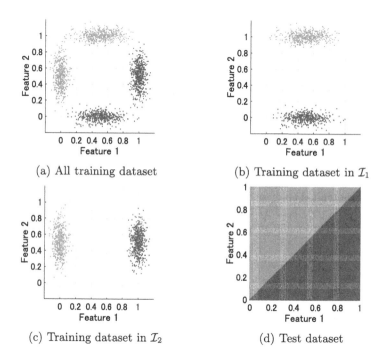

Fig. 3. Features 1 and 2 of the training and test dataset for the artificial problem.

4.1   Experiment I: For Artificial Data

Herein, we used a 20-dimensional artificial data for two-class classification. Figure 3(a) depicts the first two dimensions of all the training dataset, where the number of samples is $n = 2000$. The other 18 dimensions were random values.

We considered the case in which the dataset in Fig. 3(a) is distributed into four parties: $c = 2$ and $d_1 = d_2 = 2$. Figures 3(b) and (c) demonstrate the first two dimensions of training datasets in $\mathcal{I}_1$ and in $\mathcal{I}_2$, respectively. For the feature (vertical) partitioning, we set

$$\mathcal{I}_{11} = \mathcal{I}_{21} = \{1, 3, 5, \ldots, 19\}, \quad \mathcal{I}_{12} = \mathcal{I}_{22} = \{2, 4, 6, \ldots, 20\}.$$

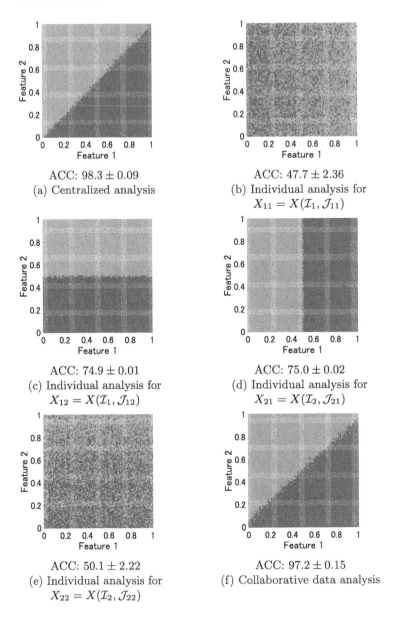

Fig. 4. Recognition results of the centralized, individual and collaborative data analyses for the artificial problem.

Note that only features 1 and 2 are necessary for recognition. Figure 3(d) illustrates the first two dimensions of test dataset. For the proposed method, we set the dimensionality of the intermediate representations $\widetilde{m}_{ij} = 4$ for all parties.

Figure 4 presents the recognition results and accuracy (ACC). From these results, we can observe that individual analysis cannot obtain good recognition results. This is because of the following reasons. Since X_{11} has feature 1 of $\mathcal{I}_1$ shown in Fig. 3(b) and X_{22} has feature 2 of $\mathcal{I}_2$ shown in Fig. 3(c), the distributions of two classes are overlapped. Therefore, only using X_{11} or X_{22}, we cannot separate two classes. Moreover, X_{12} has feature 2 of $\mathcal{I}_1$ and X_{21} has feature 1 of $\mathcal{I}_2$. Therefore, the classification boundaries for X_{12} and X_{21} are horizontal and vertical, respectively.

On the other hand, when compared with individual analysis, the proposed method (Fig. 4(f)) achieves a good recognition result as well as centralized analysis (Fig. 4(a)).

4.2 Experiment II: vs. Number of Parties

We used a 10-class classification of handwritten digits (MNIST) [19], where $m = 784$. We set the number of samples for each institution $|\mathcal{I}_i| = n_i = 25$ and the number of partitions based on features $d_i = 2$. Then, we evaluated the recognition performance for 1,000 test data samples by increasing the number of partitions based on samples c from 1 to 20, i.e., the number of parties $d = \sum_{i=1}^{c} d_i$ from 2 to 30. We evaluated 10 trials with randomly selected $\mathcal{I}_i, \mathcal{J}_{ij}$. For the proposed method, we set $\tilde{m}_{ij} = 20$.

Figure 5 depicts recognition performance regarding normalized mutual information (NMI) [26] and accuracy (ACC). It is observed that the recognition performance of the proposed method increases with an increase in the number of parties and achieves a significantly higher recognition performance than individual analysis and competitive to centralized analysis.

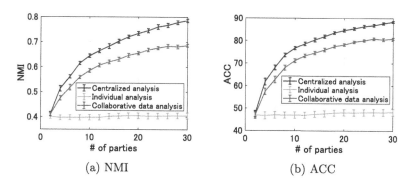

(a) NMI   (b) ACC

Fig. 5. Recognition performance (NMI and ACC) vs. number of parties on MNIST.

Table 2. Recognition performance (average ± standard error) for real-world problems. The values m, n and l denote the number of features, samples and classes, respectively.

	Name of dataset and size		Name of dataset and size	
	NMI	ACC	NMI	ACC
Method	ALLAML $(m, n, l) = (7129, 72, 2)$		Carcinom $(m, n, l) = (9182, 174, 11)$	
Centralized analysis	0.83 ± 0.03	95.71 ± 0.81	0.93 ± 0.01	93.13 ± 0.55
Individual analysis	0.53 ± 0.04	86.72 ± 1.34	0.89 ± 0.01	87.18 ± 1.07
Collab. data analysis	0.69 ± 0.04	91.80 ± 1.12	0.90 ± 0.01	88.75 ± 1.01
Method	GLA-BRA-180 $(m, n, l) = (49151, 180, 4)$		GLI-85 $(m, n, l) = (22283, 85, 2)$	
Centralized analysis	0.43 ± 0.02	71.11 ± 0.77	0.35 ± 0.03	85.88 ± 0.85
Indivisual analysis	0.41 ± 0.02	68.01 ± 1.05	0.32 ± 0.03	81.98 ± 1.41
Collab. data analysis	0.42 ± 0.02	69.56 ± 0.94	0.36 ± 0.04	84.94 ± 1.13
Method	Jaffe $(m, n, l) = (676, 213, 10)$		Leukemia $(m, n, l) = (7070, 72, 2)$	
Centralized analysis	1.00 ± 0.00	99.52 ± 0.13	0.83 ± 0.03	95.71 ± 0.81
Indivisual analysis	0.98 ± 0.00	98.33 ± 0.32	0.57 ± 0.04	87.82 ± 1.36
Collab. data analysis	1.00 ± 0.00	99.62 ± 0.17	0.71 ± 0.04	92.68 ± 1.01
Method	Lung $(m, n, l) = (3312, 203, 5)$		Lymphoma $(m, n, l) = (4026, 96, 9)$	
Centralized analysis	0.89 ± 0.01	96.54 ± 0.36	0.92 ± 0.00	90.58 ± 0.87
Indivisual analysis	0.84 ± 0.01	94.29 ± 0.44	0.80 ± 0.01	81.17 ± 1.20
Collab. data analysis	0.86 ± 0.01	95.39 ± 0.41	0.85 ± 0.01	85.46 ± 0.97
Method	pixraw10P $(m, n, l) = (10000, 100, 10)$		Prostate_GE $(m, n, l) = (5966, 102, 2)$	
Centralized analysis	0.98 ± 0.00	97.00 ± 0.57	0.58 ± 0.02	90.18 ± 0.45
Individual analysis	0.96 ± 0.00	92.93 ± 0.95	0.50 ± 0.03	87.04 ± 0.94
Collab. data analysis	0.98 ± 0.00	96.20 ± 0.64	0.58 ± 0.02	89.99 ± 0.76
Method	warpAR10P $(m, n, l) = (2400, 130, 10)$		warpPIE10P $(m, n, l) = (2420, 210, 10)$	
Centralized analysis	0.95 ± 0.01	93.85 ± 1.01	0.99 ± 0.00	99.05 ± 0.16
Indivisual analysis	0.81 ± 0.01	74.81 ± 1.28	0.95 ± 0.00	95.51 ± 0.41
Collab. data analysis	0.92 ± 0.01	90.46 ± 1.02	0.98 ± 0.00	98.19 ± 0.31

4.3   Experiment III: For Real-World Data

Now, we evaluate the performance for the binary and multi-class classification problems obtained from [19, 24] and feature selection datasets[1].

---

[1] Available at http://featureselection.asu.edu/datasets.php.

We consider the case that the dataset is distributed into six parties: $c = 2$ and $d_1 = d_2 = 3$. The performance of each method is evaluated by utilizing a five-fold cross-validation. In each training set of the cross-validation, we evaluated 10 trials with randomly selected $\mathcal{I}_i, \mathcal{J}_{ij}$. For the proposed method, we set $\widetilde{m}_{ij} = 50$.

The numerical results of centralized analysis, an average of individual analyses and the proposed method for 12 test problems are presented in Table 2. We can observe from Table 2 that the proposed method has a recognition performance higher than that of individual analysis and competitive to that of centralized analysis on the most datasets.

4.4   Remarks on Numerical Results

The numerical results demonstrated that the proposed method achieves higher recognition performance than individual analysis and competitive to centralized analysis for artificial and real-world datasets. Note that centralized analysis is just ideal since one cannot share the original datasets X_{ij} in our target situation.

In all the numerical experiments of this paper, we evaluate the performance with IID local data. For federated learning, it is shown that, with non-IID local data, the performance can be greatly reduced [32]. We will evaluate the performance of the proposed method with non-IID local data in the future.

5   Conclusions

In this study, we proposed a novel non-model sharing-type collaborative learning method for distributed data analysis, in which data are partitioned based on both samples and features. The proposed method realized collaborative analysis by utilizing the intermediate representation without using privacy-preserving computations and centralizing model. By applying the practical operation strategy under some assumptions, the proposed method preserves the privacy of the original data X_{ij} in each party.

The proposed method addressed the issue of centralized and individual analyses and achieved high-quality recognition for artificial and real-world datasets. It is inferred that the proposed method would become a breakthrough technology for distributed data analysis in the real-world including distributed medical data analysis and distributed manufacturing data analysis.

In our future studies, the authors will further analyze the privacy and confidentiality concerns of the proposed method and investigate practical techniques to construct a suitable anchor data. The authors will also apply the proposed method to large-scale distributed data in real-world applications, e.g., the application in medical or manufacture fields, and evaluate its recognition performance.

References

1. Abadi, M., et al.: Deep learning with differential privacy. In: Proceedings of the 2016 ACM SIGSAC Conference on Computer and Communications Security, pp. 308–318. ACM (2016)

2. Bishop, C.M.: Pattern Recognition and Machine Learning (Information Science and Statistics). Springer, Heidelberg (2006)
3. Bogdanova, A., Nakai, A., Okada, Y., Imakura, A., Sakurai, T.: Federated learning system without model sharing through integration of dimensional reduced data representations. In: International Workshop on Federated Learning for User Privacy and Data Confidentiality in Conjunction with IJCAI 2020 (FL-IJCAI 2020) (2020, accepted)
4. Chillotti, I., Gama, N., Georgieva, M., Izabachène, M.: Faster fully homomorphic encryption: bootstrapping in less than 0.1 seconds. In: Cheon, J.H., Takagi, T. (eds.) ASIACRYPT 2016. LNCS, vol. 10031, pp. 3–33. Springer, Heidelberg (2016). https://doi.org/10.1007/978-3-662-53887-6_1
5. Cho, H., Wu, D.J., Berger, B.: Secure genome-wide association analysis using multiparty computation. Nat. Biotechnol. **36**(6), 547 (2018)
6. Dwork, C.: Differential privacy. In: Bugliesi, M., Preneel, B., Sassone, V., Wegener, I. (eds.) ICALP 2006. LNCS, vol. 4052, pp. 1–12. Springer, Heidelberg (2006). https://doi.org/10.1007/11787006_1
7. Fisher, R.A.: The use of multiple measurements in taxonomic problems. Ann. Hum. Genet. **7**(2), 179–188 (1936)
8. Gentry, C.: Fully homomorphic encryption using ideal lattices. In: Stoc, vol. 9, pp. 169–178 (2009)
9. Gilad-Bachrach, R., Dowlin, N., Laine, K., Lauter, K., Naehrig, M., Wernsing, J.: CryptoNets: applying neural networks to encrypted data with high throughput and accuracy. In: International Conference on Machine Learning, pp. 201–210 (2016)
10. He, X., Niyogi, P.: Locality preserving projections. In: Advances in Neural Information Processing Systems, pp. 153–160 (2004)
11. Imakura, A., Matsuda, M., Ye, X., Sakurai, T.: Complex moment-based supervised eigenmap for dimensionality reduction. In: Proceedings of the AAAI Conference on Artificial Intelligence, vol. 33, pp. 3910–3918 (2019)
12. Imakura, A., Sakurai, T.: Data collaboration analysis for distributed datasets. arXiv preprint arXiv:1902.07535 (2019)
13. Imakura, A., Sakurai, T.: Data collaboration analysis framework using centralization of individual intermediate representations for distributed data sets. ASCE-ASME J. Risk Uncertain. Eng. Syst. Part A Civil Eng. **6**, 04020018 (2020)
14. Ito, S., Murota, K.: An algorithm for the generalized eigenvalue problem for nonsquare matrix pencils by minimal perturbation approach. SIAM J. Matrix. Anal. Appl. **37**, 409–419 (2016)
15. Jha, S., Kruger, L., McDaniel, P.: Privacy preserving clustering. In: di Vimercati, S.C., Syverson, P., Gollmann, D. (eds.) ESORICS 2005. LNCS, vol. 3679, pp. 397–417. Springer, Heidelberg (2005). https://doi.org/10.1007/11555827_23
16. Ji, Z., Lipton, Z.C., Elkan, C.: Differential privacy and machine learning: a survey and review. arXiv preprint arXiv:1412.7584 (2014)
17. Konečnỳ, J., McMahan, H.B., Ramage, D., Richtarik, P.: Federated optimization: distributed machine learning for on-device intelligence. arXiv preprint arXiv:1610.02527 (2016)
18. Konečnỳ, J., McMahan, H.B., Yu, F.X., Richtarik, P., Suresh, A.T., Bacon, D.: Federated learning: strategies for improving communication efficiency. In: NIPS Workshop on Private Multi-Party Machine Learning (2016). https://arxiv.org/abs/1610.05492
19. LeCun, Y.: The MNIST database of handwritten digits (1998). http://yann.lecun.com/exdb/mnist/

20. Li, X., Chen, M., Nie, F., Wang, Q.: Locality adaptive discriminant analysis. In: Proceedings of the 26th International Joint Conference on Artificial Intelligence, pp. 2201–2207. AAAI Press (2017)
21. van der Maaten, L., Hinton, G., Visualizing data using t-SNE: J. Machine Learn. Res. **9**, 2579–2605 (2008)
22. McMahan, H.B., Moore, E., Ramage, D., Hampson, S., et al.: Communication-efficient learning of deep networks from decentralized data. arXiv preprint arXiv:1602.05629 (2016)
23. Pearson, K.: LIII. On lines and planes of closest fit to systems of points in space. London Edinburgh Dublin Philos. Mag. J. Sci. **2**(11), 559–572 (1901)
24. Samaria, F., Harter, A.: Parameterisation of a stochastic model for human face identification. In: Proceeding of IEEE Workshop on Applications of Computer Vision (1994)
25. Saunders, C., Gammerman, A., Vovk, V.: Ridge regression learning algorithm in dual variables (1998)
26. Strehl, A., Ghosh, J.: Cluster ensembles-a knowledge reuse framework for combining multiple partitions. J. Mach. Learn. Res. **3**, 583–617 (2002)
27. Sugiyama, M.: Dimensionality reduction of multimodal labeled data by local Fisher discriminant analysis. J. Mach. Learn. Res. **8**(May), 1027–1061 (2007)
28. Tibshirani, R.: Regression shrinkage and selection via the lasso. J. Royal Stat. Soci. (Series B) **58**, 267–288 (1996)
29. Yang, Q.: GDPR, data shortage and AI (2019). https://aaai.org/Conferences/AAAI-19/invited-speakers/. Invited Talk of The Thirty-Third AAAI Conference on Artificial Intelligence (AAAI-19)
30. Yang, Q., Liu, Y., Chen, T., Tong, Y.: Federated machine learning: concept and applications. ACM Trans. Intell. Syst. Technol. **10**(2), Article 12 (2019)
31. Ye, X., Li, H., Imakura, A., Sakurai, T.: Distributed collaborative feature selection based on intermediate representation. In: The 28th International Joint Conference on Artificial Intelligence (IJCAI-19). pp. 4142–4149 (2019)
32. Zhao, Y., Li, M., Lai, L., Suda, N., Civin, D., Chandra, V.: Federated learning with non-iid data. arXiv preprint arXiv:cs.LG/1806.00582 (2018)

ERA: Extracting Planning Macro-Operators from Adjacent and Non-adjacent Sequences

Sandra Castellanos-Paez$^{(\boxtimes)}$ ⓘ, Romain Rombourg, and Philippe Lalanda

Univ. Grenoble Alpes, CNRS, Grenoble INP Institute of Engineering Univ. Grenoble Alpes, LIG, 38000 Grenoble, France
sandra.castellanos@univ-grenoble-alpes.fr

Abstract. Intuitively, Automated Planning systems capable of learning from previous experiences should be able to achieve better performance. One way to build on past experiences is to augment domains with macro-operators (i.e. frequent operator sequences). In most existing works, macros are generated from chunks of adjacent operators extracted from a set of plans. Although they provide some interesting results this type of analysis may provide incomplete results. In this paper, we propose ERA, an automatic extraction method for macro-operators from a set of solution plans. Our algorithm is domain and planner independent and can find all macro-operator occurrences even if the operators are non-adjacent. Our method has proven to successfully find macro-operators of different lengths for six different benchmark domains. Also, our experiments highlighted the capital role of considering non-adjacent occurrences in the extraction of macro-operators.

Keywords: Automated planning · Macro-operators · Learning · Data mining

1 Introduction

Planning systems have long been the subject of important research activities in the AI community, be it industrial or academic [8,12]. They are actually key components of intelligent agents that need to make timely decisions in complex environments, like for instance autonomous robots, smart vehicles, or pervasive systems supporting human beings. Developing such systems however remains challenging for a number of reasons. Performance is one of the main challenges. Indeed, despite remarkable progress in recent years, many planning systems fail to meet timing requirements imposed by demanding domains.

We believe that an interesting approach to improve performance is to use past experiences. With the development of pervasive applications, for instance, large organised collections of plans are available. They can then be inspected, analysed, evaluated and even modified by human experts or automated reasoning

© Springer Nature Switzerland AG 2021
H. Uehara et al. (Eds.): PKAW 2020, LNAI 12280, pp. 30–45, 2021.
https://doi.org/10.1007/978-3-030-69886-7_3

systems if needed. Knowledge extracted in those plans repositories can be used to speed up and improve the quality of the planning process in a given domain.

In some domains, especially in industry, plans are stored. So, they can be used to extract knowledge about the system. A particular type of knowledge that can be extracted are the routines, i.e. sequences of actions regularly used by the system. Routines are present in real-life applications or closely related systems.

In AI planning, macros can model system routines. A *macro* consists of a sequence of actions that occurs frequently in solution plans. Once learned, they can be re-injected directly into the planning domain. Thus, the domain benefits from the knowledge extracted from previous problem solving. The system applies a macro in the same way that a primitive action. However, macros allow jumping into the search space by building deep and promising states to reach a goal state. Learning macros from previously acquired knowledge has proven to be beneficial for improving a planner's performance [2–4].

Macros have been widely studied to speed-up planning processes [1,3,5,10, 11]. These approaches consist of two main phases: extraction and selection. Extraction consists in identifying sequences of actions that could be potential candidates to augment the domain. The selection phase must find a trade-off between the benefit expected by adding macros and the additional cost induced by the branching factor increase.

Literature about macros presents various techniques to build them, ranging from simple combination of primitive actions and the use of chunks of plans to the use of genetic learning algorithms or statistical analyses based on n-grams.

In this paper, we investigate an automatic extraction of macro-operators from a set of solution plans. This approach should be domain-independent and particularly adapted to the extraction of recurrent patterns (i.e. the routines). Besides, we want to exploit the extraction of sequences of non-adjacent actions. Only a few works have explored this path [2,3]. Interestingly, they have shown that this allows more routines to be extracted and therefore, would be more profitable for the system.

Precisely, we propose *ERA*, a pattern mining inspired algorithm to mine macro-operators directly from a set of solution plans. This algorithm allows to find all macro-operators satisfying a set frequency threshold even if its actions are non-adjacent in some or all of its occurrences. We see this work as a first step towards a macro-learning method allowing to exploit a large amount of solution plans.

The paper is structured as it follows. First, we introduce the concepts of classical planning, macro-operators and sequential pattern mining. Then, we present the ERA algorithm, describe each of its steps and analyse its complexity. We then present an evaluation of our method quantifying the impact of a gap parameter over six benchmark domains. After, we discuss our results and compare our method to other works. Finally, we provide a conclusion and some perspectives.

2   Background Theory

We are interested in plan synthesis, a particular form of planning which takes a description of the world state, all its known actions and a goal [8]. As a result, we get an organised set of actions whose execution makes it possible to solve the planning task. In this work, we address sequential planning in the STRIPS framework [6].

A state is defined as a set of predicates. A planning task is composed of a *planning domain* and a *planning problem* and the purpose of this task is to find a *plan* to solve this problem. A planning domain describes the world through a set of predicates and a set of planning operators. A planning problem describes the initial state of the world and the goal state to be attained. A planning operator is a triple $o = $ *(name(o), pre(o), effects(o))* where its elements are defined as follows:

- *name(o)* is in the form $name(x_1, ..., x_n)$ where $x_1, ..., x_n$ are the object variable symbols that appear in o.
- *pre(o)* is the set of predicates involving the variables of o and that must be satisfied when o is instantiated.
- *effects(o)* is the set of predicates involving the variables of o to be applied to a state when o is instantiated.

A grounded operator is an instance of a planning operator (i.e. a *lifted* operator for which variables are instantiated). A ground operator a is applicable in a state s if and only if all predicates in the preconditions of a belong to s. A state s' is reached from s if a grounded operator can be applied. Finally, a (solution) plan π is an ordered sequence of grounded operators to reach a goal state s_g from an initial state s_i.

Macros are based on the idea of composing a sequence of primitive operators and viewing the sequence as a single operator. For our purposes, we distinguish two related but different terms: grounded macros and lifted macros. A grounded macro is related to a lifted macro as a ground operator is related to a lifted operator. We use these terms according to literature common terminology.

The problem of identifying recurrent sequences of grounded operators in AI planning is analogous to the sequential pattern mining problem. Sequential pattern mining (SPM) is a sub-field of data mining that consists in analysing data, encoded as sequences of symbols, to detect sub-sequences of symbols [7,9]. SPM is commonly used to detect recurrent sub-sequences.

In the following, we define a set of concepts (borrowed from SPM) necessary for the understanding of this work.

A sequence database C is a set of pairs $< sid, s >$, where sid is a sequence identifier and s is a sequence.

A sequence $S_A = X_1, X_2, \ldots, X_k$, where $X_1, \ldots, X_k$ are ground operators, is a sub-sequence of another sequence $S_B = Y_1, Y_2, \ldots, Y_m$, where $Y_1, \ldots, Y_m$ are ground operators, if and only if there exists integers $1 \leq e_1 < e_2 \cdots < ek \leq m$ such that $X_1 = Y_{e_1}, X_2 = Y_{e_2}, \ldots, X_k = Y_{e_k}$.

The absolute support of a sequence S is the number of sequences S_i, in the sequence database C, where S is a sub-sequence of S_i. The relative support of a sequence S is the absolute support of S divided by the total number of sequences in C. A frequent sequence is a sequence whose relative support satisfies a given relative support threshold. Thereafter, we will call this threshold *minsup*.

Besides, notice that a frequent sequence can occur in several other sequences but not necessarily in a contiguous fashion, as the definition of sub-sequence implies. So, we define a *gap* as the number of operators allowed between two consecutive operators of a sequence and it can take values in $[0, \infty]$. A sub-sequence $S = Y_{e_1}, Y_{e_2}, \ldots, Y_{e_k}$ satisfies a gap constraint g if $\forall i \in [2, k], e_i - e_{i-1} \leq g + 1$.

3   ERA

In the following, we will present ERA, our pattern mining inspired algorithm to mine macro-operators (lifted macros) directly from a set of solution plans. ERA stands for **E**xtraction of **R**ich patterns with **A**ttribute structures.

3.1   Overview

In planning, each plan is composed of an ordered sequence of grounded operators which in turn are composed of parameters (objects). An example of plan is: $\pi = \langle$ unstack blockA blockC, put-down blockA, pick-up blockB, stack blockB blockA$\rangle$.

Mining macro-operators from a set of plans requires an approach which ensures to find the frequent sequences of operators without a loss of information about their characteristics. Then, neither an operator can be dissociated from its objects nor a sequence of operators can disregard the relationship between operators' objects. In other words, the problem is to look for the most frequent sequences of operators with a specific set of object relationships. Thus, it should be noted that for a same sequence of operators, different sets of object relationships lead to the construction of different macro-operators.

Our approach extracts (lifted) macro-operators from a set of sequences of grounded operators (See Fig. 1). Besides, it can detect the occurrence of a macro-operator even if the actions composing it are not adjacent.

3.2   ERA Algorithm

ERA mines all macro-operators (regardless of their length or up to a maximum length) satisfying a frequency threshold and under a gap constraint from a set of solution plans. Additionally, for each macro-operator m, this algorithm yields the following characteristics:

- support [integer]: the number of plans containing at least one occurrence of m.

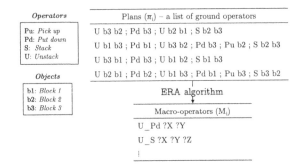

Fig. 1. A sample of extracted macro-operators from a set of plans

– sequence ids [list]: the plan identifiers where m appears.
– number of occurrences [list]: the number of occurrences of m in each plan.

For processing purposes, plans are encoded into a sequence database in two different ways. First, an action wise encoding where each distinct action is assigned a single number, yielding a dictionary A (for example {1:pick-up b, 2:stack b a, 3:pick-up c, ...}) and second an element wise encoding where every single element is assigned a single number, yielding a dictionary E (for example {1:pick-up, 2:b, 3:a, ...}.

ERA pseudo code is described in Algorithm 1. It takes as input the two previously described encodings A and E of the set of plans, a *minsup* threshold, a gap g, and the maximal length of sequences to extract.

First, it searches the set of macro-operators of length two in A by using the procedure *MINE* (line 6, described in Algorithm 2). Second, for each macro-operator of this set, if it does not satisfy the *minsup* threshold it is removed, otherwise the macro-operator and its characteristics are kept (line 11, 12, 13). Finally, if no macro-operator has been found for the current length, it stops. Otherwise, it increases the length by one (line 14) and it continues to loop until it reaches the maximal length (line 5). It gives as a result a set of frequent macro-operators of different lengths with their respective characteristics.

3.3 Mining Procedure

The objective of the mining procedure is to obtain the set of macro-operators of length l and their characteristics from the set of solution plans. To do so, it analyses for each plan all sub-sequences of length l satisfying the gap constraint g and determines if the sub-sequence is a valid occurrence[1] of a macro-operator. If the algorithm finds a valid macro-operator occurrence, it stores this occurrence and updates the characteristics related to this macro-operator. To speed up its computation, it uses previous information obtained when mining length $l - 1$.

---

[1] The operators of the macro can be moved contiguously in the plan without an impact on the final state or without impeding its execution.

The pseudo code of this procedure, called MINE, is described by Algorithm 2. It takes as input both sequence databases A and E from the main algorithm, the gap parameter g, the length l to be evaluated and a dictionary M of all found macro-operators (of different lengths less than l) and their support. The purpose of the first loop (line 3) is to go through all combinations of ordered sub-sequences satisfying the gap constraint for each sequence in A (line 7) and for each sub-sequence, determine if it is a valid macro-operator and if it is valid in a number of sequences greater than the *minsup* parameter. To accomplish this, the following steps are performed:

- It moves on to the next sub-sequence,
  - if the sub-sequence of length $l-1$ does not satisfy the *minsup*. For that, the current sub-sequence length should be greater than two in order to be able to build its identifier[2] of length $l-1$. Then, it checks if this identifier is found in the general dictionary of pairs <macro-operator,support> (line 10).
  - if there are not enough plans left to ensure that the sub-sequence is valid in a number of sequences greater than the *minsup* (line 13).
- Otherwise,
  - it removes from the current plan δ the individual grounded operators of the sub-sequence sp, it builds a grounded macro-operator from sp (line 14) and puts it, each time, at a different position in the plan (line 20, 21). It tries δ (line 22) from the calculated initial state S_i for the original plan ρ (line 6). If the result state ϵ is a superset (line 23) of the calculated final state S_g from the original plan ρ (line 6), then it stops trying positions for this sub-sequence. If it finds at least one valid position for the built grounded macro-operator, it stores the modified plan with the lifted macro-operator identifier μ as the key access (line 26) and μ is added to the list of the macro-operators found in the plan (line 27). To analyse new occurrences of an already found macro-operator, the algorithm uses the corresponding modified plan (line 16, 17).

Once it has analysed all combinations of sub-sequences of length l from ρ, it moves to the second loop (line 28). The purpose here is to compute and save or update, the characteristics of each found macro-operator. Thus, it updates the set of plans where the macro-operator with identifier μ appeared (denoted K_o) by adding the index of the current plan *indexPlan* (line 29). Also, it computes and stores the number of occurrences in the plan for the analysed macro-operator (line 30, 31). Finally, if the current macro-operator appears in the plan at least once, the support value is incremented by one (line 33) or added with a value of 1 if it did not appear before (line 35).

The mining procedure gives as a result a set of frequent macro-operators of length l with its respective characteristics. They will be filtered, by using the *minsup* parameter in the main algorithm, before being added to the final set of mined macro-operators.

---

[2] See description in the subsection *Identifier construction*.

Algorithm 1. ERA algorithm - Main algorithm

Input A sequence database A of grounded operators, a sequence database E of ele-
     ments of an operator, a $minsup$ parameter, a gap parameter g and a maximal
     length $maxLength$.
Output A dictionary M of pairs $<m, s>$, m is a macro-operator and s is its support;
     a dictionary K of pairs $< m, k >$ k is the id of the sequence where m appears; a
     dictionary J of pairs $<m, j>$, j is the number of occurrences of the macro-operator
     m for each sequence.
1: **function** MININGMACROS($A, E, minsup, g, maxLength$)
2:      Mo, Ko, Jo ← empty dictionaries
3:      M, K, J ← empty dictionaries
4:      $stop$ ← False, l ← 2
5:      **while** $(l \leq maxLength) \wedge (stop$ is False$)$ **do**
6:          Mo, Ko, Jo ← MINE(A,E,M,l)
7:          $stop$ ← True
8:          **for each** macro-operator m in Mo **do**
9:              **if** support(m) $\geq minsup$ **then**
10:                 $stop \leftarrow False$
11:                 add the key m with value s to M
12:                 add the pair $<m, k>$ to K from Ko
13:                 add the pair $<m, j>$ to J from Jo
14:         increase l by one
15:     **return** M,K,J

Identifier Construction. The identifier construction procedure takes as input
a sub-sequence of grounded operators sp and a length l. Only the first l elements
of sp are kept in this procedure. A string identifier is built as follows. First, each
element e is translated by using E. Next, the first sub-element of each e is
used together with a character representing the operators. After, we use another
character and a incremental number for each other sub-element of e because
they represent the parameters. Notice that the incremental number is reset to
zero with each new identifier construction and a same parameter will have the
same incremental number.

Example 1. Let us consider the length $l = 2$, the sub-sequence {pick-up b, stack
b a, pick-up c} and the element encoding $E = \{1 : pick - up, 2 : b, 3 : stack, 4 :
a, 5 : c\}$. We only keep the first two operators since $l = 2$ and by using E,
we translate them into {1 2, 3 2 4}. We chose the character 'o' to represent
operators and the character 'p' to represent parameters. We obtain the identifier
{o1p0o3p0p1}.

3.4   Complexity Analysis.

The main task of the ERA algorithm is the analysis of a sub-sequence which in
the worst case has a complexity $O(l(\rho))$ where $l(\rho)$ is the length of the plan ρ.
In the case of an infinite gap, this task is repeated for each sub-sequence in a

---

Algorithm 2. Mining macro-operators of length l

Input The sequence database A, the sequence database E, a dictionary M of pairs $< m, s >$, m is a macro-operator and s is its support and a length l and a gap parameter g.

Output A dictionary Mo of pairs $< m, s >$, m is a macro-operator of length l and s is its support; a dictionary Ko of pairs $< m, k >$, k is the id of the sequence where m appears; and a dictionary Jo of key $<m, iP>$, iP is the index of the sequence where m appears, and value j, the number of occurrences of the macro-operator m in each sequence.

```
 1: function MINE(A, E, M, g, l)
 2:     Mo, Ko, Jo ← empty dictionaries
 3:     for each plan ρ in A do
 4:         D, macroPlan ← empty dictionaries
 5:         idsPlan ← {∅}
 6:         S_i, S_g ← calculate initial and final state from ρ
 7:         P ← all combinations of sub-sequences of length l from ρ            ▷ †
 8:         for each ordered sub-sequence sp in P satisfying g do
 9:             if l > 2 then
10:                 if computeId(sp, l − 1) ∉ M then skip sp
11:             else  μ ← computeId(sp, l)
12:                 if len(A)-indexPlan < minsup−supp(μ) then skip sp
13:                 else
14:                     add the key-value < k, {actions(sp)} > to D          ▷ k ∈ Z*_−
15:                     i ← 0
16:                     if μ ∈ macroPlan then
17:                         δ ← macroPlan[μ]
18:                     else  δ ← ρ
19:                     while (not ok)∧(i < len(δ) − len(sp) + 1) do
20:                         remove sp from δ
21:                         insert k in δ in position i
22:                         ε ← execute(S_i, δ)
23:                         if S_g ⊂ ε then ok ← True
24:                         reset δ
25:                     if ok then
26:                         add < μ, δ > to macroPlan
27:                         add μ to idsPlan
28:             for each identifier μ in idsPlans do
29:                 add the key μ with value indexPlan to Ko
30:                 nbA ← (len(ρ)−len(macroPlan[μ])) / (l−1)
31:                 add < μ, indexPlan > with value nbA to Jo
32:                 if (nbA > 0) ∧ (μ in Mo) then
33:                     increase support of μ by one
34:                 else
35:                     if nbA > 0 then add the key μ with value nbA to Mo
36:     return Mo, Ko, Jo
```

† : the combinations keep the order of occurrence in the original plan.

plan, for each plan in the set of solution plans and for each sub-sequence length. In (1), we first compute the number of sub-sequences n_{sp} of length k in a plan ρ of length $l(\rho)$.

$$n_{sp} = \binom{l(\rho)}{k} \tag{1}$$

Then, if n_{MINE} is the number of sub-sequences analysed in a execution of the MINE procedure at length k, we have:

$$n_{MINE} = \sum_{\rho_i \in C} \binom{l(\rho_i)}{k} \tag{2}$$

In the worst case, the ERA algorithm will mine up to the maximal length l_{max}. Considering that all plan lengths are equal to the maximum plan length L, i.e. $L = \max_{\rho_i \in C} l(\rho_i)$, we have N, the total number of sub-sequences analysed given by (3).

$$N = \sum_{\rho_i \in C} \sum_{k=2}^{l_{max}} \binom{L}{k} \tag{3}$$

$$N = O\left(|C| \sum_{k=2}^{l_{max}} O\left(L^k\right)\right) \tag{4}$$

$$N = O\left(|C| L^{l_{max}}\right) \tag{5}$$

From (4), we show in (5) the number of sub-sequences to be analysed. Then, in the worst case with an infinite gap, the complexity is $O\left(|C| L^{l_{max}+1}\right)$, i.e. polynomial in L and linear in the size of the solution plan set C.

In the case of a finite gap g, the analysis of a sub-sequence is repeated for each sub-sequence in a plan satisfying the gap constraint and for each plan and sub-sequence length.

We recall that a sub-sequence $S_A = Y_{e_1}, \ldots, Y_{e_k}$ of a sequence $S_B = Y_1, \ldots, Y_L$ satisfies a gap constraint g if $\forall i \in [2, k], e_i - e_{i-1} \le g + 1$. Notice that the sub-sequence S_A can be uniquely identified by the list of indices $\{e_1, \ldots, e_k\}$ of the elements in S_B, but it can also be equivalently represented as a list $\{e_1, e_2 - e_1, \ldots, e_i - e_{i-1}, \ldots, e_k - e_{k-1}\}$. Under this last representation, one can easily see if a given sub-sequence satisfies the gap constraint. Then the maximal number of sub-sequences N_{gap} with first element Y_{e_1} and length k, can be computed as one plus the biggest number in base $g + 1$ with $k - 1$ digits (see (6)).

$$N_{gap} = 1 + g \sum_{i=0}^{k-2} (g+1)^i = (g+1)^{k-1} \tag{6}$$

In the worst case, the ERA algorithm will mine up to the maximal length l_{max}. Similar to the infinite gap case, we consider that all plan lengths are equal to the maximum plan length L.

In (7), we show that an upper bound on the number N of sub-sequences to be analysed can be computed by considering that for each possible first element $Y_i, i \in [1, L-k]$, k the sub-sequence length, the maximal number of sub-sequences N_{gap} will be analysed.

$$N < \sum_{\rho_i \in C} \sum_{k=2}^{l_{max}} (L - k) N_{gap} \tag{7}$$

$$N = O\left(|C| L (g + 1)^{l_{max} - 1}\right) = O\left(|C| L\right) \tag{8}$$

We show in (8) an upper bound on the number of sub-sequences to be analysed. Then, in the worst case with a finite gap, the complexity is $O\left(|C| L^2\right)$, i.e. quadratic in L and linear in the size of the solution plan set C.

4   Evaluation

In the following, we aim to show the impact of the gap when extracting macro-operators with ERA. For this purpose, we used six benchmarks domains[3] taken from the International Planning competition (IPC-2011): `barman`, `blocksworld`, `depots`, `gripper`, `rover` and `satellite`.

4.1   Experimental Setup

To the best of our knowledge, no open plan database is available. Thus, for each benchmark domain, we generated a set of 50 distinct problem instances using the generators[4] from the International Planning Competition. Then, we solved the problems by using the FastDownward planner with an A* search strategy and the FF heuristic as the evaluator for the h-value. As a result, we obtained a set of 50 sub-optimal solution plans, for each benchmark domain, with a length between 20 and 50 ground operators.

To evaluate the gap impact, for each benchmark, we used ERA with a fixed frequency threshold *minSup* of 0.85, an infinite maximum length and a finite gap varying between 0 and 15 plus the infinite gap case. Experiments were performed on an Intel Core i7-4710MQ quad-core CPU clocked at 2.5 GHz and with 8 GB of RAM.

---

[3] Further details can be found at http://www.plg.inf.uc3m.es/ipc2011-learning/Domains.html.

[4] https://bitbucket.org/planning-tools/pddl-generators.

4.2   Results of the ERA Algorithm

We present in Fig. 2, for each domain, the number of extracted macro-operators as a function of the gap. We observe that the number of extracted macro-operators increase consistently with the gap for all domains. In most domains, a gap of at least 9 was necessary to extract all macro-operators, i.e. the number of extracted macro-operators with an infinite gap. Among the six domains, Barman and Satellite were exceptions. For Barman, all macro-operators were found for all gaps greater or equal to 1. And for Satellite, not all macro-operators were found even with a gap of 15.

We show in Fig. 3, for each domain, the length of the longest macro-operator found as a function of the gap. We observe that our method is able to recover long macros (e.g. a size of 6 for the longest macro in Barman and a size of 5 for the longest macro in Satellite) since we did not have any restriction on macro length. Also, similar to the number of extracted macros, higher gap values allow for longer macros.

Finally, we have in Fig. 4 the time used by ERA to extract macro-operators for each domain, as a function of the gap. We observe that the time increases with the gap. Also, we find two different behaviours: either polynomial, for barman, blocksworld, depots and satellite or almost linear, for gripper and rover. Notice that this behaviour is unrelated to the complexity shown in Sect. 3.4, since the complexity was given in terms of plan length and plan set size.

5   Discussion

The ERA algorithm checks, for each plan, every sub-sequence satisfying the gap constraint. If an infinite gap is used, the algorithm is then guaranteed to find all macro-operators, satisfying the frequency threshold, and all their occurrences. Also, macro-operator occurrences (even non-adjacent occurrences) registered by ERA are valid. Indeed, to be registered, an occurrence must be composed of grounded operators that can be moved contiguously in the analysed plan without impacting its final state or impeding its execution. Finally, if the macro-operator occurrences satisfy the frequency threshold, a macro-operator is built as a contiguous sequence of lifted operators.

Intuitively, one could think that high gap values would not impact significantly the mining results since two distant operators should be less related than two close operators. Indeed, that would be true if the planning system was focused on accomplishing sequentially disconnected groups of sub-goals, e.g. preparing and serving a specific cocktail in barman. However, every plan (even optimal) can be reordered in hundreds or even thousands of different ways from which only a few correspond to a configuration where all disconnected goals are accomplished sequentially. Our results clearly show that mining with a non-zero gap allows to extract much more information. Precisely, in five domains out of six, to extract as much information as an infinite gap, a gap value ranging from 9 to 14 was needed. To the best of our knowledge, our work is the only one focused on the extraction of macro-operators from a set of plans by considering

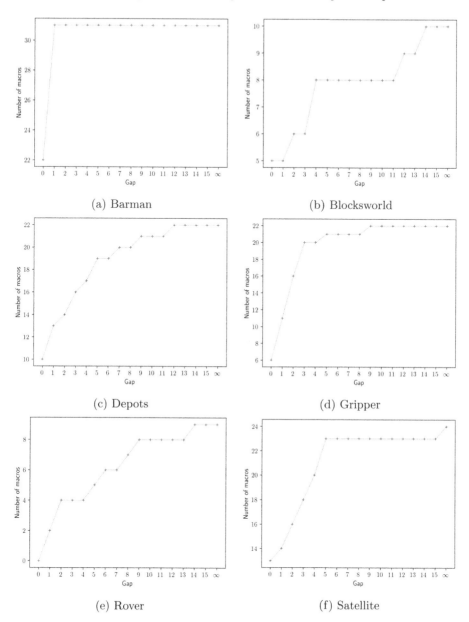

(a) Barman

(b) Blocksworld

(c) Depots

(d) Gripper

(e) Rover

(f) Satellite

Fig. 2. Number of macro-operators extracted for each benchmark domain.

adjacent and non-adjacent operators. Other works also included an approach to handle non-adjacent operators to build macro-operators [2,3]. Botea et al. [2] extract macros from solution graphs of training problems. They enumerate and select sub-graphs from the solution graphs and build one macro for each selected

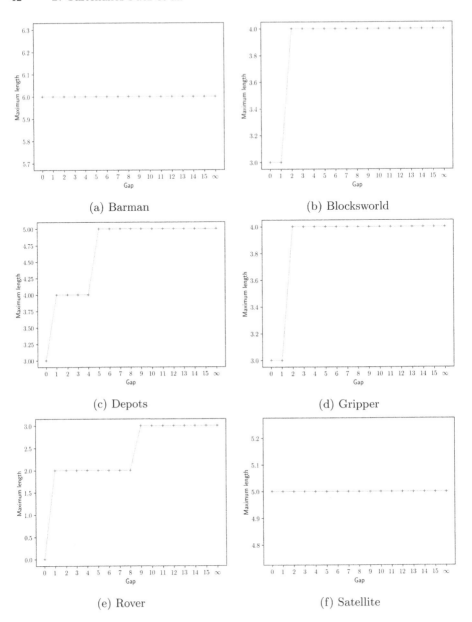

Fig. 3. Maximum length of macro-operators extracted for each benchmark domain.

sub-graph. They introduce a k parameter as the maximal number of operators that can be skipped between the first and the last element of the sub-graph (we can roughly see a sub-graph as a sub-sequence). Their work differs from ours because their handling of the gap does not allow an exhaustive search and can then miss many macro-operator occurrences. Also, they set a hard limit on the

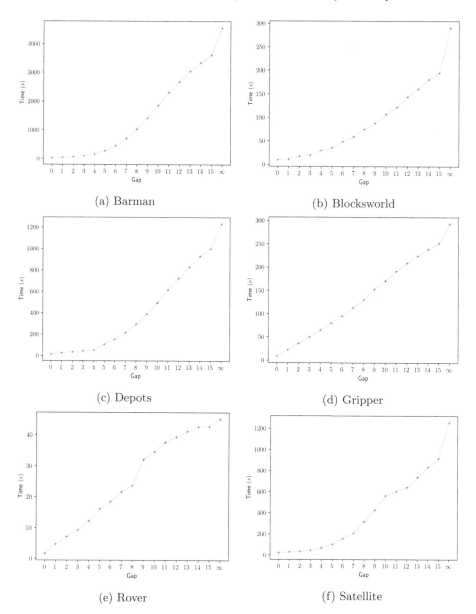

Fig. 4. Time to extract macro-operators using ERA for each benchmark domain.

upper bound of the maximal length of the extracted macro-operators. Chrpa et al. [3] extract macros by iteratively combining operators (even non-adjacent) in plans that share some parameters while keeping the plan valid. However, their technique is not guaranteed to find all macro-operator occurrences.

The macro-operators extracted by ERA can be composed either by repeated operator sequences, e.g. in Depots a macro-operator of length 4 is composed of a repeated sequence of `lift` and `load` operators, or by different operators, e.g. in Barman a macro-operator of length 5 is composed of five different operators.

6   Conclusion

We provided an algorithm to analyse sequences of operators (even non-adjacent) from past solution plans. Precisely, ERA algorithm extracts all macro-operators, satisfying a frequency threshold parameter and under a gap constraint, from existing plans. Our algorithm has a quadratic complexity with a finite gap and a polynomial complexity with an infinite gap. Below, we highlight the advantages of our work:

- *Planner independent*, our algorithm can be used on existing plans from a given domain regardless any domain characteristic or the planner used to obtain those plans.
- *Domain-independent*, our method does not need *a priori* knowledge on the domain.
- *Non-adjacent operators*, we can identify macros from a sequence of adjacent and non-adjacent operators.
- *Completeness*, with an infinite gap our algorithm is guaranteed to find all occurrences of any macro-operator.

Our method has proven to successfully find macro-operators of different lengths for six different benchmark domains. Also, our experiments highlighted the capital role that plays the gap in the extraction of macro-operators.

We see this work as a first step towards a macro-learning method allowing to exploit solution plans. As a future work, we would like to analyse the link between the gap and (1) the correctness of the support and (2) the number of occurrences. More precisely, we would like to investigate if a finite gap could ensure in most cases that all occurrences were found. Another interesting perspective would be to analyse the effect of the gap with plans obtained through different search strategies. Finally, we would like to include ERA in a full macro-learning method including a macro selection phase.

References

1. Botea, A., Enzenberger, M., Müller, M., Schaeffer, J.: Macro-FF: improving AI planning with automatically learned macro-operators. J. Artif. Intelli. Res. **24**, 581–621 (2005)
2. Botea, A., Müller, M., Schaeffer, J.: Learning partial-order macros from solutions. In: Proceedings of the Fifteenth International Conference on International Conference on Automated Planning and Scheduling, pp. 231–240. AAAI Press (2005)

3. Chrpa, L., Vallati, M., McCluskey, T.L.: MUM: a technique for maximising the utility of macro-operators by constrained generation and use. In: Proceedings of the Twenty-Fourth International Conference on Automated Planning and Scheduling (2014)
4. Coles, A., Smith, A.: Marvin: a heuristic search planner with online macro-action learning. J. Artif. Intell. Res. **28**, 119–156 (2007)
5. Dulac, A., Pellier, D., Fiorino, H., Janiszek, D.: Learning useful macro-actions for planning with n-grams. In: 2013 IEEE 25th International Conference on Tools with Artificial Intelligence, pp. 803–810 (2013). https://doi.org/10.1109/ICTAI.2013.123
6. Fikes, R., Nilsson, N.: STRIPS: a new approach to the application of theorem proving to problem solving. Artif. Intell. **3–4**(2), 189–208 (1971)
7. Fournier-Viger, P., Lin, J.C.W., Kiran, R.U., Koh, Y.S., Thomas, R.: A survey of sequential pattern mining. Data Sci. Pattern Recogn. **1**(1), 54–77 (2017)
8. Ghallab, M., Nau, D., Traverso, P.: Automated Planning: Theory and Practice. Elsevier, Amsterdam (2004)
9. Han, J., Pei, J., Kamber, M.: Data Mining: Concepts and Techniques. Elsevier, Amsterdam (2011)
10. Hofmann, T., Niemueller, T., Lakemeyer, G.: Initial results on generating macro actions from a plan database for planning on autonomous mobile robots. In: Twenty-Seventh International Conference on Automated Planning and Scheduling (2017)
11. Newton, M.A.H., Levine, J.: Implicit learning of macro-actions for planning. In: Proceedings of the 19th European Conference on Artificial Intelligence (ECAI 2010) (2010)
12. Vukovic, M., et al.: Towards automated planning for enterprise services: opportunities and challenges. In: Yangui, S., Bouassida Rodriguez, I., Drira, K., Tari, Z. (eds.) ICSOC 2019. LNCS, vol. 11895, pp. 64–68. Springer, Cham (2019). https://doi.org/10.1007/978-3-030-33702-5_6

Deep Neural Network Incorporating CNN and MF for Item-Based Fashion Recommendation

Taku Ito, Issei Nakamura, Shigeki Tanaka, Toshiki Sakai, Takeshi Kato, Yusuke Fukazawa$^{(\boxtimes)}$, and Takeshi Yoshimura$^{(\boxtimes)}$

NTT DOCOMO, INC., Chiyoda, Japan
taku.itou.ws@nttdocomo.com, yusuke.fukazawa@gmail.com

Abstract. In fashion electronic commerce services, two item-based recommendation approaches, image similarity-based and click likelihood-based, are used to improve the revenue of a website. To improve accuracy, in this paper, we propose a hybrid model, a deep neural network (DNN) that predicts click probability of a target fashion item by incorporating both image similarity and click likelihood. To create an image similarity feature, we acquire a latent image feature through a CNN-based classification of fashion color, type and pattern. To create a click likelihood feature, we calculate matrix factorization (MF) and use decomposed item features as latent click log feature. To solve a cold-start problem (recommendation of new items), we complement the latent log features of new items with those of existing ones. An offline evaluation shows that the accuracy of proposed model (both log and image) improved by 14% compared with matrix factorization (log only) and 56% the image-only model. Moreover, the complement of latent log features changes the new item ratio to six times.

Keywords: Fashion recommendation · Item-based recommendation · Deep Neural Network (DNN) · Convolutional Neural Network (CNN) · Matrix factorization

1 Introduction

In fashion electronic commerce (EC) services, the recommender system plays a crucial role in improving the revenue of a website. Especially, item-based recommendation, which is recommendation for a target fashion item on an original item's page, is widely used. Two approaches are mainly used in item-based recommendation: appearance similarity-based and click likelihood-based. Appearance similarity-based recommendation recommends items that look similar to the original one based on calculated image similarity [8,15,18]. Many studies have proposed derivative forms of DNN models such as convolutional neural network (CNN). These studies recommend similar items from the viewpoint of appearance and do not consider user interest that is hidden in click logs. We

© Springer Nature Switzerland AG 2021
H. Uehara et al. (Eds.): PKAW 2020, LNAI 12280, pp. 46–57, 2021.
https://doi.org/10.1007/978-3-030-69886-7_4

hypothesize that users want to click on recommended items for two reasons: one is to look for exactly the same appearance with different metadata (brand, cost etc.), and the other is to look for items whose images are not exactly the same but have slightly different taste. Appearance similarity-based recommendation can cover for the former's needs but not the latter. On the contrary, click log similarity-based recommendation recommends items that are likely to be clicked on or bought using users' clicking or buying logs [4,19]. However, this approach has a drawback of not being able to recommend new items. This problem is more serious in the fashion field, because new fashion items appear one after another on a daily basis [14]; new fashion items reflect seasonality and trend so users tend to purchase them; and the number of stocks of existing items is limited compared with digital contents. Therefore, except for log, other information such as image features must be considered to recommend new items.

From the above-mentioned background, two requirements must be satisfied in item-based recommendation for fashion EC websites. One is recommendation of items with high click probability for accuracy, and the other is recommendation of new items for novelty. Accuracy and novelty are usually in a trade-off relationship; hence, both of them must be maintained. We satisfy both requirements by constructing a DNN model that incorporates both image similarity and click likelihood. We use the output of middle layers of the three CNN models for fashion attribute classification as latent image feature. We represent images by fashion color (e.g., red/blue), type (e.g., skirt/t-shirt) and pattern (e.g., stripe/check) using a CNN-based classification model. We create latent log features calculated by MF as click likelihood feature. As we cannot output MF-based features for new items, we thus, propose a method to complement for the MF-based features of new items by selecting an item whose image features are closest to those of the new item and replacing the latent log features of the item with those of the new item.

Contributions of this study are as follows:

1. Propose a DNN model that considers both latent log and latent image features. We calculate item latent log features by MF. We represent latent image features acquired through CNN-based classification of fashion color, type and pattern.
2. Propose a method that recommends new items without log by complementing with the latent log feature of new items using an item whose latent image features are closest to those of new items.
3. An offline evaluation shows that the accuracy of proposed model (both log and image) exhibits best score (0.025) between MF (0.022) and the image-only model (0.017). As for the new item ratio, the proposed method also shows best score (0.19) compared with MF + complementation (0.19) and image-only model (0.16). We show that the proposed method achieves recommendation of novel items while maintaining accuracy.

We describe related works in Sect. 2. We present details of our proposed method in Sect. 3. We describe experiments in Sect. 4. We conclude this paper in Sect. 5.

2 Related Works

Fashion recommendation can be classified into two types: one is outfit recommendation, which is used to recommend several combinations of clothes that look good from a set of clothes [1,5,6,9,16,17,21], and the other is item-based recommendation, which is used to recommend other products that are likely to be bought by users interested in an original item [2,3,8,10,15,18]. This research targets the latter type of recommendation.

2.1 Outfit Recommendation

Appearance of items is key in fashion recommendation. He et al. [6] proposed a model that can recommend new items without logs and consider how items look by combining latent and visual factors as item feature. Yu et al. [21] used "the aesthetic score" learned from using an aesthetic visual analysis dataset containing 250,000 images with aesthetic ratings to recommend aesthetic items. Meanwhile, Guo et al. [5] proposed a cross-category recommendation model that considered visual compatibility that is calculated by the Siamese CNN. Packer et al. [16] proposed a recommendation that models the dynamics of an individual user's visual preferences. In addition, Agarwal et al. [1] proposed a personalized similar item recommendation by learning user-item interactions.

2.2 Item-Based Recommendation

Here we describe image-similarity based recommendation. Huang et al. [8] proposed a dual attribute-aware ranking network for retrieval feature learning to retrieve same or attribute-similar clothing items from online shopping stores when given a user photo depicting a clothing image. Wang et al. [18] proposed a framework to tackle the problem of automatic clothing search in consumer photos when photos are usually taken under completely uncontrolled realistic imaging conditions by leveraging the low-level (e.g., color) and high-level features of clothes. Manfredi et al. [15] proposed a general approach for automatic segmentation, color-based retrieval and classification of garments in fashion store databases, exploiting shape and color information.

Click log similarity-based recommendation is recommendation of items that are likely to be clicked on or bought by using user clicking or buying logs [4,19]. Most of relevant studies have adopted traditional approaches such as extended matrix factorization (MF) [7].

3 Methodology

Algorithm 1 presents the proposed fashion recommendation procedure. The proposed algorithm consists of two phases: the first one is offline training phase and the second is recommendation phase. We detailed both phases in Sect. 3.1 and 3.2.

Algorithm 1: Fashion Recommendation Algorithm

Input:

$a_i \in A$ denotes image (RGB) of item i.

$b_{u,i} \in B$ denotes click log whether user (or session) u clicked item i (=1) or not (=0).

$c_{i,j} \in C$ denotes click log whether item j was clicked (=1) or not (=0) at item i's page.

Output:

$s_{i,j} \in S$ denotes click probability of item j on item i's page.

Notations:

k_i denotes features of item i.

$f(a_i)$ denotes function that outputs latent image features of a_i by CNN.

$g(B,i)$ denotes function that outputs latent log features of item i computed by matrix factorization with input of user-item click log matrix B.

$h(k_i, k_j)$ denotes function that outputs click probability of item j on item i's page computed by DNN with input of item feature k_i and k_j.

$sim(a_i, a_j)$ denotes function that outputs similarity of images between item i and item j.

Procedure:

1) Offline training phase:

  for all item $i \in I_{training}$ (training item set)

    $k_i = \{f(a_i), g(B,i)\}$

  for all pairs of items $i \in I_{training}$ and $j \in I_{training}$

    minimize $e = c_{i,j} - h(k_i, k_j)$

2) Item recommendation phase:

  for all pairs of item $i \in I_{training}$ and $j \in I_{target}$ (recommendation item set)

    $k_i = \{f(a_i), g(B,i)\}$

    if item $j \in I_{training}$

      $k_j = \{f(a_j), g(B,j)\}$

    else

      $k_j = \{f(a_j), g(B,m)\}$ where $m = \underset{m}{\arg\min} \, sim(a_j, a_m)$

    $s_{i,j} = h(k_i, k_j)$

3.1   Offline Training Phase

Figure 1 shows the outline of offline training phase. In this step, we create latent image and latent log features using MF and the CNN model and train DNN by click history.

Latent Image Features. In general, image data is extremely high-dimensional. As is well known as the curse of dimensionality, increase in the number of features causes overlearning, which makes it difficult to improve generalization performance. To solve this problem, we reduce the dimensionality by feature selection and dimensionality reduction. In recent years, a number of methods have been studied to use the intermediate layer of deep learning trained in the image classification problem as a method of dimensionality compression [13,20]. Kavukcuoglu et al. [11] and Zeiler et al. [22] show that common image features

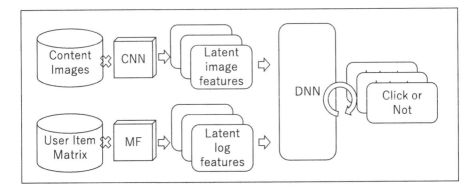

Fig. 1. Overview of offline training step. We create latent log and latent image features using MF and CNN model and train DNN by click history.

such as line segments and points are learned in the intermediate layer. Therefore, in this paper, in order to extract fashion-specific latent image features, the intermediate layer is extracted as a feature from deep neural networks that learn the classification problem of clothing color, type and pattern.

We will explain here how to extract latent image features. When extracting image features, the model must learn what users focus on when viewing related items. We assumed here that the point was "fashion color (e.g., red/blue)/fashion type (e.g., skirt/t-shirt)/fashion pattern (e.g., stripe/check)" and constructed a CNN model to classify these elements and use middle layers of the model as latent image feature.

Figure 2 shows the model. The input is images of the item, and each model predicts the item's fashion type, color and pattern. Each model consists of five convolutional layers followed by three fully connected layers and finally output a one-hot vector. We train these CNN models using the dataset from fashion EC site "d fashion" provided by NTT DOCOMO, Inc. We label the type/ color/ pattern for each item (e.g., blue stripe t-shirt). We prepare about 100,000 labeled items and train three CNN models independently. We extracted latent image features from the middle layer, thereby enabling obtainment of features that indicate the color, type and pattern of the item with rich information.

We use CaffeNet[1], which is one of the deep learning frameworks, to learn each classification model of color, type and pattern. The parameters are optimized using the SGD (stochastic gradient descent) method. In FC (Fully Connected) 6, 7, and 8 layers, the number of dimensions of FC7 layer is changed from the default 4,096 dimensions to 1,024 dimensions and this is used as latent image features. Since there are three models, the image feature amount is $1,024 \times 3 = 3,072$ dimensions.

---

[1] https://caffe.berkeleyvision.org/.

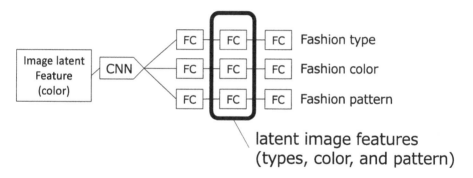

Fig. 2. We extract middle layers of three classification models as latent image feature.

Latent Log Features. We used MF when extracting latent log features. We assumed that users tend to click on related items from currently viewed ones. Assuming that similar users clicked these items, we used the item latent log features obtained by MF as latent log feature. We created a user-item click log matrix $R(M \times N)$ with rows of users and columns of items from the log. We decomposed the matrix into a user matrix $U(M \times K)$ and an item matrix $P(N \times K)$ by MF. As a result of the decomposition, a $P_j(K \times 1)$ vector is generated for item j.

Learning DNN Model. In this section, we will explain the recommendation model using extracted features. Figure 3 illustrates the model. The model input each feature of the pair of original and target items and then calculated the score of the pair. In the learning phase, if some users browsed from the original item to the target item in the past, the model learns the score as 1, otherwise as 0. By learning this score, it is able to learn which items users tend to click on from currently viewed items.

In DNN, we take both latent image features and latent log feature of the original item i and the recommended target item j as input. The number of input dimensions is $3 \times 2 \times 1024$-dimensional features output by CNN and $2 \times K$-dimensional vector by MF. Here we use $K=16$. For the latent image feature input, the dimensions of latent image features are reduced with three dense layers (1024, 256 and 16 dimensions). After that, 6×16 dimensions are combined and finally made into 16 dimensions through the dense layer. For the latent log feature input, the inner product of the latent log feature of the original item and that of the target item is calculated. Finally, we calculate summation of the 16-dimensional vector and the result of inner product to output the click probability. We learn the network weights of the DNN with the ground truth whether the target item j was clicked (=1) or not (=0) on the original item page i. We used Adam [12] for optimization.

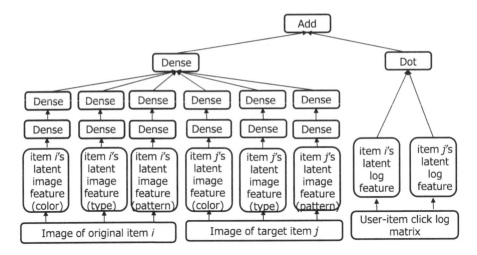

Fig. 3. DNN model is learned using both latent image features and latent log feature of the original item i and the recommended target item j as input.

3.2 Item Recommendation Phase

In the item recommendation phase, we recommend items j to be displayed on their own page i. Here we suppose item i exists in a training set. On the other hand, we suppose that a set of recommendation target items includes new items that do not exist in the training set. As for item j in the training set, we can calculate both image and latent log features, and then calculate click probability. On the other hand, as for new item j which does not exist in the training set, we can calculate latent image feature, but we cannot calculate latent log feature as nobody clicked on the item beforehand. To complement latent log feature, we use an item whose latent image features are most similar to those of item j.

4   Experiments

We conducted an experiment using the logs collected from fashion EC website "d fashion" operated by NTT DOCOMO, Inc. to evaluate the effectiveness of proposed model. First, we will explain the dataset we experimented on, then the evaluation methodology and finally the evaluation results.

4.1 Datasets

On "d fashion," many logs are not associated with a user ID, because users can browse without a user account. Therefore, in this study, we treated a session ID linked with cookie data as a user unit. The lifetime of a cookie was treated as one session. Table 1 lists the basic statistics of the dataset.

Table 1. Basic statistics of the fashion item dataset

Timespan	Training: 1st Nov 2018 – 30th Nov 2018 Test: 1st Dec 2018 – 16th Dec 2018
# of Products	280,076
# of Sessions	228,495
# of Logs	9,407,223

4.2 Evaluation Method

We conducted the experiments having two viewpoints; the first is of recommendation accuracy, and the second is of novelty (degree of new item recommendation). The model is also required to be able to recommend new items without losing accuracy in fashion EC websites.

We explain here the evaluation metrics of the first viewpoint. As eight items are displayed as similar on "d fashion," the model calculated eight most similar items from the session, and we evaluated whether or not these items were actually clicked on next. We specifically used MAP@8 and AUC score as evaluation methodologies. The AUC score indicates that items with higher recommendation score were actually clicked, while MAP@8 is the probability that one of the recommended items was actually clicked on.

We then explain the evaluation methodology of the second viewpoint here. As an indicator of novelty, we evaluate whether we are able to recommend content that users have not yet seen. As described in the previous section, because of the different time periods covered by training data and test data, there is new release content in test data that does not exist in the training data. We evaluate whether we are able to recommend new release content that only exists in the test data among the eight items recommendation. Specifically from the eight items obtained by the model, evaluation was made according to the ratio of items that did not exist in the training data.

4.3 Comparison Methods

We compared the following models to verify the effects of using latent log and latent image features and complement latent log features by latent image features:

1. Popularity (POP): items are ranked according to their popularity.
2. Image-only: items are ranked by latent image feature cosine distance with the original image.
3. MF: items are ranked by the cosine distance of log features obtained by MF with the original item.
4. MF + complement: items are ranked by the cosine distance of log features obtained by MF with the original item. the latent log features of new items are complemented by the item with most similar latent image features.

5. DNN: the model described in Sect. 3.1 using log and latent image features. We do zero padding to the log feature of new items.
6. DNN + complement (proposed): the model described in Sect. 3.1 using log and latent image features. The latent log features of new items are complemented by the items whose latent image features are closest.

Table 2 shows comparison of models from four viewpoints.

Table 2. Comparison methods

Model	Use latent log feature	Use latent image feature	Complement latent log feature
POP	No	No	No
Image-only	No	Yes	No
MF	Yes	No	No
MF + complement	No	No	Yes
DNN	Yes	Yes	No
DNN + complement (proposed)	Yes	Yes	Yes

4.4 Performance

We present results and discuss our findings here. The following are obtained from the results shown in Table 3.

Table 3. Evaluation results

Model	MAP@8	AUC	New item ratio
POP	0.020	0.68	0
Image only	0.017	0.71	0.16
MF (log only)	0.022	0.66	0
MF + complementation	0.022	0.7	0.19
DNN	0.025	0.71	0.03
DNN + complementation	0.025	0.71	0.19

1. The MAP@8 of the DNN (0.025) increased by 14% compared with MF (0.022), and AUC of the DNN (0.71) increased by 8% compared with MF (0.66). The MAP@8 of the DNN also increased by 56% compared with the image-only model (0.017). These results indicate that considering the log and latent image features is key in fashion recommendation.

2. The new item ratio of the DNN + complement (19%) was six times compared to that of the DNN (3.0%), while that of the MF + complement was 19%. Meanwhile, that of the MF was 0%. The accuracy of the complement model was still maintained.

As can be from the above findings, we have shown that the proposed method achieves the recommendation of novel items while maintaining accuracy. Figure 4 displays five items similar to the original item. The image-only model exhibited items that looked similar to the original item. On the contrary, many items that looked completely different from the original item were displayed by MF because it used only the latent log features for similarity calculation. The DNN model displayed candidates with a mixture of similar and non-similar appearances, which was considered to improve accuracy by broadly matching the user's interest.

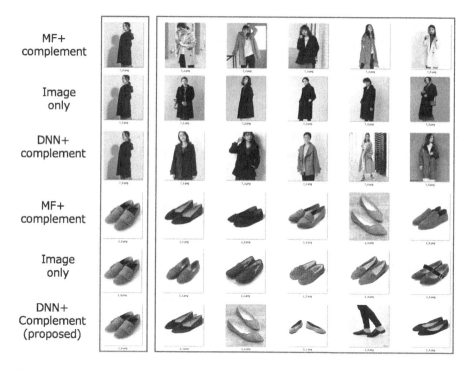

Fig. 4. Results of recommended items for query items are shown. Upper results are for color black women's coat, while those below are for brown shoes. (Color figure online)

4.5   Online Evaluation

This model has been adapted to the online test in real e-commerce service "d fashion" from April 2019. We have tuned the model several times by correction of brand bias in recommended items and narrowing down of candidates using latent image features. We are going to show the result of model tuning in the workshop.

5   Conclusion

Many fashion EC websites have recommended items in recent years. In item-based fashion recommendations, no studies have considered image similarity and user click logs in the DNN framework. Here we constructed a CNN model for extracting latent image features representing three elements (color/type/pattern) that are considered to be important when users select items. We also used MF to extract latent log features to learn which items are often clicked on after currently viewed items. The log features of new items were then complemented with the item with similar latent image features to recommend new ones. We also constructed a pair of original item and candidate items that were browsed on next and built a model to calculate click probability. With this model, the accuracy was improved compared with the model that used only images/logs. In addition, the proposed model was able to recommend new items. In the future, we would like to incorporate user feature and time-series data to the model.

References

1. Agarwal, P., Vempati, S., Borar, S.: Personalizing similar product recommendations in fashion e-commerce. ArXiv abs/1806.11371 (2018)
2. Bell, S., Bala, K.: Learning visual similarity for product design with convolutional neural networks. ACM Trans. Graph. **34**, 98:1–98:10 (2015)
3. Boureau, Y.L., Bach, F.R., LeCun, Y., Ponce, J.: Learning mid-level features for recognition. In: 2010 IEEE Computer Society Conference on Computer Vision and Pattern Recognition, pp. 2559–2566 (2010)
4. Fard, K., Nilashi, M., Salim, N.: Recommender system based on semantic similarity. Int. J. Electr. Comput. Eng. (IJECE), **3** (2013)
5. Guo, H., Tang, R., Ye, Y., Li, Z., He, X.: Deepfm: a factorization-machine based neural network for CTR prediction. In: Proceedings of the 26thInternational Joint Conference on Artificial Intelligence, pp. 1725–1731. IJCAIf17, AAAI Press (2017)
6. He, R., McAuley, J.: VBPR: Visual Bayesian personalized ranking from implicit feedback. In: AAAI, pp. 144–150 (2016)
7. Hu, Y., Koren, Y., Volinsky, C.: Collaborative filtering for implicit feedback datasets. In: 2008 Eighth IEEE International Conference on Data Mining, pp. 263–272 (2008)
8. Huang, J., Feris, R., Chen, Q., Yan, S.: Cross-domain image retrieval with a dual attribute-aware ranking network. In: 2015 IEEE International Conference on Computer Vision (ICCV), pp. 1062–1070 (2015)
9. Iwata, T., Watanabe, S., Sawada, H.: Fashion coordinates recommender system using photographs from fashion magazines. In: Proceedings of the Twenty-Second International Joint Conference on Artificial Intelligence, pp. 2262–2267 (2011)
10. Jing, Y., et al.: Visual search at pinterest, pp. 1889–1898 (2015)
11. Kavukcuoglu, K., Sermanet, P., lan Boureau, Y., Gregor, K., Mathieu, M., Cun, Y.L.: Learning convolutional feature hierarchies for visual recognition. Adv. Neural Inf. Process. Syst. **23**, 1090–1098 (2010)
12. Kingma, D.P., Ba, J.: Adam: a method for stochastic optimization. In: 3rd International Conference on Learning Representations, ICLR (2015)

13. Kiros, R., Salakhutdinov, R., Zemel, R.: Multimodal neural language models. In: Proceedings of the 31st International Conference on International Conference on Machine Learning, ICMLf14 (2014)
14. Kula, M.: Metadata embeddings for user and item cold-start recommendations. In: CBRecSys@RecSys 2015 (2015)
15. Manfredi, M., Grana, C., Calderara, S., Cucchiara, R.: A complete system for garment segmentation and color classification. J. Mach. Vis. Appl. **25**(4), 955–969 (2014)
16. Packer, C., McAuley, J.J., Ramisa, A.: Visually-aware personalized recommendation using interpretable image representations. ArXiv abs/1806.09820 (2018)
17. Sembium, V., Rastogi, R., Saroop, A., Merugu, S.: Recommending product sizes to customers. In: Proceedings of the Eleventh ACM Conference on Recommender Systems (2017)
18. Wang, X., Zhang, T.: Clothes search in consumer photos via color matching and attribute learning. In: Proceedings of the 19th ACM International Conference on Multimedia, pp. 1353–1356 (2011)
19. Ying, Y.: The personalized recommendation algorithm based on item semantic similarity. In: Communication Systems and Information Technology, pp. 999–1004 (2011)
20. Yosinski, J., Clune, J., Bengio, Y., Lipson, H.: How transferable are features in deep neural networks? Adv. Neural Inf. Process. Syst. **27**, 3320–3328 (2014)
21. Yu, W., Zhang, H., He, X., Chen, X., Xiong, L., Qin, Z.: Aesthetic-based clothing recommendation. In: WWW (2018)
22. Zeiler, M.D., Fergus, R.: Visualizing and understanding convolutional networks. In: Fleet, D., Pajdla, T., Schiele, B., Tuytelaars, T. (eds.) ECCV 2014. LNCS, vol. 8689, pp. 818–833. Springer, Cham (2014). https://doi.org/10.1007/978-3-319-10590-1_53

C-LIME: A Consistency-Oriented LIME for Time-Series Health-Risk Predictions

Taku Ito$^{(\boxtimes)}$, Keiichi Ochiai, and Yusuke Fukazawa

NTT DOCOMO, INC., Tokyo, Japan
taku.itou.ws@nttdocomo.com

Abstract. Predicting health risk from electronic health records (EHRs) is increasingly demanded in the medical and health fields. Many studies have pursued prediction accuracy while ignoring the interpretability of their developed models. To encourage lifestyle changes by patients and employees, an appropriate explanation of why the model outputs high risk is as important as accurately predicting the health risk. In this study, we construct 33 predictive models (11 health-checkup items checked after one, two, and three years). We also clarify a problem in the existing Local Interpretable Model-agnostic Explanations (LIME), namely, inconsistency among the health-risk predictions of the three target years. To resolve this problem, we find and exclude an anomalous sample that deteriorate the interpretation, and output a consistent interpretation of the health-risk predictions over the three years. We evaluate proposed method using more than 10,000 medical examination data. Accuracy was improved by 16% at the maximum compared to the baseline that output the risk at year $Y + 1,2,3$ equaling to that at year Y. Also, proposed LIME called C-LIME improve number of employees whom we can provide consistent lifestyle advice over the years three times compared to LIME. We have released a health-risk prediction and lifestyle recommendation service using proposed method for employees of the Nippon Telegraph and Telephone Group from April of 2019.

Keywords: Health-risk prediction · LIME · Health-checkup data

1 Introduction

The amount of digital information stored in electronic health records (EHRs) has exploded over the past decade [23]. This growth has been accompanied by an expansion of research and business applications related to EHR data mining. Yadav et al. [24] reviewed the major application areas of EHR mining, namely, understanding the natural history of disease, cohort identification, risk prediction [9], biomarker discovery, adverse event detection, and constructing evidence-based guidelines.

Under Japanese governmental law, companies are required to conduct annual health check-ups of their employees. In recent years, the records of these check-ups have provided the data for promoting the health of employees. Like the

© Springer Nature Switzerland AG 2021
H. Uehara et al. (Eds.): PKAW 2020, LNAI 12280, pp. 58–69, 2021.
https://doi.org/10.1007/978-3-030-69886-7_5

EHR data, employee health-checkup data are valuable because they are the historical records of many employees collected over many years. Accordingly, health-risk prediction models based on EHR or periodical health check-up data are actively sought. For example, Kanegae et al. developed a risk-prediction model for new-onset hypertension using the 2005–2016 health-checkup data of 18,258 individuals [13]. However, prediction models based on machine learning are often black boxes that do not explain why the displayed health risk was predicted. To improve employees' awareness of their risk and encourage lifestyle changes, the prediction result must be convincing and the underlying cause must be clearly understood.

Some researchers have proposed machine learning methods that output an interpretable result from the prediction model. However, the existing interpretation approach employs simple models such as linear regression. The integration of the prediction and interpretation models introduces an inevitable trade-off between accuracy of prediction and ease of interpretation. This problem has been resolved by a concept called explainable artificial intelligence (XAI). In XAI models such as Local Interpretable Model-agnostic Explanations (LIME) [21] and Shapley value solutions [14], the prediction and interpretation models are learned independently. Such models improve the interpretability without lowering the prediction accuracy.

In this study, we develop an interpretable health-risk prediction model that recommends changes in lifestyle habits that will benefit health several years later. First, we construct prediction models of employee at year $Y + N$ ($N = 1, 2$ and 3) by inputting the health examination result of the employee at year Y. Then, for each of 1,2 and 3 year forecast models, we construct interpretation model to interpret the health risk using XAI. However, we face the interpretation problem between models caused by XAI. As we create multiple different models for each of 1, 2 and 3 year, there is a possibility that the explanations will be inconsistent among those models. Here, we assume to interpret the reason why an employee's BMI increases using amount of alcohol consumption. There is a possibility that one-year forecast model explains that BMI increases when the amount of drinking increases, whereas the two-year forecast model explains that BMI increases when the amount of drinking decreases. This is caused by sparseness of the health examination datasets. If there are few samples near target employee in a training dataset of one of the 3 forecast target years, the interpretation model is more likely to be distorted by anomalous samples. As a result, there have a possibility to output inconsistent interpretation between health risk predictive models of three forecast target years.

The contributions of this paper are as follows:

1. We construct $11 \times 3 = 33$ predictive models consisting of 11 health-checkup items and three target years (i.e. health risk assessments after one, two, and three years), and evaluate it using more than 10,000 medical examination data. Accuracy was improved by 16% at the maximum compared to the baseline that output the risk at year $Y + 1,2,3$ equaling to that at year Y.

2. We clarify that LIME outputs inconsistent results of the same employee during the first, second, and third target years.
3. We solve the LIME problem by finding and excluding the anomalous samples that deteriorate the interpretation, and thereby output a consistent interpretation among the health-risk predictive models of the three target years. Proposed LIME called C-LIME improve number of employees whom we can provide consistent lifestyle advice over the years three times compared to LIME.
4. We release a health-risk prediction and lifestyle recommendation service for employees of the NTT Group. The service combines C-LIME with a health-risk prediction algorithm.

The remainder of this paper is constructed as follows. Related works are reviewed in Sect. 2. Section 3 explains our risk-prediction model, and presents our proposed consistency-oriented LIME (C-LIME). In Sect. 4, we describe evaluation results on both accuracy and interpretation of health risk prediction. In Sect. 5, we describe the service using C-LIME. We conclude this paper in Sect. 6.

2   Related Works

This section explains the related research on risk prediction based on electronic health records and explainable artificial intelligence.

2.1   Risk Prediction Based on Electronic Health Records (EHRs)

Rahimian et al. developed machine learning models for predicting first emergency admissions using the electronic health records of 4.6 million patients [19]. Chen et al. proposed a multimodal disease-risk-prediction algorithm based on a convolutional neural network (CNN)-based, which uses the structured and unstructured data from hospitals [4]. Huang et al. [12] developed a regularized stacked denoising auto-encoder model that stratifies the clinical risks of patients with acute coronary syndrome. To build the training model, they accessed a large volume of electronic health records. Kanegae et al. developed a risk-prediction model for new-onset hypertension using XGBoost, and tested it on the 2005–2016 health-checkup data of 18,258 individuals [13]. Pham et al. introduced an end-to-end deep dynamic neural network that infers current illness states from medical records and previous illness histories, and predicts the future medical outcomes [18]. Cheng et al. proposed a deep learning approach that predicts chronic disease occurrence from patient EHRs [5]. Suo et al. also predicted the risk of potential diseases from EHRs by incorporating the prior medical knowledge into predictive models [15]. Rajkomar et al. showed that by representing patients' entire raw EHR records using deep learning methods, multiple medical events can be accurately predicted [20]. The unsupervised deep-feature learning method of Miotto et al. [16] derives a general-purpose patient representation from EHR data, which facilitates clinical predictive modeling. Nguyen et al. presented an end-to-end deep learning system that extracts features from medical records and automatically predicts the future risk [17].

2.2   Explainable Artificial Intelligence (XAI)

In the business context, a prediction model must be both accurate and interpretable. To resolve the trade-off between these equally important requirements, some researchers have proposed that the interpretation model be separated from the prediction model. This method improves the interpretability without lowering the prediction accuracy. In addition, consumer analysis should provide not only precise predictions, but also the reasons for each user prediction. Hall et al. [10] recognized three types of explainable machine learning methods. The first type outputs the feature importance, and includes gradient-based feature attribution [1] and the Shapley values [14]. The second type outputs a surrogate classification or regression results, and includes decision tree variants [3], Craven and Shavlik tree-structured representations [6], anchors [22], and LIME [21]. The third type outputs visualizations of trained model predictions, and includes accumulated local effects [2], partial dependence [11], and individual conditional expectation [8].

2.3   Summary

As revealed in the above review, most of the current researches focus on improving the accuracy of health-risk prediction models using state-of-the-art machine learning technologies such as deep learning. As a research topic, the interpretability of predictive models is only just emerging [7], and the inconsistency problem among the interpretabilities of different target years in health-risk prediction has not been discussed.

Table 1. Risk thresholds of official health indicators

Inspection items	Risk threshold
BMI	25-
Diastolic blood pressure	85-
Systolic blood pressure	130-
Neutral fat	149-
GOT	35-
GPT	35-
HDL cholesterol	40-
LDL cholesterol	140-
γ-GTP	50-
Uric acid	7-
Fasting blood sugar	100-

3   Proposed Method

3.1   Health-Risk Prediction Algorithm

To predict the health risk of employee u in year $Y + N$ ($N = 1$, 2 and 3) from the records of 11 health inspection items, we inputted the health examination results of employee u at year Y. The explanatory variables were the 11 health-checkup items and the responses to a lifestyle questionnaire (13 items) in year Y. The binary classification problem determined whether or not the level of each of the 11 health inspection items posed a health risk in years $Y + 1$, $Y + 2$, and $Y + 3$. To define the risk value, we referred to the health guidance judgment values[1] of the Ministry of Health, Labor, and Welfare. The risk levels of each health inspection item are listed in Table 1. As the learning model, we employed Python's library XGBoost. We set the space of parameter maxdepth of the library as {2,3,4,5} and the space of parameter subsample as {0.2,0.4,0.8,0.95}, and automatically searched for the optimum parameter value using Python's library called GridSearchCV.

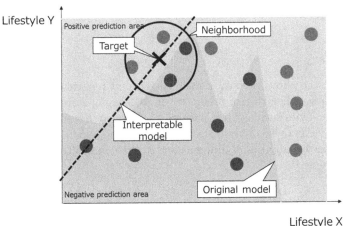

Fig. 1. Explanation of LIME. Shown are the classification results of body mass index (BMI) risk after one year of following lifestyles X and Y. LIME determines the target point and interprets the points in its vicinity to explain whether lifestyle A or B significantly decreases the BMI risk. Blue and red circles indicate negative and positive BMI risk, respectively. The boundary between the red and blue areas is the positive-negative classification boundary obtained by the learning model. (Color figure online)

3.2   Interpretation of Health-Risk Prediction by LIME

This section explains interpretation of health-risk prediction by LIME. Figure 1 visualizes the classification results of the body mass index (BMI) risk one year after following lifestyles X and Y, predicted by XGBoost as the learning model. When the classification boundary line separating the positive and negative risks is nonlinear, as in Fig. 1, the lifestyle factors that largely contribute to the BMI value are not easily interpreted. LIME first extracts a target data point and the

[1] https://www.jpm1960.org/exam/exam01/exam15.html.

points in its vicinity, and performs a linear regression analysis of those points. The resulting linear regression model (interpretation model) reveals the explanatory variables that greatly contribute to the prediction among the combinations of explanatory variables and partial regression coefficients. Note that the generated interpretation model depends on the selection of the target data. In other words, employees can personally interpret the important lifestyles that reduce the BMI risk.

Algorithm 1: C-LIME. We added (1), (2) and (3) to the algorithm of original LIME [21].

Require:
    Classifier f, Number of samples N
    Instance x, and its interpretable version x'
    Similarity kernel π_x, length of explanation K
Procedure:
    $Z \leftarrow \{\}$
    for $i \in \{1, 2, 3, ..., N\}$ **do**
        $z_i' \leftarrow sample\_around(x')$
        $\alpha = f(x' + \Delta(z_i' - x)) - f(x') \cdots \cdot(1)$
        $\beta = f(z_i') - f(x') \cdots \cdots \cdots \cdots (2)$
        if $\text{sgn}(\alpha) = \text{sgn}(\beta) \cdots \cdots \cdots \cdots \cdot(3)$
            $Z \leftarrow Z \cup \langle z_i', f(z_i), \pi_x(z_i) \rangle$
        end if
    end for
    $w \leftarrow$ K-Lasso(Z, K) with z_i' as features, $f(z)$ as target
    return w

3.3 C-LIME: Consistently Explainable LIME

The interpretation model built by LIME depends on the data points near the target data. If the nearby dataset includes points that are extremely deviated from the general tendency in the neighboring dataset, the model will be distorted. For example, suppose that the nearby dataset contains the data of one employee whose BMI declined after a sudden illness, regardless of lifestyle (X or Y). In this case, the interpretation model created by LIME will not provide a correct recommendation for lifestyle improvement.

To solve this problem, our C-LIME check whether interpretation model around target sample will be distorted by overfitting to anomalous samples. We show the procedure in Algorithm 1. First, for each of the neighboring sample candidates z_i' around target sample x', we compute the change in the output of the prediction model when moving a small amount from x' to z_i' by $\alpha = f(x' + \Delta(z_i' - x')) - f(x')$. α represents the general dynamics of prediction model around target sample x'. We assume this general dynamics is consistent around target sample even if the target year is different. Second, we compute the difference between the outputs of the prediction models for x' and z'_i by $\beta = f(z'_i) - f(x')$. β represents the specific dynamics of the prediction model between x' and z'_i. If the specific dynamics β is equals to general dynamics of α, we consider the neighboring sample z'_i follow the general tendency around x'. Otherwise, we consider the neighboring sample is extremely deviated from the general tendency. Here, we regard the sign of β that does not match that of α as an anomalous sample that distorts interpretation model around target sample by overfitting. We exclude the candidate data from the sample when generating the interpretation model. Figure 2 shows a comparison between the interpretation model that includes the anomalous samples generated by LIME and the interpretation model that excludes the anomalous samples calculated by C-LIME. In the figure on the left, an interpretation model that is significantly different from the prediction model is generated due to the overfitting to anomalous sample. On the other hand, in the right figure, by removing the anomalous that cause overfitting, we can obtain an interpretation model close to the prediction model.

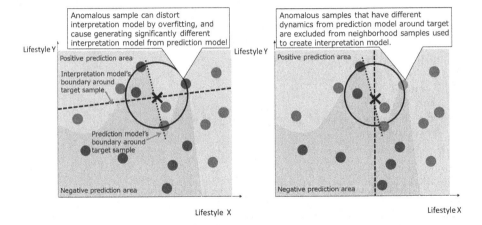

Fig. 2. Left: Explanation of the LIME problem. The anomalous sample distorts the interpretation. Right: Solution to the LIME problem. After removing the anomalous sample, the interpretation model approximates the prediction model.

4   Evaluation

4.1   Accuracy of Health-Risk Prediction Model

We evaluated our prediction models on the medical examination data of employees with 4 consecutive years (more than 10,000 data points) owned by NTT DOCOMO, Inc. As the baseline case, we assumed that the risk of most employees at years $Y + 1, 2, 3$ equals the risk at year Y. Table 2 compares the area under the curve (AUC) results of the prediction model and the baseline. We split the datasets into set of 20% and 80%, and use former set as test set and latter set as training set. We repeat this split 5 times and calculated the average AUC. The AUC, which estimates the probability of randomly selecting a test result (true positive) over a control event (false positive), was 7% to 16% higher in all 33 XGBoost prediction models than in the baseline case.

Table 2. Comparison of prediction model and baseline (AUC of 11 × 3 predictive models: 11 health-checkup items after 1, 2, and 3 years).

	Proposed method			Baseline		
	1 yr later	2 yrs later	3 yrs later	1 yr later	2 yrs later	3 yrs later
BMI	0.98	0.97	0.96	0.91	0.89	0.88
Diastolic blood pressure	0.88	0.87	0.85	0.75	0.74	0.72
Systolic blood pressure	0.9	0.89	0.87	0.76	0.75	0.73
Neutral Fat	0.89	0.88	0.87	0.77	0.76	0.75
HDL cholesterol	0.94	0.93	0.92	0.76	0.75	0.75
LDL cholesterol	0.9	0.88	0.87	0.79	0.76	0.75
GOT	0.86	0.84	0.82	0.7	0.68	0.66
GPT	0.89	0.87	0.85	0.78	0.75	0.75
γ-GTP	0.95	0.94	0.93	0.86	0.84	0.82
Uric acid	0.9	0.88	0.87	0.78	0.77	0.76
Fasting blood sugar	0.86	0.85	0.83	0.74	0.73	0.71

4.2   Interpretation of Health Risk Prediction Model Using C-LIME

Tables 3 and 4 compare the output results of LIME and C-LIME for a specific employee. The models classify the risk of metabolic syndrome after one, two, and three years. The contents show the lifestyles that highly contribute to the metabolic risk. In the LIME predictions (Table 3) the contributions of "Fast eating" after two years were reversed after three years. The BMI of fast eaters is unlikely to decrease after two years, but will probably increase after three years. The anomalous result probably arose from sudden BMI changes in the nearby employee data, which were unrelated to their lifestyle. On the other hand, the C-LIME predictions (Table 4) excluded these data points, avoiding the above-mentioned counter-intuitive prediction. Removing the anomalous sample is thus essential for providing a convincing risk-prediction result.

We randomly selected 100 people from the data and examined the number of employees who do not have the above inconsistent lifestyle advice. Specifically, we evaluated the number of employees who meet the following two conditions.

- Employees whose BMI are predicted to be greater than the risk value in one of the health risk prediction models of 1, 2, or 3 years later.
- Employees who found consistency in lifestyle advice during the first, second, and third target years by LIME or C-LIME

As a result, in LIME, 5 employees met the above criteria. On the other hand, C-LIME had 16 employees who met the criteria. These results suggest that C-LIME has enabled consistent lifestyle advice over the years.

Table 3. Health-risk prediction of an employee interpreted by LIME

Impact on BMI 1 yr later		Impact on BMI 2 yrs later		Impact on BMI 3 yrs later	
Lifestyle habit	Impact score	Lifestyle habit	Impact score	Lifestyle habit	Impact score
Amount of drinking	−0.14	Physical activity	−0.17	Weight gain	0.08
Frequency of drinking	0.09	Fast eating	−0.08	Fast eating	0.03
Physical activity	−0.06				

Table 4. Health-risk prediction of an employee interpreted by C-LIME

Impact on BMI 1 yr later		Impact on BMI 2 yrs later		Impact on BMI 3 yrs later	
Lifestyle habit	Impact score	Lifestyle habit	Impact score	Lifestyle habit	Impact score
Late supper	0.05	Late supper	0.04	Sleep	0.03
Frequency of drinking	−0.03	Physical activity	−0.04	Amount of drinking	0.03
		Sleep	0.03		

5   Health-Risk Prediction and Lifestyle Recommendation Service

In April of 2019, we released our health-risk prediction and lifestyle recommendation service for employees of the NTT Group[2]. Our service combines a health-risk prediction algorithm with C-LIME. Figure 3 shows the user interface when predicting the risks of hypertension and metabolic syndrome. The health-risk prediction model computes the employees' health risks in the upcoming year from their health-checkup data in the current year. C-LIME also obtains and displays the lifestyle tips that will enhance the employees' awareness of their health risks and encourage them to change their lifestyles.

---

[2] https://www.nttdocomo.co.jp/binary/pdf/info/news_release/topics_190531_00.pdf.

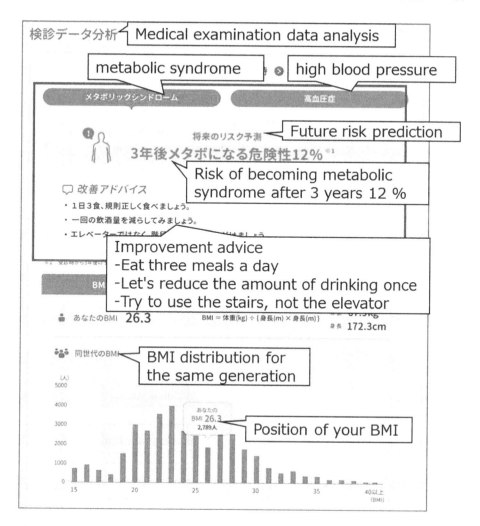

Fig. 3. Display example of our health-risk prediction and lifestyle recommendation service for NTT Group employees.

6 Conclusions

This paper discussed the predictability and interpretability of health risks determined from health-checkup data. Our health-risk prediction model comprises 33 predictive models (11 health-checkup items assessed after one, two, and three years) constructed from more than 10,000 annual health check-up records. To improve the interpretability of health prediction, we proposed our C-LIME method that identifies and removes anomalous sample before proceeding with LIME, and consistently explains the predictions of three target years. We have also provided a health-risk prediction and lifestyle recommendation service to employees of the NTT Group. In future work, we will improve the accuracy of our method using a state-of-the-art machine learning algorithm, and generate advice that encourages behavioral changes in the employees.

References

1. Ancona, M.B., Ceolini, E., Öztireli, C., Gross, M.: Towards better understanding of gradient-based attribution methods for deep neural networks. In: ICLR (2018)
2. Apley, D.W.: Visualizing the effects of predictor variables in black box supervised learning models. arXiv:1612.08468 (2016)
3. Bastani, O., Pu, Y., Solar-Lezama, A.: Verifiable reinforcement learning via policy extraction. In: NeurIPS (2018)
4. Chen, M., Hao, Y., Hwang, K., Wang, L., Wang, L.: Disease prediction by machine learning over big data from healthcare communities. IEEE Access **5**, 8869–8879 (2017)
5. Cheng, Y., Wang, F., Zhang, P., Hu, J.: Risk prediction with electronic health records: a deep learning approach. In: Proceedings of the 2016 SIAM International Conference on Data Mining (2016)
6. Craven, M.W., Shavlik, J.W.: Extracting tree-structured representations of trained networks. In: Proceedings of the 8th International Conference on Neural Information Processing Systems, pp. 24–30 (1995)
7. Elshawi, R., Al-Mallah, M.H., Sakr, S.: On the interpretability of machine learning-based model for predicting hypertension. BMC Med. Inf. Decis. Making **19** (2019)
8. Goldstein, A., Kapelner, A., Bleich, J., Pitkin, E.: Peeking inside the black box: visualizing statistical learning with plots of individual conditional expectation (2013)
9. Goldstein, B.A., Navar, A.M., Pencina, M.J., Ioannidis, J.P.A.: Opportunities and challenges in developing risk prediction models with electronic health records data: a systematic review. J. Am. Med. Inf. Assoc. **24**(1), 198–208 (2016)
10. Hall, P., Gill, N., Schmidt, N.: Proposed guidelines for the responsible use of explainable machine learning (2019)
11. Hastie, T.J., Tibshirani, R., Friedman, J.H.: The elements of statistical learning (2001)
12. Huang, Z., Dong, W., Duan, H., Liu, J.: A regularized deep learning approach for clinical risk prediction of acute coronary syndrome using electronic health records. IEEE Trans. Biomed. Eng. **65**(5), 956–968 (2018)
13. Kanegae, H., Suzuki, K., Fukatani, K., Ito, T., Harada, N., Kario, K.: Highly precise risk prediction model for new onset hypertension using artificial intelligence techniques. J. Clin. Hypertension (2019)
14. Lundberg, S., Lee, S.I.: A unified approach to interpreting model predictions. In: NIPS (2017)
15. Ma, F., Gao, J., Suo, Q., You, Q., Zhou, J., Zhang, A.: Risk prediction on electronic health records with prior medical knowledge. In: Proceedings of the 24th ACM SIGKDD International Conference on Knowledge Discovery and Data Mining, pp. 1910–1919 (2018)
16. Miotto, R., Li, L., Kidd, B.A., Dudley, J.T.: Deep patient: An unsupervised representation to predict the future of patients from the electronic health records. Sci. Rep. **6** (2016)

17. Nguyen, P., Tran, T., Wickramasinghe, N., Venkatesh, S.: D*eepr*: a convolutional net for medical records. IEEE J. Biomed. Health Inf. **21**(1), 22–30 (2017)
18. Pham, T., Tran, T., Phung, D., Venkatesh, S.: Predicting healthcare trajectories from medical records: a deep learning approach. J. Biomed. Inf. **69**, 218–229 (2017)
19. Rahimian, F., et al.: Predicting the risk of emergency admission with machine learning: development and validation using linked electronic health records. PLOS Medicine **15**, e1002695 (2018)
20. Rajkomar, A., et al.: Scalable and accurate deep learning with electronic health records. NPJ Digit. Med. **1** (2018)
21. Ribeiro, M.T., Singh, S., Guestrin, C.: "Why should I trust you?": explaining the predictions of any classifier. In: Proceedings of the 22nd ACM SIGKDD International Conference on Knowledge Discovery and Data Mining, pp. 1135–1144 (2016)
22. Ribeiro, M.T., Singh, S., Guestrin, C.: Anchors: High-precision model-agnostic explanations. In: AAAI (2018)
23. Shickel, B., Tighe, P.J., Bihorac, A., Rashidi, P.: Deep EHR: a survey of recent advances in deep learning techniques for electronic health record (EHR) analysis. IEEE J. Biomed. Health Informatics **22**(5), 1589–1604 (2018)
24. Yadav, P., Steinbach, M., Kumar, V., Simon, G.: Mining electronic health records (EHRs): a survey. ACM Comput. Surv. **50**(6) (2018)

Discriminant Knowledge Extraction from Electrocardiograms for Automated Diagnosis of Myocardial Infarction

Girmaw Abebe Tadesse[1,2]($\boxtimes$), Komminist Weldemariam[1], Hamza Javed[2],
Yong Liu[3], Jin Liu[3], Jiyan Chen[3], and Tingting Zhu[2]

[1] IBM Research - Africa, Nairobi, Kenya
girmaw.abebe.tadesse@ibm.com
[2] University of Oxford, Oxford, UK
[3] Department of Cardiology, Provincial Key Laboratory of Coronary Disease,
Guangdong Cardiovascular Institute, Guangzhou 510100, China

Abstract. Visual inspection of electrocardiograms (ECGs) is a common clinical practice to diagnose heart diseases (HDs), which are still responsible for millions of deaths globally every year. In particular, myocardial infarction (MI) is the leading cause of mortality among HDs. ECGs reflect the electrical activity of the heart and provide a quicker process of diagnosis compared to laboratory blood tests. However, still it requires trained clinicians to interpret ECG waveforms, which poses a challenge in low-resourced healthcare systems, such as poor doctor-to-patient ratios. Previous works in this space have shown the use of data-driven approaches to predict HDs from ECG signals but focused on domain-specific features that are less generalizable across patient and device variations. Moreover, limited work has been conducted on the use of longitudinal information and fusion of multiple ECG leads. In contrast, we propose an end-to-end trainable solution for MI diagnosis, which (1) uses 12 ECG leads; (2) fuses the leads at data-level by stacking their spectrograms; (3) employs transfer learning to encode features rather than learning representations from scratch; and (4) uses a recurrent neural network to encode temporal dependency in long duration ECGs. Our approach is validated using multiple datasets, including tens of thousands of subjects, and encouraging performance is achieved.

Keywords: Myocardial infarction · Electrocardiograms · Deep learning · Fusion

1 Introduction

Myocardial infarction (MI), commonly known as a heart attack, is the leading cause of cardiovascular deaths worldwide [24]. Severity of MI relates to its damaging perfusion impact resulting from blocks in coronary arteries, which

H. Uehara et al. (Eds.): PKAW 2020, LNAI 12280, pp. 70–82, 2021.
https://doi.org/10.1007/978-3-030-69886-7_6

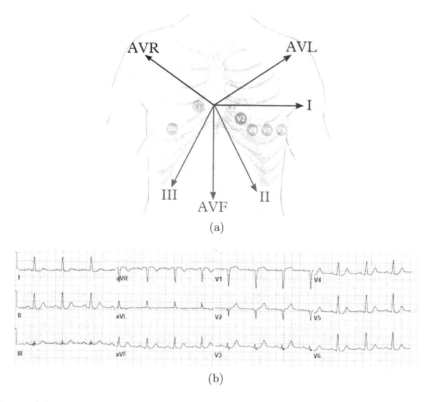

Fig. 1. (a) Conventional mounts for the 12 ECG leads, (b) Clinical visualisation of 12-lead ECG by radiologists ©ecgpedia.org.

interrupts the supply of oxygen and nutrients to the body [12]. It often takes hours to observe the impact of MI in blood samples as the cardiac enzymes are elevated [6]. As a result, electrocardiogram (ECG) waveform inspection (by cardiologists) has become a common clinical practice to screen MI, which partly benefits from quicker and non-invasive acquisition of these waveforms, especially in settings with less equipped laboratories to analyse blood samples. ECG waveforms represent the electrical activity of the heart from continuous polarisation and depolarisation of the atria and ventricle over time. The conventional 12-lead ECG waveforms contain the electrical signals acquired from different perspectives (see Fig. 1 (a)). An example of visualisation of these ECG signals as seen by a cardiologist is shown in Fig. 1 (b).

Inspection of ECGs provides a faster diagnosis process compared to blood sample analysis. However, the manual inspection of ECG signals is highly subjective depending on the expertise of the clinicians. This problem becomes severe in healthcare systems associated with inadequate medical experts, particularly in developing countries. Thus, the development of an intelligent diagnosis support system that can analyse ECG waveforms automatically is a practically well motivated task in healthcare [10, 20, 23].

The majority of existing methods for automated detection of MI from ECG traces, have focused on analysing morphological changes of the signal, such as QRS complex and P- and T-waves [9, 16]. In these methods, handcrafted features are extracted from the ECG waveforms in order to make the classification using domain-expert rule-based thresholding [1], or by using data-driven machine learning (ML) models [14]. These manual feature encoding techniques necessitate extensive pre-processing steps aimed at filtering artefacts from the waveforms. Moreover, manual design (handcrafting) of features requires domain-specific expertise, resulting in a time-consuming and tedious model development process. The handcrafted features proposed to classify HDs often vary across existing works in the literature, which suggests the lack of common and generalisable features to detect HDs across variations in patient and device characteristics.

On the other hand, deep learning methods can avoid the manual feature engineering step as they can automatically learn discriminative features for a specific task. Deep learning methods have achieved state-of-the-art performance in a wide range of application domains such as natural language processing and computer vision. Clinical tasks that involve medical image analysis, have been reported to benefit from automated decision support systems that employ deep learning [15]. Existing works on HD detection from ECG readings have also reported high accuracies whilst at the same time reducing the level of expert input required [3, 5, 8, 13, 22]. Different architectures of deep learning could be considered for HD detection, but convolutional neural networks (CNNs) have been the most frequently employed [5, 13, 18]. Generally, existing deep learning methods for HD detection are limited to using only a single or a few leads of ECG waveforms, despite the fact that multiple ECG leads are understood to contain more heart-related information that can be used for improved diagnoses [18]. Moreover, effectively combining the distinctive characteristics offered by each ECG lead, e.g., using fusion techniques, is not well studied in the literature [4]. Though ECG waveforms involve periodic patterns over time, longer ECG duration might help to understand the temporal dynamics of the waveforms, e.g., through using recurrent neural networks (RNNs). In addition, existing methods are mostly validated using a small cohort of patients, which is often a bottleneck in proving the generalisability of existing methods [2, 21]. Automatic learning of features from raw ECG waveforms could also necessitate a need for larger training datasets and computational overhead.

In this paper, we propose an end-to-end trainable MI diagnosis system that employs a spectral-longitudinal model from ECG waveforms. The transfer learning approach, applied through the use of existing computer vision networks to encode discriminative features to detect MI patients, circumventing the need to manually craft features. In order to utilise the multi-perspective information available in conventional 12-lead ECG waveforms, we employ early fusion by stacking the frequency-time representations of the ECG leads. Additionally, we use recurrent neural networks to exploit the temporal information available in long ECG waveforms. For validation, we have used a large and private collection of ECG waveforms of more than 15,000 MI patients. For comparative purposes, we have also validated our proposed model on the publicly available and commonly used PTB Diagnostic ECG database [11].

The remainder of this paper is organised as follows: Sect. 2 formulates the problem and presents the proposed spectral-longitudinal framework and describes its components in detail. Section 3 describes the experiments, that is the datasets considered and model parameter setup, as well as the results obtained and discussion. Finally, concluding remarks are presented in Sect. 4.

2   Our Approach

In this section, we present our end-to-end machine learning pipeline to model and predict MI diagnosis from 12-lead ECG waveforms, by circumventing the need to manually craft features.

2.1   Overview

Figure 2 shows the overview of our proposed approach. Let $\mathcal{D}$ denote a dataset that contains the 12-lead ECG waveforms of N patients who have been tested for MI, i.e., $\mathcal{D} = \{R_i\}_{i=1}^N$, we develop an ML binary classification algorithm to identify the subset of patients with MI, from those who do not have MI. The 12 leads are composed of the six limb leads (I, II, III, aVR, aVL, and aVF) and the six precordial leads ($V_1, \cdots, V_6$), as illustrated in Fig. 1 (a)). Thus, the ECG data of the ith patient can be expressed as $R_i = (\mathbf{r}_i^1, \cdots, \mathbf{r}_i^{12})$. The proposed approach outputs s_i, which is the prediction probability of a patient being diagnosed with MI. We also employ early fusion of information from multiple leads, by combining or stacking their spectrograms similarly to how a clinician would view a 12 lead ECG trace (as shown in Fig. 1 (b)) which is then followed by either a spectral $\mathcal{S}(\cdot)$, longitudinal $\mathcal{L}(\cdot)$ or joint spectral-longitudinal $\Psi(\cdot)$ model.

The pre-processing step concerns removing noise and movement artefacts from the ECGs, using a band-pass filter. Furthermore, an overlapping window was applied to generate samples from each lead waveform. Given a time series of ECG waveform for a particular lead, $\mathbf{r}_i^l \in R_i$, we extracted multiple samples (windows) from each lead in a patient, i.e., $\mathbf{r}_i^l = (\mathbf{u}_{i1}^l, \mathbf{u}_{i2}^l, \cdots, \mathbf{u}_{iw}^l, \cdots, \mathbf{u}_{iW}^l)$, where W is the number of windows extracted from $\mathbf{r}_i^l$. Note that for the purposes of readability, we hereafter drop the subscript i.

We then employ a fast Fourier transform, $\mathcal{T}(\cdot)$, to map the ECG waveform, $\mathbf{t}_w^l$, into a frequency-time representation as a spectrogram, i.e. $\Omega_w^l = \mathcal{T}(\mathbf{t}_w^l)$ (see Fig. 3). A spectrogram encodes the frequency-time characteristics of the ECG waveforms, and it is hypothesised that a spectrogram of an MI ECG would exhibit different patterns than that from a healthy subject. Another advantage of using a spectral-based data representation is the generalisation it can offer, as it would eliminate variations in ECG device specifications such as sampling

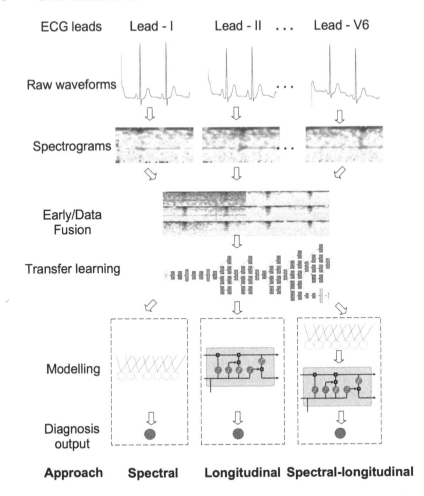

Fig. 2. Overview of the proposed approach. First, a spectral representation is obtained from each lead followed by early data fusion of these spectrograms via stacking. Next, existing computer vision networks are utilised to extract features from their hidden layers via transfer learning. Finally, modelling is performed by either a spectral, longitudinal or our proposed joint spectral-longitudinal model.

rates and mounting positions [17]. Furthermore, the 2-D representation of spectrograms produces a visualisation of the ECG signals, enabling the application of image-based CNNs architectures. These models are well suited to encode discriminative features from the captured ECGs, and importantly, transfer learning can be employed by taking advantage of powerful pre-trained networks from the computer vision application domain. Thereby reducing the amount of data that would have been required if models were trained from scratch.

Moreover, each ECG lead measures the electrical activity of the heart from different angles or orientations [18]. Consideration of multiple leads therefore

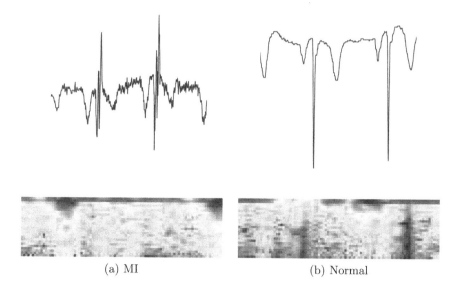

(a) MI   (b) Normal

Fig. 3. Examples of a 2-second aVR lead ECG waveform (top) and its corresponding spectrograms (bottom) for a MI and healthy subject, respectively.

offers increased diagnostic information, which could be effectively utilised to better discriminate between MI and non-MI. For this purpose, we employ a data-level fusion scheme at the early stages of the pipeline as shown in Fig. 2, which avoids the need to model each lead separately. The stacking of spectrograms for the different leads has been motivated by the standard ECG manufacture format as shown in Fig. 1 (a). Moreover, early data fusion enables feature encoding step to learn joint features from multiple leads. The output of the early fusion is represented by λ_w:

$$
\Lambda_w = \begin{bmatrix} \Omega_w^I, & \Omega_w^{aVR}, & \Omega_w^{V1}, & \Omega_w^{V4} \\ \Omega_w^{II}, & \Omega_w^{aVL}, & \Omega_w^{V2}, & \Omega_w^{V5} \\ \Omega_w^{III}, & \Omega_w^{aVF}, & \Omega_w^{V3}, & \Omega_w^{V6} \end{bmatrix},
$$

where Λ_w is the output of the early fusion.

Finally, after early fusion is performed, spectral modelling - $\mathcal{S}(\cdot)$, is applied through the use of CNNs to encode the frequency-time characteristics of the stacked spectrogram - Λ_w. We propose employing cross-domain transfer learning by using existing computer vision networks, e.g., GoogLeNet [19], to encode dense features taken from their hidden layers, i.e. $\mathbf{t}_w = \mathcal{S}(\Lambda_w)$. This helps to avoid training a dedicated spectral-based CNN from scratch, which is a process that requires enormous amount of training data, computational resources and time.

2.2   Modelling Spectral and Longitudinal Characteristics

A high-dimensional feature vector, $\mathbf{t}_w \in \mathbb{R}^\kappa$, is obtained for each sample (stacked spectrogram of multiple-leads) using GoogLeNet via transfer learning. This feature vector is then served as input to the classification model to provide prediction of the diagnosis. Three approaches of the classification model will be discussed below: *Spectral*, *Longitudinal* and *Spectral-longitudinal*.

Spectral Model - $\mathcal{S}(\cdot)$, takes $\mathbf{t}_w$ as input and only involves a dense layer (with κ neurons) followed by the softmax layer to provide the diagnosis output. The dense layer projects $\mathbf{t}_w \in \mathbb{R}^\kappa$ into $\mathbf{l}_w \in \mathbb{R}^\tau$, where $\tau < \kappa$ as

$$\mathbf{l}_w = \sigma(W_{lt}\mathbf{t}_w + \mathbf{b}_l), \tag{1}$$

where $\sigma(\cdot)$ is an element-wise activation function, $W_{lt} \in \mathbb{R}^{\tau \times \kappa}$ is the weight matrix associated with the dense layer and the deep feature $\mathbf{t}_w$, and $\mathbf{b}_l \in \mathbb{R}^\tau$ is a bias vector. Finally, a sigmoid-based output layer is employed that provides the prediction probability vector $s_w \in \mathbb{R}$ as

$$s_w = \frac{e^{W_{sl}\mathbf{l}_w}}{e^{W_{sl}\mathbf{l}_w} + 1}, \tag{2}$$

where $W_{sl} \in \mathbb{R}^{1 \times \tau}$ is the weight matrix associated with the softmax layer and the dense layer output $\mathbf{l}_w$.

During training, the binary cross entropy loss, L_β, is applied to iteratively minimise the classification error as

$$L_\beta = -\frac{1}{\beta} \sum_{w=1}^{\beta} y_w \times \log(s_w) + (1 - y_w) \times \log(1 - s_w), \tag{3}$$

where β is the number of samples in a specific batch, and y_w is the ground truth label associated with the wth sample.

Longitudinal Model - $\mathcal{L}(\cdot)$, is an alternative approach to the spectral model, providing the prediction probability of MI diagnosis from the deep feature representation of a sample $\mathbf{t}_w$. However, different from the spectral model, $\mathcal{S}(\cdot)$; $\mathcal{L}(\cdot)$ utilises the temporal dependency existing among subsequent windows generated from a patient, i.e., $\mathbf{t}_1, \mathbf{t}_2, \cdots, \mathbf{t}_w, \cdots, \mathbf{t}_W$. To do so, a recurrent neural network (RNN), particularly a long-short term memory (LSTM), is employed to encode the temporal information. LSTM utilises multiple gates (input, forget, and output) to control the information stored in the cell memory to mitigate the vanishing gradient problem embedded in vanilla RNN networks. The deep feature representations of consecutive samples are fed into the LSTM, which can control information flow using the gates it contains. Namely, the cell state gate $\mathbf{c}_w$ controls the flow from the current input and the previous and current hidden state (denoted by $\mathbf{t}_w$, $\mathbf{h}_{w-1}$ and $\mathbf{h}_w$ respectively). Additionally, the contribution of the previous state information, $\mathbf{c}_{w-1}$ is controlled by the forget gate $\mathbf{f}_w$. The input gate, $\mathbf{i}_w$, naturally controls the new candidate cell state, $\bar{\mathbf{c}}_w$. Finally, the output gate $\mathbf{o}_w$, evaluates $\mathbf{c}_w$ in order to predict the current hidden state, $\mathbf{h}_w$ as

$$\mathbf{h}_w = \mathbf{o}_w \odot \phi(\mathbf{f}_w \odot \mathbf{c}_{w-1} + \mathbf{i}_w \odot \bar{\mathbf{c}}_w), \tag{4}$$

where $\odot$ is an element-wise multiplication and ϕ is a tanh activation function. $\mathbf{h}_w$, $\mathbf{i}_w$, $\mathbf{c}_w$, $\mathbf{c}_{w-1}$, $\bar{\mathbf{c}}_w$ and $\mathbf{o}_w \in \mathbb{R}^\eta$. To obtain the MI diagnosis prediction, a sigmoid-based wrapper is applied on the hidden layer output of the LSTM, $\mathbf{h}_n$, similarly to Eq. (2), upon which a cross-entropy loss in Eq. (3) is applied to train the model.

Spectral-Longitudinal Model - $\Psi(\cdot)$, comprises both the spectral and longitudinal models discussed above in cascading fashion. Note that separate use of spectral and longitudinal models each poses distinct challenges for effective modelling, i.e., the former model is unable to account for the obvious temporal dependencies that would be present among consecutive samples; on the other hand, though the longitudinal model is capable of encoding such temporal information, training of the LSTM model is often associated with computational challenges and introduction of performance bias as a result of taking the high-dimensional $\mathbf{t}_w$ as its input. Hence, to circumvent these individual limitations, we propose the joint spectra-longitudinal model, $\Psi(\cdot)$, which addresses the above challenges by jointly utilising the advantages provided by these two separate model paradigms.

Given a subsequent of deep feature vectors as $\mathbf{t}_w \in \mathbb{R}^\kappa$, $\Psi(\cdot)$ first employs a dense layer as in Eq. (1) resulting $\mathbf{l}_w \in \mathbb{R}^\tau$. Then an LSTM network is employed to encode the temporal dependency similarly to Eq. (4). Note the input to the LSTM is output of the dense layer, $\mathbf{l}_w$, not $\mathbf{t}_w$. The hidden layer prediction of the LSTM is then wrapped to provide the MI diagnosis prediction vector s_w using the sigmoid-based wrapped in Eq. (2). The cross-entropy loss function as in Eq. (3) is used to jointly train the spectral and longitudinal components of $\Psi(\cdot)$ model.

3 Experiments

The proposed discriminant knowledge extraction for MI detection using deep learning is validated in both private and public datasets. This section presents the details of these datasets followed by the set up of parameters used in the spectral and longitudinal models. Finally, the result of the proposed method is presented across the two datasets and modelling techniques.

3.1 Datasets

We used two datasets, GCI (proprietary) and PTB (public), to validate the proposed spectral-longitudinal model. The GCI dataset contains 10-s 12-lead ECG waveforms from 11,853 MI and 5,528 Normal (a total of 17,381) records with a sampling rate 500 Hz, collected from the Provincial Key Laboratory of Coronary Heart Disease, Guangdong Cardiovascular Institute (GCI). Similarly, the PTB Diagnostic ECG database contains collected 12-lead ECGs from patients diagnosed with multiple heart diseases, sampled 1000 Hz [7, 11]. Here we consider cases which relate to MI (148 subjects) and health (52 subjects) with a total of 200 subjects. As the duration of ECG data may vary across subjects, we used only the first 10-second segment of each patient.

3.2   Setup

In the pre-processing step, a moving window with duration of 1 s with a 50% overlap is applied to each ECG lead, resulting a total of 19 samples extracted from a 10 s ECG lead signal. In the spectrogram generation step, a short time Fourier transform (STFT) is applied with a chunk duration of 0.1 s with 90% overlap in order to obtain smooth frequency-time representation. In the transfer learning step of exploiting existing computer vision networks, we use the GoogLeNet [19] to encode features from the stacked spectrograms. Particularly, the penultimate hidden layer of GoogLeNet (Inception - v3) framework is used that provides a feature of dimension $\kappa = 2,048$. The dense layer in the spectral model is designed with 16 neurons. Similarly, the longitudinal model is designed to be simple with a single-layered LSTM network of 8 neurons at the input, output, and forget gates. The temporal duration of the LSTM is set to 19 samples equivalent to the number of windows generated from a 10 s patient signal. During the training of the joint spectral and longitudinal model, we employ a learning rate of 0.001 with a batch size of 76, which contains two patients per class in each iteration. A five-fold stratified cross-validation is applied to each dataset to partition the data into train and test sets. Area under the receiver operating curve (AUROC), Sensitivity and Specificity are employed as evaluation metrics to compare the performance of MI detection averaged across the five-folds. Moreover, confusion matrices are also presented, when necessary, to assess the misclassification error of MI cases.

3.3   Results and Discussion

The area under receiver operating characteristic curve (AUROC) values obtained for the detection of MI in the two validation datasets (GCI and PTB) are shown in Table 1. The spectral, $\mathcal{S}(\cdot)$, and longitudinal, $\mathcal{L}(\cdot)$, models as baseline methods are compared with the joint spectral-longitudinal, $\psi(\cdot)$, model. As expected, the baseline methods have inferior performance when compared to the joint spectral-longitudinal model proposed in this work, where the $\psi(\cdot)$ achieves the highest AUROC values of 85% and 94% on the GCI and PTB datasets, respectively. The higher classification performance on the PTB dataset can be attributed to the simplicity of MI cases in this dataset, whereas there is a higher degree of patient variation in the GCI dataset. Furthermore, GCI MI cases are different

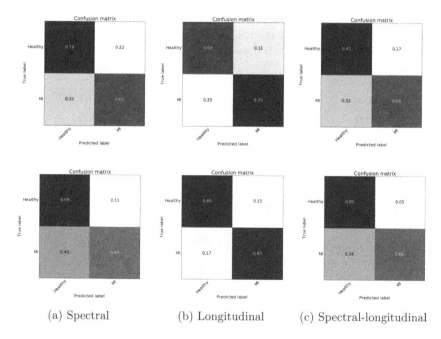

(a) Spectral   (b) Longitudinal   (c) Spectral-longitudinal

Fig. 4. Confusion matrices of spectral, longitudinal and the proposed spectral-longitudinal models. Top row: GCI results; bottom row: PTB results. Higher MI detection performance in the PTB deataset is partially due to the simplicity of the dataset.

in their onset time, i.e., acute, recent and old, which increases the variation in patient samples even further.

The longitudinal model, $\mathcal{L}(\cdot)$, alone can not achieve significant improvement over the spectral model, i.e., 80% vs. 81% in the GCI dataset and 88% vs. 90% in the PTB dataset. This can likely be attributed to the longitudinal model overfitting when taking the high dimensional ($\mathbf{R}^{2048}$) inception feature vector ($\mathbf{t}_w$), extracted from GoogleNet, as input. Further evidence of this is provided by the confusion matrices shown in Fig. 4, which can be used to analyse in more detail the misclassification rates of MI cases in the two datasets. The longitudinal models achieve the highest detection sensitivity of the MI cases (75% in GCI and 83% in PTB). However, this performance comes at the cost of lowest precision (84% in GCI and 96% in PTB) and specificity particularly in the GCI dataset (69% Specificity). By contrast, the joint spectral-longitudinal model achieves the highest AUROC with an effective trade-off between sensitivity and specificity, by using the dense layer outputs of the spectral models to reduce the high feature dimension of the inception features from 2048-D to 8-D. This approach reduces the overfitting issue which hinders the longitudinal models, and consequently the highest specificity values are achieved using spectral-longitudinal models (83% in GCI and 95% in PTB). As a result, spectral-longitudinal models are able to achieve the lowest misclassification rate of healthy cases to MI, with only 17% in GCI - compared to the 22% and 31% when using spectral and longitudinal

Table 1. Precision, Sensitivity, Specificity and Area under receiver operating characteristics, AUROC (%), results of the proposed framework for MI detection validated on the private GCI and public PTB datasets.

GCI Dataset				
Methods	Precision	Sensitivity	Specificity	AUROC
Spectral	87%	67%	78%	81%
Longitudinal	84%	**75%**	69%	80%
Spectral-longitudinal	**90%**	68%	**83%**	**85%**
PTB Dataset				
Methods	Precision	Sensitivity	Specificity	AUROC
Spectral	**99%**	60%	89%	88%
Longitudinal	96%	**83%**	85%	90%
Spectral-longitudinal	98%	66%	**95%**	**94%**

models, respectively. Similarly, only a 5% misclassification rate of healthy cases to MI occurs in PTB using longitudinal model compared to 11% using spectral and 15% using longitudinal models. Similar pattern of reducing the misclassifications of MI cases to Healthy cases occurs, particularly for PTB dataset as the spectral-longitudinal model reduced the MI misclassification by 6% in PTB compared to the Spectral model. The misclassification rate of MI cases was not reduced significantly in GCI datasets compared to the PTB dataset, due to the higher imbalance and variation of these cases in the former.

4   Conclusions

Heart diseases (HDs), and myocardial infarction (MI) in particular, continue to be responsible for millions of deaths worldwide. Clinically, inspection of electrocardiograms (ECGs) by the cardiologists has become acceptable and common practice to provide screening of MI. However, the inter-subject variability associated with ECG interpretation poses a challenge, in addition to the cumbersomeness of the inspection for many patients and longer ECG recordings. These problems are most pronounced in low-resourced environments, in which there are an insufficient number of trained clinical professionals. In this context, machine learning algorithms can be employed to assist in the diagnosis process, by providing a data-driven decision support tool to healthcare professionals. While most existing methods that automate HD diagnosis utilise domain specific features, e.g. morphological changes in ECGs, they often do not generalise well across variation in patient characteristics and device specifications. In this paper, we propose an end-to-end deep learning system to detect MI cases from healthy patients using a transfer learning approach and early fusion of multiple leads. The former allows the need for large amounts of training data to be avoided, whilst the latter enables the information across all 12 leads to effectively be exploited through joint-feature encoding. The proposed framework was validated on both private (>15,000 patients) and public datasets and encouraging performance is achieved. Generally, the spectral-longitudinal model that encodes deep spectral representations as well as the temporal dependency in ECG signals, achieved the highest performance over the baseline spectral or longitudinal models on both datasets. Future work includes the exploration of more efficient integration of multiple-leads, as well as identifying the time onset of a heart attack.

Acknowledgements. This project was supported by the EPSRC "FAST" Healthcare NetworkPlus initiative. TZ was supported by the RAEng Engineering for Development Research Fellowship.

References

1. Abubakar, S.M., Saadeh, W., Altaf, M.A.B.: A wearable long-term single-lead ECG processor for early detection of cardiac arrhythmia. In: 2018 Design, Automation and Test in Europe Conference and Exhibition (DATE), pp. 961–966. IEEE (2018)
2. Acharya, U.R., Fujita, H., Oh, S.L., Hagiwara, Y., Tan, J.H., Adam, M.: Application of deep convolutional neural network for automated detection of myocardial infarction using ECG signals. Inf. Sci. **415**, 190–198 (2017)
3. Al Rahhal, M.M., Bazi, Y., AlHichri, H., Alajlan, N., Melgani, F., Yager, R.R.: Deep learning approach for active classification of electrocardiogram signals. Inf. Sci. **345**, 340–354 (2016)
4. Ansari, S., et al.: A review of automated methods for detection of myocardial ischemia and infarction using electrocardiogram and electronic health records. IEEE Rev. Biomed. Eng. **10**, 264–298 (2017)
5. Baloglu, U.B., Talo, M., Yildirim, O., San Tan, R., Acharya, U.R.: Classification of myocardial infarction with multi-lead ECG signals and deep CNN. Pattern Recogn. Lett. **122**, 23–30 (2019)
6. Bax, J.J., et al.: Third universal definition of myocardial infarction. J. Am. Coll. Cardiol. **60**(16), 1581–1598 (2012)
7. Bousseljot, R., Kreiseler, D., Schnabel, A.: Nutzung der ekg-signaldatenbank cardiodat der ptb über das internet. Biomedizinische Technik/Biomed. Eng. **40**(s1), 317–318 (1995)
8. Darmawahyuni, A., et al.: Deep learning with a recurrent network structure in the sequence modeling of imbalanced data for ECG-rhythm classifier. Algorithms **12**(6), 118 (2019)
9. Dash, S., Chon, K., Lu, S., Raeder, E.: Automatic real time detection of atrial fibrillation. Ann. Biomed. Eng. **37**(9), 1701–1709 (2009)
10. Duong, H.T.H., et al.: Heart rate variability as an indicator of autonomic nervous system disturbance in tetanus. Am. J. Trop. Med. Hyg. **102**(2), 403–407 (2020)
11. Goldberger, A.L., et al.: PhysioBank, PhysioToolkit, and PhysioNet: components of a new research resource for complex physiologic signals. Circulation **101**(23), e215–e220 (2000)
12. Goldberger, A.L., Gold-berger, E.: Clinical electrocardiography, a simplified approach. Critical Care Med. **9**(12), 891–892 (1981)
13. Han, C., Shi, L.: Ml-resnet: a novel network to detect and locate myocardial infarction using 12 leads ECG. Comput. Methods Programs Biomed. **185**, 105138 (2020)

14. Kumar, M., Pachori, R., Acharya, U.: Automated diagnosis of myocardial infarction ECG signals using sample entropy in flexible analytic wavelet transform framework. Entropy **19**(9), 488 (2017)
15. Litjens, G., et al.: A survey on deep learning in medical image analysis. Med. Image Anal. **42**, 60–88 (2017)
16. Mehta, S., Lingayat, N., Sanghvi, S.: Detection and delineation of P and T waves in 12-lead electrocardiograms. Expert Syst. **26**(1), 125–143 (2009)
17. Ravi, D., Wong, C., Lo, B., Yang, G.Z.: A deep learning approach to on-node sensor data analytics for mobile or wearable devices. IEEE J. Biomed. Health Inf. **21**(1), 56–64 (2017)
18. Strodthoff, N., Strodthoff, C.: Detecting and interpreting myocardial infarction using fully convolutional neural networks. Physiol. Meas. (2018)
19. Szegedy, C., et al.: Going deeper with convolutions. In: Proceedings of the IEEE Conference on Computer Vision and Pattern Recognition, pp. 1–9 (2015)
20. Tadesse, G.A., et al.: Multi-modal diagnosis of infectious diseases in the developing world. IEEE J. Biomed. Health Inf. (2020)
21. Tadesse, G.A., Javed, H., Weldemariam, K., Zhu, T.: A spectral-longitudinal model for detection of heart attack from12-lead electrocardiogram waveforms. In: Proceedings of Annual International Conference of the IEEE Engineering in Medicine and Biology Society (EMBC) to appear (2020)
22. Tadesse, G.A., et al.: Cardiovascular disease diagnosis using cross-domain transfer learning. In: Proceedings of Annual International Conference of the IEEE Engineering in Medicine and Biology Society (EMBC), pp. 4262–4265 (2019)
23. Tadesse, G.A., Zhu, T., Thanh, N.L.N., Hung, N.T., Duong, H.T.H., Khanh, T.H., Quang, P.V., Tran, D.D., Yen, L.M., Doorn, H.R.V., andJohn Prince, N.V.H., Javed, H., Kiyasseh, D., Tan, L.V., Thwaites, L., Clifton, D.A.: Severity detection tool for patients with infectious disease. arXiv preprint arXiv:1912.05345 (2019)
24. WHO: Cardiovascular diseases (CVDs). www.who.int/news-room/fact-sheets/detail/cardiovascular-diseases-(cvds). Accessed 13 Aug 2020

Stabilizing the Predictive Performance for Ear Emergence in Rice Crops Across Cropping Regions

Yasuhiro Iuchi[1(✉)], Hiroshi Uehara[1], Yusuke Fukazawa[2],
and Yoshihiro Kaneta[1]

[1] Akita Prefectural University, Akita, Japan
{b19d001,uehara,ykaneta}@akita-pu.ac.jp
[2] Tokyo University, Tokyo, Japan
yusuke.fukazawa@gmail.com

Abstract. Several studies have demonstrated a good predictive performance of ear emergence in rice crops. However, significant regional variations in performance have been discovered and they remain unsolved. In this study, we aim to realize a stable predictive performance for ear emergence in rice crops regardless of its regional variations. Although a variety of data that represents regional characteristics have been adopted as the variables for prediction in related work, stability of the predictive performance has not been attained. These results imply that explicit regional data is insufficient for stabilizing the regional variances of the prediction. This study proposes to use engineered variables that uncover hidden regional characteristics behind the explicit regional data. Pre-examinations of the regional data indicate distinctive patterns of time dependency according to each region. Based on the findings, hidden Markov models are applied to the micro climate data to create engineered variables that represent the implicit time dependent regional characteristics. The efficiency of these variables is empirically studied, and the results show a significant improvement in the regional predictive variance.

Keywords: Crop prediction · Machine learning · E-agriculture

1 Introduction

Recently, a data-driven approach to agriculture has received global attention [1], owing to critical situations such as the declining farmer population, unexpected climate extremes, and the lack of food security. Applying machine learning to agricultural data is expected to produce results to overcome these issues. In this respect, several studies on data engineering for agriculture have been conducted. Among them, predicting the growth stages (i.e., stages of germination, tillering, heading, etc.) are important topics to be studied in terms of achieving adaptive

© Springer Nature Switzerland AG 2021
H. Uehara et al. (Eds.): PKAW 2020, LNAI 12280, pp. 83–97, 2021.
https://doi.org/10.1007/978-3-030-69886-7_7

farming operations such as fertilization and watering. These topics are independent of the implicit knowledge of experienced farmers. Research on growth stages is mainly concentrated on staple foods; several studies have successfully gained good predictive performances [2,3]. Most of them adopt regional characteristics such as a regional climate, soil ingredients, and the elevation as explanatory variables. This suggests that the predictive performance may depend on the divergence of regional characteristics [4]. However, predicting regional variances has not been sufficiently pursued [5]; in fact, there still does not exist a method by which the predictive stability can be achieved regardless of the regional varieties.

This study proposes to predict the ear emergence of rice, which is a growth stage in the crop with a stable performance regardless of the regional differences. By applying the proposed technique to "Akita-Komachi" (a major cultivar of Japanese rice plants), we will empirically ensure the method's efficiency. Akita-Komachi is mainly produced in the Akita prefecture, which is a rural area in Japan. Obtaining precise predictions of ear emergence is crucial to optimize the timing of farming controls, which can lead to a good harvest.

Section 2 provides an overview of the literature on crop predictions to shed light on the issue that is the focus of our study. The source of the data, which is used for the predictive variables, is introduced in Sect. 3. Section 4 presents our proposal, followed by the prediction procedure in Sect. 5. Thereafter, the empirical study to evaluate the proposed method is described in Sect. 6. Finally, Sect. 7 presents the discussion.

2   Related Studies

Predicting the stages of crop growth has been the focus of considerable research attention in recent years [2–9]. Among the crop growth stages, predicting ear emergence is crucial as it helps farmers determine the precise timing for farming operations, which includes fertilization, pest control, and water control. Timely farming operations affect the amount and quality of the harvest [7]. As a result, several studies have dealt with predicting ear emergence, especially for staple crops such as wheat [6,7] and rice [10]. These studies make use of regional characteristics such as locally partitioned weather information (hereafter referred to as micro climate) and the latitude. Ying-Xue et al. [5] determined that the predictive performance differs significantly depending on the regional characteristics of each field. In addition, these differences are not sufficiently explained by the explicit regional characteristics such as the micro climate, latitude, longitude, and elevation. This study aims to determine the hidden regional variables that affect the the predictive performance for each region; thus, achieving a stable prediction regardless of the regional diversity. To verify our proposal, we focus on predicting the ear emergence in "Akita-Komachi." This is one of the major cultivars of Japanese rice crops, which is mainly produced in the Akita prefecture. Within the prefecture, there are regional diversities in terms of climate and soil types.

Table 1. Cropping records of Akita-Komachi

Year	Address	Regional cropping environments		Stages of crop growth		Growing condition					
		Elevation (m)	Soil type	Planting date	Ear emergence date	Planting density (stump/ m^2)	Plant height (cm)	Number of stems	Number of leaves	SPAD	Seedling condition
2007	Masuda, Yokote city	200	Fine grain, gley	May 24	August 5	21	26.4	5.7	6.4	46.3	Medium seedling
1995	Kurooka, Noshiro	10	peat	May 19	August 7	23.2	22.6	5.1	5.1	40.6	Young seedling
2002	Shinjyo, Akita city	28	Coarse grain strong, gley	May 14	August 7	18.7	24	8.3	6.2	44.5	Medium seedling
1999	Nihata, Noshiro city	10	Lowland soils, brown	May 9	August 1	18.1	26.5	7.8	7.4	47.8	Medium seedling
2018	Gomihori, Northen Akita city	80	Lowland, gray	May 13	July 30	21.6	27.6	13	7.2	45.4	Young seedling

Table 2. Micro climatic data from the National Agriculture and Food Research Organization (NARO)

Date	Latitude	Longitude	Average temperature ($^\circ$C)	Rainfall (mm/day)	Solar radiation (hour/day)
May 10, 1985	39.577	140.227	8.9316	0	10.9768
May 11, 1985	39.577	140.227	10.3436	0	1.9772
May 12, 1985	39.577	140.227	10.0606	8.1610	9.7421
May 13, 1985	39.577	140.227	13.3962	2.5448	10.0046
May 14, 1985	39.577	140.227	15.3084	0	1.6698
May 15, 1985	39.577	140.227	15.2721	0	3.6441
May 16, 1985	39.577	140.227	13.3131	0	4.8949
May 17, 1985	39.577	140.227	10.3242	0.9029	0.2165
May 18, 1985	39.577	140.227	13.6470	0.8789	2.6986
May 19, 1985	39.577	140.227	14.2983	0	0.0041
May 20, 1985	39.577	140.227	12.5507	0	1.4538

3   Data

Most studies for predicting the crop growth stages make use of explicit regional data, which includes explanatory variables such as micro climate data and soil types in each region [4,6,9–11]. The current study makes use of similar regional data. In this section, all the data that are used as the source of the explicit regional variables are described.

3.1   Cropping Records

For over three decades, municipal institutions for agricultural research in Japan have accumulated regional agricultural records for the purpose of generating

Table 3. Partitioned cropping regions in the Akita prefecture

Region name	Number of samples in each region	Earliest planting date	Latest planting date
Yuri-Honjyo city (S,H)	32	May 14	May 31
Yuri-Honjyo city (N,H)	22	May 15	May 30
Hiraka county (S,H)	28	May 17	May 28
Yokote city (N,L)	37	May 12	May 31
Hiraka county (N,H)	36	May 16	May 29
Yokote city (N,H)	51	May 18	June 2
Yuzawa city (N,H)	37	May 17	May 29
Ogachi county (S,H)	46	May 16	June 2
Yuzawa city (S,H)	46	May 17	June 2
Ogachi county (N,H)	75	May 16	May 29
N, Akita city (N,H)	46	May 10	May 22
Odate city (N,H)	28	May 13	May 25
N, Akita city (N,L)	71	May 11	May 28
N, Akita city (S,L)	31	May 17	May 28
N, Akita city (S,H)	39	May 13	May 29
S, Akita county (N,L)	56	May 7	May 23
S, Akita county (S,L)	44	May 6	May 21
Oga city (S,L)	32	May 5	May 23
Oga city (N,L)	27	May 9	May 23
Akita city (N,L)	42	May 8	May 25
Senboku city (N,H)	89	May 10	May 28
Senboku city (S,L)	48	May 15	May 27
Senboku city (S,H)	40	May 13	May 26
Kazuno city (S,H)	48	May 13	May 22
Kazuno city (N,H)	71	May 16	May 28
Yokote city (S,L)	24	May 19	May 26
Odate city (S,L)	22	May 14	May 24
Yamamoto county (N,L)	49	May 9	May 27
Yamamoto county (S,L)	61	May 10	May 25
Yokote city (S,H)	75	May 16	June 3
Noshiro city (N,L)	60	May 8	May 23
Akita city (S,L)	44	May 9	May 27
Daisen city (S,L)	28	May 17	May 25
Total	1485	-	-

*The parentheses following the name of the municipal areas represent the information of the partitioned area as follows.
S: Southern area below the average latitude of the municipal area
N: Northern area above the average latitude of the municipal area
H: Area above 50 m elevation
L: Area below 50 m elevation

historical statistics. This study makes use of the records for Akita-Komachi. These records have been recorded by the institution of agricultural research in the Akita prefecture. They have been collected from 115 diversified observation points to cover all the regions in the prefecture because the regional cropping environments, such as climate and soil, vary within the prefecture. As such, the records reflect the regional diversity. This is suitable for the purpose of our study.

In Table 1, an example of cropping records of Akita-Komachi is shown. The table reveals that the records cover a variety of aspects of cropping such as the location of cropping, regional cropping environments, and the stages of crop growth. The current investigation makes use of the data on regional cropping environments. This includes the data on elevation and soil types that have accumulated over 25 years from 1993 to 2018, which amounts to 1,485 records.

Apart from the explanatory variables, the crop growth stages in the records are used as objective variables. These variables are discussed in detail in Sect. 5, under, "Engineering variables".

3.2 Micro Climate Data

Climatic data have been recognized as important variables; they are generally applied to study crop predictions. As described in the previous subsection, the climatic characteristics in the Akita prefecture dynamically differ depending on each region. Therefore, micro climatic data (i.e., regionally partitioned climatic data) are indispensable in this study.

The National Agriculture and Food Research Organization[1](referred to as NARO, hereafter) has developed a micro climate database specifically for agriculture. The data are characterized by their small meshed boundary. This data, together with data estimation, reflect the regional characteristics such as elevations. As the data format in Table 2 shows, the data consist of a daily time series including the temperature, rainfall, and solar radiation for each $1\,km^2$ meshed area, which covers all of Japan.

3.3 Partitioned Regions

Because the regional characteristics vary even within the same municipal areas in the Akita prefecture, in this study, we further partitioned each area into small regions so that each region would have similar characteristics. The planting dates in Table 1 were used to find the actual regional partition because they reflect the long-term experiences of the farmers based on the individual cropping environment in each region. Regions with similar planting dates imply environmental similarities. In Table 3, the results of the partitioned regions that have similar planting dates that range around $15\,d$ are shown. The latitudes and elevations enable the partition. Specifically, we set thresholds for the latitudes and elevations for each municipal area. The former threshold is the average latitude of the municipal area, and the latter is $50\,m$; these thresholds result in a maximum of four partitioned areas within each municipal area. The parentheses following the municipal names in Table 3 represent the information of the partitions as described in the footnote under Table 3. Therefore, the cropping fields of Akita-Komachi in the Akita prefecture are divided into 33 regions, and the average number of cropping records belonging to each region is 45.

---

[1] https://amu.rd.naro.go.jp/.

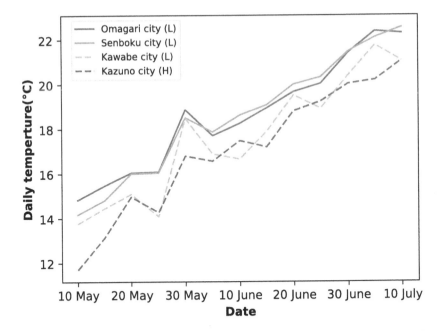

Fig. 1. Time series of the regional temperature

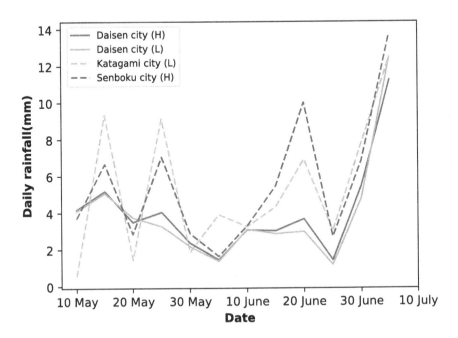

Fig. 2. Time series of the regional rainfall

4   Proposal - Engineering Variables

As described in the literature, the reason for the significant variance of the predictive performance for each region remains unresolved [5] due to the variety of regional variables that have been applied to previous studies [4,6,9–11]. Moreover, the applied regional variables seem to be exhausted in terms of using the readily accessible explicit data. By taking this situation into consideration, this study proposes to create effective variables by engineering the variables that were used in previous studies.

The engineering variables approach makes use of the statistics that represents the patterns of the time series fluctuations of the micro climatic data. For example, the daily temperature of the basin area is characterized by its sharp rise in early summer, whereas the temperature curve of the sea-side area is gently sloping. This example implies that there may be a time series dependency in the micro climatic data. This characterizes each region. Nevertheless, most previous studies deal with these time series data as if they are independent of the time sequence. To the best of our knowledge, none of them have explicitly defined the variables that reflect the time series dependency. In the following subsections, we describe the procedures that were performed to create the engineered variables that reflect the time series dependency characterizing the partitioned regions.

4.1   Clustering Regional Time Series Patterns

In Fig. 1 and Fig. 2, the daily temperature and rainfall, which is an average of more than 25 years in some of the partitioned regions, respectively, are illustrated. Both figures exhibit an apparent difference in the time series patterns between the regions that are represented by continuous lines and the ones represented by dotted lines. From this implication, we analyzed every time series pattern of the temperature and rainfall belonging to the 20 partitioned regions in Table 3. In addition, we defined two time series clusters for the temperature and rainfall as follows.

1. Time series clusters of the regional temperature.
      *temp*1 Patterns of sharp rise with transitioning to summer.
      *temp*2 Patterns of gentle sloping with transitioning to summer.
2. Time series clusters of the regional rainfall.
      *rain*1 Patterns of dynamic fluctuation with transitioning to summer.
      *rain*2 Patterns of gentle fluctuation with transitioning to summer.

4.2   Deriving the Time Series Statistics

The statistics representing the patterns of the time series dependency are derived as a form of likelihood, i.e., each regional time series (daily temperature and daily rainfall) likely belongs to the time series clusters that were introduced earlier. For this purpose, the hidden Markov model (HMM) is adopted. Once the HMM is trained by the time series data with the supervised labels, the algorithm is able to evaluate the likelihood, which represents each testing time series that is classified into the labels.

Taking the series of daily temperature as an example, each series is labeled by either the cluster, temp1, or temp2 as mentioned earlier. The HMM is individually trained by each cluster of the datasets to maximize the likelihood function $L(\pi_i, A_i, \phi_i, Z_i | obsTrain_{i,t})$. Thereafter, two sets of parameters, $\{A_{temp1}, \phi_{temp1}, \pi_{temp1}\}, and \{A_{temp2}, \phi_{temp2}, \pi_{temp2}\}$ are optimized to represent the characteristics of each cluster's time series dependency.

$$L(\pi_i, A_i, \phi_i, Z_i | obsTrain_{i,t})$$
$$= \underset{\pi_i, A_i, \phi_i}{\arg\max} \, p(z_{i,1} | \pi_i) \left[\prod_{t=2}^{T} p(z_{i,t} | z_{i,t-1}, A_i) \right] \prod_{t=1}^{T} p(obsTrain_{i,t} | z_{i,t}, \phi_i) \qquad (1)$$

Here,

i: ID of the cluster.

t: Each time point of the observed data, i.e., daily temperature and daily rainfall.

$obsTrain_{i,t}$: Observed training data belonging to i at t.

$z_{i,t}$: Hidden state behind the observation for each cluster.

π_i: Initial probability of the hidden state $z_{i,1}$.

A_i: Transition probability of the hidden state from $z_{i,t}$ to $z_{i,t+1}$.

ϕ_i: Probability of the hidden state $z_{i,t}$.

Once the HMM is trained, the likelihood of each series of testing data can be evaluated by the likelihood function $L(Z_i | \pi_i, A_i, \phi_i)$. In the case of the daily temperature, each series is evaluated by two trained HMMs with the parameters $\{A_{temp1}, \phi_{temp1}, \pi_{temp1}\}$, and $\{A_{temp2}, \phi_{temp2}, \pi_{temp2}\}$, which generates a pair of likelihoods. The larger the value of the likelihood, the more likely it is that the temperature series belongs to the corresponding cluster that is represented by the trained parameters $\{A_{temp_i}, \phi_{temp_i}, \pi_{temp_i}\}$ of the HMM. Therefore, the larger value is adopted as the statistics that characterizes the regional time series dependency for each series of the daily temperature. The same procedure is applied to each series of the daily rainfall.

This study proposes two kinds of time series statistics as engineering explanatory variables: one is the likelihood of the time series temperature, and the other is the likelihood of the time series rainfall. Both of these are engineered variables that are based on the micro climatic data, and they reflect the hidden regional characteristics that are specialized in the time series dependency.

$$L(Z_i | \pi_i, A_i, \phi_i) = \underset{z_{i,1}, \ldots, z_{i,T}}{\max} \ln p(obsTest_{i,1}, ..obsTest_{i,T}, z_{i,1}, .., z_{i,T} | \pi_i, A_i, \phi_i)$$
$$(2)$$

Here,

$obsTest_{i,t}$: Observed testing data belonging to i at t

5   Predicting Procedure

We applied the same machine learning algorithm to two kinds of datasets to evaluate the efficiency of our proposal while incorporating engineering explanatory variables that reflect the hidden regional characteristics. One comprises the conventional explanatory variables that were used in the previous studies [4, 6, 9–11]. The other incorporates the engineering explanatory variables with conventional explanatory variables. The following subsection elaborates the datasets and the predicting procedure.

5.1   Datasets

5.1.1   Objective Variable

An objective variable for our study is defined as the number of days between the planting date and the date of ear emergence; both are listed in Table 1. This variable has been considered as, practically, the duration rather than the date of ear emergence is of concern to the farmers. As described in the previous section, the number of acquired objective variables is 1,485 based on the cropping records. Hereafter, the objective variable (i.e., the duration) is referred to as the heading dates for simplicity.

Table 4. Explanatory variables for the baseline and proposed predictions

		Variables	Description	Source
Baseline prediction		Daily temperature	Daily temperature every five days from May 10 to July 10 (13 variables in total)	Micro climate
		Elevation	Elevation of observation point	Cropping records
		Soil type	19 type of soil ingredients	
		Planting date		
Proposed prediction		Likelihood of rainfall	Engineered variables by applying HMM to time series of rainfall and temperature	Micro climate
		Likelihood of temperature		

5.1.2   Explanatory Variables

Based on the previous studies on crop predictions [4, 6, 9–11], this study made use of the typical explanatory variables that have been used in the literature. The variables are: the daily temperature, daily rainfall, soil type, and planting date. All these variables reflect the regional characteristics. The relevant daily temperature and rainfall are specified, and they are retrieved from the micro climatic database based on the address and the year of each record for the cropping records. The other variables are the ones that are described for the cropping records. As such, 1,485 sets of explanatory variables were prepared with the corresponding objective variables as mentioned above. Whereas the conventional predictions are executed based on these explanatory variables(referred as base line predictions hereafter), the prediction based on our proposal also adopts engineering variables that are elaborated in Sect. 4(referred as proposed predictions hereafter),.

5.2 Executing Predictions

Out of the 1,485 datasets that are described above, 80% are allocated as training data, and the rest are allocated as testing data. The training and testing data were evenly sampled from the aforementioned regionally partitioned data to avoid regional bias. XGBoost, which is a decision tree algorithm, ensembles under the gradient boosting framework; it is applied for predicting the heading dates. We adopted this algorithm along with several learning algorithms because it demonstrates outstanding performance for small datasets [12]; thus, it is suitable for our datasets that amounts to 1,485. XGBoost enables feature importance analysis, which clarifies the contribution of each explanatory variable that is introduced in Sect. 7. The predictions are executed with five-fold cross validations.

5.3 Evaluating Predictive Performance

The variance of the regional root mean squared error (RMSE) is adopted to evaluate the performance of the proposed method. The RMSE is the average difference between the predicted heading dates and actual ones (i.e., the objective variables as above). The regional RMSE is the RMSE derived from each partitioned region, and the predictive performance in terms of the regional variance is represented as the variance of the regional RMSE that is formulated in Eq. 3.

$$Var_{regionalRMSE} = \frac{1}{K}\sum_{k=1}^{K}(r_k - \bar{r})^2 \tag{3}$$

Here,

K: The number of partitioned regions.
r_k: Regional RMSE defined as (4).
$\bar{r}$: Average of the regional RMSE.

$$r_k = \sqrt{\frac{1}{N_k}\sum_{n_k=1}^{N_k}(y_{n_k} - \hat{y_{n_k}})^2} \tag{4}$$

Table 5. RMSE with the predicted region

AREA	RMSE		Value of improvement
	Baseline	Proposed	
Yuri-Honjyo city (S, H)	4.45	3.31	1.14
Yuri-Honjyo city (N, H)	5.35	3.98	1.37
Hiraka county (S, H)	1.63	1.90	−0.27
Yokote city (N, L)	3.39	1.86	1.53
Hiraka county (N, H)	3.23	3.07	0.16
Yokote city (N, H)	2.92	2.72	0.20
Yuzawa city (N, H)	2.93	2.97	−0.04
Ogachi county (S, H)	5.69	4.82	0.87
Yuzawa city (S, H)	2.61	2.24	0.37
Ogachi county (N, H)	3.33	2.92	0.41
N, Akita city (N, H)	4.36	2.61	1.75
Odate city (N, H)	2.21	4.17	−1.96
N, Akita city (N, L)	2.08	2.99	-0.91
N, Akita city (S, L)	3.02	1.94	1.08
N, Akita city (S, H)	2.30	2.29	0.01
S, Akita county (N, L)	2.58	2.22	0.36
S, Akita county (S, L)	3.83	3.32	0.51
Oga city (S, L)	4.09	4.18	−0.09
Oga city (N, L)	3.35	3.47	−0.12
Akita city (N, L)	4.05	2.99	1.06
Senboku city (N, H)	4.50	3.41	1.09
Senboku city (S, L)	2.61	2.12	0.49
Senboku city (S, H)	4.31	3.58	0.73
Kazuno city (S, H)	3.75	2.91	0.84
Kazuno city (N, H)	2.77	2.47	0.30
Yokote city (S, L)	2.56	2.45	0.11
Odate city (S, L)	3.05	2.61	0.44
Yamamoto county (N, L)	3.05	2.98	0.07
Yamamoto county (S, L)	2.35	2.24	0.11
Yokote city (S, H)	2.70	2.17	0.53
Noshiro city (N, L)	2.84	2.97	−0.13
Akita city (S, L)	3.68	3.22	0.46
Daisen city (S, L)	2.92	2.48	0.44
Variance of regional RMSE	0.83	0.49	−
Overall RMSE	3.38	2.94	−
Average value of improvement	−	−	0.39

*The parentheses following the name of the municipal areas represent the information of the partitioned area as follows.
*Value of improvement: Baseline RMSE − Proposed RMSE
S: Southern area below the average latitude of the municipal area
N: Northern area above the average latitude of the municipal area
H: Area above the elevation of 50 m
L: Area below the elevation of 50 m

Here,

N_k: The number of testing data in the kth region.

y_{n_k}: Actual heading dates of the ith testing data in the kth region.

$\hat{y_{n_k}}$: Predicted heading dates of the ith testing data in the kth region .

6   Evaluation

Based on the aforementioned procedure for the prediction, the performance in terms of regional predictive variance of the heading dates is compared between the baseline and the proposed method. Table 4 lists the explanatory variables that are used in the baseline and the proposed method. The table shows that adopting the engineered variables is the only difference between the proposed method and the baseline.

Table 5 lists the regional RMSEs (Eq. 4). Apparently, the regional RMSEs of the proposed method fall in a more narrow range of values than those of the baseline. Therefore, the variance of the regional RMSE (Eq. 3) of the proposed method indicates a significantly small value of 0.49. This is smaller than the baseline, which is 0.83. In addition, the overall RMSE also significantly improved from ±3.38 d to ±2.94 d. For both improvements, the variance of the regional RMSE and the overall RMSE strongly support the efficiency of the proposed engineered variables that reflect the hidden regional time series characteristics.

Table 6. Most important 15 explanatory variables

Explanatory variables	Importance
Base date	170
Elevation	146
May 10	134
June 10	119
June 5	113
May 25	111
July 10	108
June 15	106
May 15	105
May 20	92
Likelihood of rainfall	91
May 30	88
June 20	83
Likelihood of temperature	76
June 30	69

7   Discussion

In Table 6, the top 15 explanatory variables from the 34 variables are presented in order of their contributions to the prediction. The contributions of the likelihood of the time series temperature and the likelihood of the time series rainfall are ranked as 14 and 11, respectively, and both are not necessarily high among all of the explanatory variables. Meanwhile, if the contributions of the variables are ranked by each partitioned region, the ranking of the contribution differs from each other. This is demonstrated in Table 7. Table 7(a-1), (a-2) are the rankings of the variables with respect to the regions. This indicates a significant predictive improvement for the proposed method. Comparatively, Table 7(b) results in a small improvement. As demonstrated by these tables, the engineered variables tend to be ranked higher in the regions, which indicates a significant predictive improvement and vice versa.

These analyses imply that the proposed variables are complementary for the region that is insufficiently predicted by the baseline variables.

Table 7. Top 10 important explanatory variables by each partitioned region

(a-1) Northern Akita city (N,H) (value of improvement : 1.75)

Explanatory variables	Importance
Base date	80
Likelihood of temperature	58
Temperature June 20	51
Temperature June 15	37
Temperature June 5	29
Temperature May 20	22
Temperature May 25	22
Temperature June 30	17
Temperature June 10	17
Temperature June 25	8

(a-2) Akita city (N,L) (value of improvement : 1.06)

Explanatory variables	Importance
Base date	64
Temperature June 15	31
likelihood of rainfall	29
Temperature June 25	27
Elevation	26
Temperature May 10	25
Temperature June 10	25
Temperature June 20	24
Temperature June 5	23
Temperature July 5	22

(b) Hiraka county(N,H) (value of improvement : 0.16)

Explanatory variables	Importance
Elevation	99
Base date	88
Temperature June 30	65
Temperature May 10	58
Temperature May 30	48
Temperature June 25	43
Temperature June 10	42
Temperature May 15	41
Temperature June 20	39
Temperature July 5	32

value of improvement: Baseline RMSE − Proposed RMSE in Tab 5

8 Conclusion

In this study, engineered explanatory variables are proposed to achieve stable predictive performance of the ear emergence regardless of the cropping region. Pre-examination of the regional temperature and rainfall implies that both are time-dependent, and the patterns of dependency are distinctive, depending on the regions. From the findings, the statistics on the regional time series dependency are derived as engineered variables; such variables have not been implemented in previous studies. Prediction with the proposed variables results in a significant improvement in the regional variance of the RMSE in comparison to the conventional prediction. This result indicates the efficiency of the proposed engineered variables.

The efficiency of the proposed method was verified only for Akita-Komachi in the Akita prefecture. Expanding the data for the analysis is expected to ensure general performance of the proposed method.

Engineering the variables that represents the time series dependency might contribute to acquiring unexplored knowledge in all research concerning crop growth stages. This is because crop growths display time series phenomena in which each stage is dependent upon the preceding stages. In this respect, there remain several opportunities to pursue this approach. We expect that this study will be the first step toward novel agricultural data engineering that is focused on time series knowledge for crop growth stages.

References

1. Uehara, H., Shinjo, A.: WAGRI - the agricultural big data platform. In: ProceedingE-AGRICULTURE IN ACTION:BIG DATA FOR AGRICULTURE Food and Agriculture Organization of the United Nations and the International Telecommunication Union, pp. 73–83 (2019)
2. Streck, N.A., Albert, W., Xue, Q., Stephen, P.B.: Improving predictions of developmental stages in winter wheat: a modified Wang and Engel model. Agric. Forest Meteorol. **115**(3–4), 139–150 (2003)
3. Bogard, M., Ravel, C., Paux, E., Bordes, J.: Predictions of heading date in bread wheat (Triticum aestivum L.) using QTL-based parameters of an ecophysiological model. J. Exp. Bot. **65**(20), 5849–5865 (2014)
4. Jeong, J.H., Resop, J.P., Mueller, N.D., Fleisher, D.H.: Random forests for global and regional crop yield predictions. PLoS ONE **11**(6), e0156571 (2016)
5. Ying-xue, S., Huan, X., Li-jiao, Y.: Support vector machine-based open crop model (SBOCM): case of rice production in China. Saudi J. Biol. Sci. **24**(3), 537–547 (2017)
6. Chauhan, Y.S., Ryan, M., Chandra, S., Sadras, V.O.: Accounting for soil moisture improves prediction of flowering time in chickpea and wheat. Nature.com, vol. 7510, no.Scientific Reports, pp. 1–11 (2019)
7. Bogard, M., et al.: Predictions of heading date in bread wheat (Triticum aestivum L.) using QTL-based parameters of an ecophysiological model. J. Exp. Bot. **65**(20), 5849–5865 (2014)

8. Maeda, Y., Goyodani, T., Nishiuchi, S., Kita, E.: Yield prediction of paddy rice with machine learning. In: Proceeding The 24th Int'l Conf on Parallel and Distributed Processing Techniques and Applications, pp. 361–365 (2018)
9. Pantazi, X.E., Moshou, D., Alexandridis, T., Whetton, R.L., Mouazen, A.M.: Wheat yield prediction using machine learning and advanced sensing techniques. Comput. Electron. Agric. **121**, 57–65 (2016)
10. Horie, T., Nakagawa, H.: Modelling and prediction of developmental process in rice: I. structure and method of parameter estimation of a model for simulating developmental process toward heading. Crop Sci. Soc. Japan **59**(4), 687–695 (1990)
11. Maeda, Y., Goyodani, T., Nishiuchi, S., Kita, E.: Yield prediction of paddy rice with machine learning. In: Proceedings of the International Conference on Parallel and Distributed Processing Techniques and Applications (PDPTA), pp. 361–365 (2018)
12. Wang, Q., Shwartz, L., Grabarnik, G.Y., Nidd, M., Hwang, J.: Leveraging AI in service automation modeling: from classical AI through deep learning to combination models. In: Proceeding of Int'l Conf on Service-Oriented Computing, vol. 2019, pp. 186–201 (2019)

Description Framework for Stakeholder-Centric Value Chain of Data to Understand Data Exchange Ecosystem

Teruaki Hayashi[1]([⊠]) [iD], Gensei Ishimura[2] [iD], and Yukio Ohsawa[1] [iD]

[1] The University of Tokyo, 7-3-1, Hongo, Bunkyo-ku, Tokyo 113-8656, Japan
hayashi@sys.t.u-tokyo.ac.jp
[2] Professional University of Information and Management for Innovation, 1-18-13, Bunka, Sumida-ku, Tokyo 131-0044, Japan

Abstract. In recent years, the expectation that new businesses and economic value can be created by combining/exchanging data from different fields has risen. However, value creation by data exchange involves not only data, but also technologies and a variety of stakeholders that are integrated and in competition with one another. This makes the data exchange ecosystem a challenging subject to study. In this paper, we propose a framework for describing the stakeholder-centric value chain (SVC) of data by focusing on the relationships among stakeholders in data businesses and discussing creative ways to use them. The SVC framework enables the analysis and understanding of the structural characteristics of the data exchange ecosystem. We identified stakeholders who carry potential risk, those who play central roles in the ecosystem, and the distribution of profit among them using business models collected by the SVC.

Keywords: Market of data · Data exchange · Stakeholder · Value chain

1 Introduction

Data have been treated as economic goods in recent years, and have begun to be exchanged and traded in the market [1, 2]. Interdisciplinary business collaborations in the data exchange ecosystem have been springing up around the world, and the transaction of data among businesses has garnered the interest of researchers [3, 4]. Moreover, the expectation that personal data can be valuable has risen [5, 6], and an increasing number of businesses are entering the market that forms the ecosystem of data exchange. However, value creation in the ecosystem involves not only data, but also technologies and a variety of stakeholders that are integrated and competing against one another. This makes the ecosystem a difficult subject of research. In other words, few frameworks are available to understand and share the functions and interactions of interdisciplinary data businesses. If personal data are leaked, for example, it is difficult to determine who is responsible, what caused it, or where the bottleneck of the data business is. The deposit of data and control rights as well as the transfer to third parties increases the complexity of stakeholders related to the data business, and makes it difficult to control the

© Springer Nature Switzerland AG 2021
H. Uehara et al. (Eds.): PKAW 2020, LNAI 12280, pp. 98–105, 2021.
https://doi.org/10.1007/978-3-030-69886-7_8

value chains. Therefore, establishing an appropriate unit of analysis and framework for a comprehensive understanding of the data exchange ecosystem is an important issue.

In this study, we propose a framework for describing the stakeholder-centric value chain (SVC) of data by focusing on the relationships among stakeholders in the data businesses, and discuss creative ways to use these relationships. The contribution of this study to the literature is in describing interdisciplinary data businesses in a simple manner with minimal expression. We discuss this description and its functionality as a common language across data businesses, and the support systems that can be implemented by forming a knowledge base of data businesses collected using the SVC.

2   Data Exchange Ecosystem and Relevant Studies

As represented by digital transformation, digitization and data collaboration are expected to become prevalent in society. Unlike the conventional supply chain, the business models of interdisciplinary data exchange have been decentralized—sharing roles and values in flat and even relationships among the stakeholders. In the business model manifested by the business of e-books, for example, the computer industry, home appliances, publishers, and telecommunication companies dynamically work together to form a complex ecosystem [7]. To propose technologies and understand the characteristics of the ecosystem, several studies have attempted to tackle these challenges.

As a technology for data exchange, the Innovators' Marketplace on Data Jackets (IMDJ) provides the framework for discussion among stakeholders in the data exchange ecosystem—data holders, users, and analysts—to lead data collaboration and innovation [8]. The Data Jacket Store structures and reuses knowledge for data utilization generated in the IMDJ [9] and analyzes the relationships [10]. However, the relevant studies do not discuss human relationships in the data exchange ecosystem. As representative of research on stakeholders, action planning focuses on their roles and proposes a descriptive framework for data businesses [11]. The Industrial Value Chain Initiative (IVI) offers tools that support interdisciplinary data collaborations using the software IVI Modeler (https://iv-i.org/wp/en/), which has 16 types of charts to describe a business model. Deloitte LLP describes the relationships among stakeholders in the open-data marketplace by such roles as data enablers, suppliers, and individuals [12]. These studies provide frameworks for explaining and sharing business models, but do not discuss ways of understanding the ecosystem from a macroscopic perspective.

3   Stakeholder-Centric Value Chain of Data

The SVC is an approximate unit of analysis to understand business models in the ecosystem of data exchange that focuses on the stakeholders. In such applications of it as in knowledge representation, the SVC is based on graph representation that uses nodes, edges, and labels. Table 1 describes the elements and labels of the SVC in this context. Nodes have two types of attributes: individual and institution. Entities such as data and services exchanged among the stakeholders are defined as labels at the edges of the directed graph. An edge has six types of labels, and the data they represent are further divided into three types: a collection of non-personal data and personal data, and personal data of each individual. Many methods are available for data provision, for example, downloading data stored on a website or obtaining them by APIs such that their details are expressed in the relevant comments. There are various types of data processing, such as data cleansing, which in turn includes anonymization, visualization, and such AI techniques as machine learning. The details of the data processing are described in parentheses or in the comments. Note that the data processing is described in a self-loop in the SVC. To consider the time-series information of data businesses, time steps are attached to the edges as attributes, and if the nodes and edges require additional explanation, we can add comments to them. To describe data businesses, users can employ graphical icons (pictograms) to easily share and understand the overall structure of the business models. Yoshizawa et al. proposed a semantic network for knowledge-sharing using pictograms [13]. This method introduces a network of elements, including humans and actions, and is intended to be used in education, which is a different domain from the one considered here.

A combination of the relationships between stakeholders—the smallest unit of knowledge—allows for the description of stakeholder-centric data businesses, and the integration of these business models helps structure the ecosystem of data exchange. We use a network-based approach to analyze the characteristics of the data exchange ecosystem. To efficiently encode data businesses described by the SVC through these networks, the n-th data business G_n is represented as (V_n, E_n, A_n, T_n), which is a directed multi-attribute graph. G_n consists of nodes $v \in V_n$, a set of stakeholders, edges $e_{ij} \in E_n$, and a set of relationships between the j-th and the i-th nodes. In this framework, the values of the attribute are not numerical but given as a set of labels, where A_n represents two attribute values of the node, and T_n is a set of six attribute values of the edges (Table 1).

Table 1. Descriptive items of the SVC.

Element	Label	Icon	Description
Node	Individual		A label used when the stakeholder is an individual.
	Institution		A label used when the stakeholder is a company, an institution, or a group of individuals.
Edge	Request	R	A label indicating a request for the data.
	Service	S	A label indicating the service offered including the product.
	Payment	$	A label that indicates the exchange of money (payment).
	Data		A label that represents the data provided. "P" represents personal data, and subscript i identifies an individual if needed.
	Process	Proc()	A label that represents data processing. The name of the algorithm can be described in parentheses.
	Timestep	T_j	The time order is represented by the subscript j. If a branch occurs, hyphens or underbars can be used.
Other	Comment		Additional information about nodes and edges.

Each node has only one attribute, whereas each edge can have an unlimited number of attribute values depending on the number of its relationships.

In light of the discussion above, users of the framework of SVC and the described data businesses can be (A) partners of the data business, or (B) those who are not involved in the data business. The benefits for (A) are that the stakeholders can clarify the purposes of the business and confirm that there are no misperceptions or inconsistencies among the business partners. They can also explain the essence of the business to potential partners and look for new collaborations. By contrast, for (B), the users can understand the purpose and conditions of data businesses as well as how the stakeholders participate in their data businesses. They can also analyze the applicability of the business models and potential partnerships, thereby increasing their business values.

4   Experimental Details

One hundred-and-five participants were involved in our experiments. They consisted of engineering students and business people over 20 years of age who were interested or engaged in data businesses. We allowed them to form groups of two or three, and lectured them on the SVC framework for 30 min. We then asked each group to describe manually the outline of data businesses using the SVC framework in 30 min. This yielded 35 data business diagrams, and we converted the diagrams into the network model. We focused on a simple description of a business model, and did not rigorously evaluate the completeness and accuracy of the described business models. Therefore, note that business models do not always represent the empirical relationships among businesses.

5   Results and Discussion

5.1   Structural Characteristics of the Data Exchange Ecosystem

Figure 1 shows the relationship diagram that integrates 35 business models with 123 stakeholders as obtained in the experiment. In the diagram, companies/institutions are represented by square nodes and individuals by circular nodes. The size of each node represents the frequency of the relevant stakeholders. The labels are listed by edges, and thickness represents the number of labels. The largest business model in terms of stakeholders had 10, and the smallest had two. The average number of stakeholders in each business model was 4.97.

The network of all business models was divided into five subgraphs, and we analyzed the largest component (the number of nodes: $|V| = 93$; the number of edges: $|E| = 128$). Note that self-loops were not included, and the values were calculated as an undirected graph. From a macroscopic point of view, the average degree (k) was low at 2.75, and the power index γ was 2.44, where this represented the power distribution. The density was very small at $\rho = 0.00299$, and the stakeholder network was globally sparse. Furthermore, the value of the clustering coefficient was $C = 0.286$, and reflected the existence of hubs in local clusters. As shown in Fig. 1, the network consisted of many low-frequency stakeholders with many densely connected clusters. Data processors, data accumulators, and users appeared frequently across the business models, and were

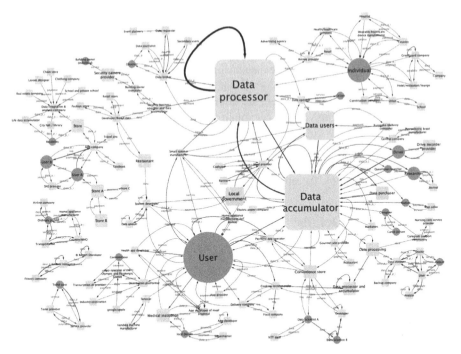

Fig. 1. The diagram of business models using the SVC framework.

located at central positions in the network. It is also noteworthy that, unlike human-related networks in general as networks of co-author or actor relationships [14], assortativity [15] did not have a high positive value at $r = -0.128$. That is, the stakeholder network of the data businesses was disassortative or neutral, and had similar characteristics to those of engineering or natural networks (representing power grids or protein interactions, respectively [14]). In these networks, nodes with a high degree tend to have linkages with low-degree nodes. In other words, hub nodes in the network are connected to avoid other hubs. In the economic system, the data providers may not sell the data to other data providers, and data analysts may have a rivalry with one another, such that the business relationships among those who have the same roles in the market are unlikely to be cultivated. Such differences may lead to a segregation of stakeholders in the ecosystem. By contrast, hubs are not connected to other hubs, as in the case of social networks [14], and the redundancy of the network is low due to its sparseness. In other words, the stakeholder network easily disintegrates when the stakeholders are removed. Whether this feature occurs because the data exchange ecosystem is not yet a mature market is debatable. To improve the understanding of the mechanism, it is necessary to compare it with the stakeholder relationships in other markets, and test with more samples of business models and the details of their business processes [16].

5.2 Knowledge Extraction from SVC

The first purpose of the SVC framework as used here was to understand the structural characteristics of the data exchange ecosystem, and the second was to reuse the structured knowledge of the data businesses. Because the knowledge unit of the SVC had a structure identical to that of linked data, such as the RDF triple, it worked as a knowledge base for a search system. Below is information that can be gleaned from structured knowledge.

(a) The most profitable stakeholder.
(b) The stakeholder who carries potential risk, for example, if personal data are leaked.
(c) The stakeholder who plays a central role in the ecosystem.
(d) Profit distribution among stakeholders.

Functioning as an ecosystem means that payments are made appropriately for the provision of data and services. Although the SVC does not include the amount of payment, it was possible to identify stakeholders who get the most money across business models. As a result, we found that data processors were paid 18 times; data accumulators: 12 times; and data integration and analysis company: 5 times. Meanwhile, let us analyze who has the highest risk in the case of leakage of personal data. We can obtain the stakeholders by those who are the end points of the flows of personal data (data(p) or data(p_i) in Fig. 1). As a result, we obtained data processors got personal data 27 times, data accumulators: 13 times; and app company: 5 times. These results suggest that the data processor was most likely to receive the highest profit, but there was a potential risk of personal data leakage for it. Moreover, using the degree and betweenness centralities, we found that data users, accumulators, and processors were the top three stakeholders that appeared frequently across business models, and may play a central role in the ecosystem.

It is also possible to create an indicator to measure whether the services provided, such as data and products, are appropriately paid for in each business model or ecosystem. We defined $k_i^{\text{in}} = \sum_{j=1}^{|V|} |e_{ij}|$ to represent the in-degree of the i-th stakeholder, $k_i^{\text{out}} = \sum_{j=1}^{|V|} |e_{ij}|$ as its out-degree, and the payment to the i-th stakeholder as $k_i^{\text{in}}(\text{payment}) = \sum_{j=1}^{|V|} |e_{ij}(\text{payment})|$. The request for data was different from that for service, and we excluded k_i^{out} from this. We also included data processing with a self-loop because this is necessary for business models. We defined the received profit sufficiency (RPS) as the degree to which the i-th stakeholder had been sufficiently paid for the service it provided, as in Eq. (1):

$$\text{RPS}_i = k_i^{\text{in}}(\text{payment}) / \left(k_i^{\text{out}} - k_i^{\text{out}}(\text{request})\right) \tag{1}$$

The calculated RPS value of each stakeholder, and RPSs of the medical institutions, hospitals, and supermarkets was one, indicating sufficient payments for the data and services that they had provided. By contrast, the RPS of the data processor was 0.75 and that of the data accumulator was 0.30. This indicates payments to the data processors and accumulators were not adequate, although they carried the risk of personal data leakage. The RPSs of residents and restaurants who were data generators were zero, which appeared to be necessary to correct the business models. We do not discuss the accuracy of the RPS here, but its concept is important in assessing the soundness of the ecosystem. The RPS can be calculated not only for each stakeholder, but also for each business model and the entire ecosystem. The RPS of the entire ecosystem using $\sum_{i=1}^{|V|} RPS_i$ was 0.32. To improve the soundness of the ecosystem, it is useful to review the business models and stakeholder relationships so that the RPS approaches one.

5.3 Limitations and Future Work

In the experiments, all participants were able to describe the model diagrams of the data businesses in a short time using the SVC framework. One participant commented that the SVC framework worked as a common language to explain and share the outlines of business models to the other members, suggesting that one of the purposes of our study was achieved. On the contrary, owing to an increase in the number of stakeholders and their relationships, the description of timesteps became complicated, and some businesses missed the information related to timesteps. Preventing excessive increases in the number of edges and excessive complexity of the timesteps are challenges for future research. Moreover, in this study, the edges had only labels, and we did not define their capacity to avoid complexity. By providing information on the frequency of data updates, task time, and flow rate at the edges, it is possible to apply methods used to solve maximum flow problems. Moreover, knowledge representation is generally based on the assumption that experts can describe the knowledge accurately and comprehensively. To understand all structures of the data exchange ecosystem, we must consider tacit knowledge in future research.

The method of analysis used here is simple but powerful in obtaining useful knowledge by applying network algorithms. Moreover, as the number of samples was small, we could not use other useful measures designed for complex networks, such as clustering or community extraction that considers multiple attributes along the edges and on nodes [17, 18]. In future research, it is important to collect more samples and verify the claims of this study.

6 Conclusion

The motivation of our study was to understand the ecosystem of data exchange and develop interdisciplinary data businesses. We proposed a framework for analyzing and understanding the structural characteristics of a data exchange ecosystem using a simple description framework that focuses on the relationships among the stakeholders using a network-based approach. In spite of the promise of interdisciplinary data collaboration, due to the diversity of stakeholders and their complex relationships, it is challenging to understand this structure. Owing to its simplicity, the SVC has the potential to function as a common language to understand data businesses. Moreover, when the number of stakeholders increases, the number of relationships exponentially increases as well. For this reason, it is difficult to consider every possible combination of stakeholders across areas. We think that SVC framework and the reutilization of structured knowledge can support the development of the ecosystem as well as data businesses.

Acknowledgement. This study was supported by the JSPS KAKENHI (JP19H05577 and JP20H02384), and the Artificial Intelligence Research Promotion Foundation.

References

1. Balazinska, M., Howe, B., Suciu, D.: Data markets in the cloud: an opportunity for the database community. The VLDB Endowment **4**(12), 1482–1485 (2011)
2. Liang, F., Yu, W., An, D., Yang, Q., Fu, X., Zhao, W.: A survey on big data market: pricing, trading and protection. IEEE Access **6**, 15132–15154 (2018)
3. Stahl, F., Schomm, F., Vossen, G.: Data marketplaces: an emerging species. In: Frontiers in Artificial Intelligence and Applications, pp. 145–158 (2014)
4. Spiekermann, M.: Data marketplaces: trends and monetisation of data goods. Intereconomics **54**(4), 208–216 (2019)
5. Xu, L., Jiang, C., Wang, J., Yuan, J., Ren, Y.: Information security in big data: privacy and data mining. IEEE Access **2**, 1149–1176 (2014)
6. Line, N., Dogru, T., El-Manstrly, D., Buoye, A., Malthouse, E., Kandampully, J.: Control, use and ownership of big data: a reciprocal view of customer big data value in the hospitality and tourism industry. Tourism Manage. **80**, 104106 (2020)
7. Yoo, Y., Henfridsson, O., Lyytinen, K.: The new organizing logic of digital innovation: an agenda for information systems research. Inf. Syst. Res. **21**(4), 724–735 (2010)
8. Ohsawa, Y., Kido, H., Hayashi, T., Liu, C., Komoda, K.: Innovators marketplace on data jackets, for valuating, sharing, and synthesizing data. In: Tweedale, J.W., Jain, L.C., Watada, J., Howlett, R.J. (eds.) Knowledge-Based Information Systems in Practice. SIST, vol. 30, pp. 83–97. Springer, Cham (2015). https://doi.org/10.1007/978-3-319-13545-8_6
9. Hayashi, T., Ohsawa, Y.: Retrieval system for data utilization knowledge integrating stakeholders' interests. In: AAAI Spring Symposium (2018)
10. Hayashi, T., Ohsawa, Y.: Context-based network analysis of structured knowledge for data utilization, In: AAAI Spring Symposium (2019)
11. Hayashi, T., Ohsawa, Y.: Processing combinatorial thinking: Innovators marketplace as role-based game plus action planning. Int. J. Knowl. Syst. Sci. **4**(3), 14–38 (2013)
12. Deloitte LLP, Open growth: Stimulating Demand for Open Data in the UK, Deloitte LLP (2012)
13. Yoshizawa-Watanabe, S., Kunigami, M., Takahashi, S., Terano, T., Yoshikawa, A.: Pictogram network: evaluating english composition skills. In: IEEE International Professional Communication Conference, pp. 1–6 (2012)
14. Barabási, A.L.: Network Science. Cambridge University Press (2016)
15. Newman, M.E.J.: Assortative mixing in networks. Phys. Rev. Lett. **89**(20), 208701 (2002)
16. Quix, C., Chakrabarti, A., Kleff, S., Pullmann, J.: Business process modelling for a data exchange platform. In: Proceedings of the 29th International Conference on Advanced Information Systems Engineering, pp. 153–160 (2017)
17. Levchuk, G., Roberts, J., Freeman, J.: Learning and detecting patterns in multi-attributed network data. In: AAAI Fall Symposium Series (2012)
18. Ito, H., Komatsu, T., Amagasa, T., Kitagawa, H.: Detecting communities and correlated attribute clusters on multi-attributed graphs. IEICE Trans. Inf. Syst. **102**(4), 810–820 (2019)

Attributed Heterogeneous Network Embedding for Link Prediction

Tingting Wang[1,2], Weiwei Yuan[1,2], and Donghai Guan[1,2(✉)]

[1] College of Computer Science and Technology,
Nanjing University of Aeronautics and Astronautics, Nanjing, China
`ttw0622@163.com`, {`yuanweiwei,dhguan`}`@nuaa.edu.cn`
[2] Collaborative Innovation Center of Novel Software Technology
and Industrialization, Nanjing, China

Abstract. Network embedding aims to embed the network into a low-dimensional vector space wherein the structural characteristic of the network and the attribute information of nodes are preserved as much as possible. Many existing network embedding works focused on the homogeneous or heterogeneous plain networks. However, networks in the real world are usually not plain since the nodes in the networks have rich attributes, and these attributes play important roles for encoding nodes' vector representations. Although some works took into account the attribute information, they could not handle the homogeneous and heterogeneous structure information of the network simultaneously. In order to solve this problem, a new network embedding method that considers both the network's homogeneous and heterogeneous structure information and nodes attribute information simultaneously is proposed in this paper. The proposed method first obtains nodes attribute information, homogeneous and heterogeneous structure information as three views of the network and learns network embeddings of the three views through different technologies respectively. Then, an attention mechanism is utilized to fuse the embedding results learned from the three views to obtain the final vector representations of nodes. We verify the performance of the proposed model through link prediction tasks on four real-world datasets, and extensive experimental results show that the proposed model outperforms the advanced baselines.

Keywords: Attributed heterogeneous information network embedding · Three views · Attention mechanism

1 Introduction

Attributed heterogeneous information networks (AHINs) are ubiquitous in the real world. It contains different types of entities and edges, and each entity is described with attributes. For example, Fig. 1 is a citation network that includes three types of entities: authors, papers and conferences, in which there is a writing relationship between authors and papers, a publishing relationship between

© Springer Nature Switzerland AG 2021
H. Uehara et al. (Eds.): PKAW 2020, LNAI 12280, pp. 106–119, 2021.
https://doi.org/10.1007/978-3-030-69886-7_9

papers and conferences and a citation relationship between papers. In addition, each entity is characteristic with attributes, such as the gender, age, affiliated institution, research direction of an author, the serial number, research topic, publication time of a paper and the title, venue and time of a conference. The analysis and research on AHINs have become a hot topic due to the progress of network embedding. Network embedding, also known as network representation learning, is a prevalent method to map nodes in a network to a low-dimensional continuous space while preserving network structure and inherent properties [4]. As an upstream technology, network embedding is helpful for many downstream network analysis tasks, such as link prediction [14], node classification [1], community detection [9] and network visualization [18], etc. [6,10,12].

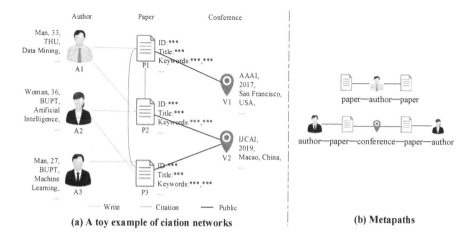

(a) A toy example of ciation networks   (b) Metapaths

Fig. 1. (a) A toy example of attributed heterogeneous network. (b) Two metapaths in the citation network.

Many network embedding methods have been proposed in the past years, but most of them rely on the assumption that the network is homogeneous and contains only one type of node and link [15]. For example, DeepWalk [16] and node2vec [11] are pioneering works that introduce random walk technique into network analysis to learn nodes representations. SDNE [23] and DNGR [3] introduce deep neural network into network embedding. Nevertheless, they were designed to handle plain networks whose nodes with no attributes. To exploit the attribute information of nodes, many attributed network embedding models were proposed. TADW [25] and HSCA [26] integrate attribute information into the process of matrix factorization. ANRL [27] and CANE [22] encode the network structure and nodes attribute information by deep learning technology. However, these methods are only applicable to homogeneous networks whose nodes and edges are single-typed while the nodes and edges are usually various in the real-world networks. More recently, PTE [19], metapath2vec [7] and HERec [17] are proposed for heterogeneous networks, which contain multi-types of nodes or edges. AHNG [15], HNE [5], HAN [24] are proposed for learning the representation of attributed heterogeneous networks or heterogeneous graphs. In addition, attention mechanism, a recent research trend in deep learning which encourages the model to focus on the most salient parts of data has been proved to be effective in heterogeneous graph neural networks [24]. However, existing network embedding methods only consider the heterogeneous network structure and nodes attribute information when processing the AHINs, and they ignore the homogeneous structure information of networks. That is to say, these methods cannot consider the three characters at the same time.

In this paper, we handle the homogeneous and heterogeneous network structure information and nodes attribute information simultaneously when learning the representations of AHINs. It faces two challenges: First, how to obtain the feature information of the three views and learn the network embedding of each view separately; Second, how to fuse the three views to learn the final vector representation of the network. To solve these two challenges, a new network embedding method for AHINs is proposed in this paper, and we name it Attributed Heterogeneous information Network Embedding (AHNE). To deal the first challenge, AHNE first utilizes the autoencoder technology to encode the attribute information of nodes to learn the attribute embedding. Then, AHNE captures the same-typed first-order and second-order neighbors of nodes to obtain the homogeneous character of the network, and utilizes the objective optimization functions to learn the homogeneous embedding of nodes. Next, AHNE regards the metapath-guided heterogeneous neighbors as the context of nodes and trains the context with the Skip-Gram [26] model to learn the heterogeneous embedding. To address the second challenge, AHNE adopts the attention mechanism to learn the attention value of each embedding learned above, and fuses them to generate the final embedding vectors of nodes. We conduct link prediction task on four real-world datasets, and experimental results show that AHNE outperforms the state-of-the-art network embedding methods. The contributions of this work are summarized as follows:

- To our best knowledge, this is the first attempt to consider both the network homogeneous and heterogeneous structure information and nodes attribute information simultaneously in the attributed heterogeneous information network embedding.
- We propose a novel attributed heterogeneous information network embedding method AHNE. AHNE captures the homogeneous and heterogeneous structure information of the network and the attribute information of nodes simultaneously and learns their embeddings separately. In addition, the attention mechanism is adopted in this work to learn the importance of different views when learning the final representatios of nodes by fusing the above three embeddings.
- We conduct link prediction experiments to evaluate the performance of the proposed model. The results show the superiority of the proposed model by comparing with the state-of-the-art models.

The remainder of the paper is organized as follows: Sect. 2 introduces related work about network embedding. Section 3 gives some definitions related to the model and describes AHNE in detail. The experimental evaluation is presented in Sect. 4. Finally, we conclude this paper in Sect. 5.

2   Related Work

Homogeneous Network Embedding. A homogeneous network refers to the nodes and edges in the network are single-typed. The pioneer of homogeneous network embedding methods mainly exploit the structural information of the network to embed the network into a low-dimensional space. For example, Deep-Walk uses random walk technology to generate context sequences of nodes, and then trains the context sequences with the Skip-Gram model to learn nodes representations. Intuitively, nodes close in the network tend to have similar contexts and thus their embedding vectors are similar. GraRep [2] converts the graph structure into linear sequences by capturing the k-step relationship between each node and its neighbors and defines different loss functions to capture the different k-step local relational information with different k values. SDNE [23] preserves the local and global network structures and deep autoencoder is used to capture the high nonlinear network structure.

However, the above methods only consider the structural information of the homogeneous network and ignore the attribute information of nodes. To compensate, TADW [25] demonstrates that the essence of DeepWalk is matrix factorization and learns the attributed network embedding by integrating the text information into the process of matrix factorization. ANRL [27] models the nodes attribute information by a neighbor enhancement autoencoder and captures the network structure by an attribute-aware skip-gram model based on the attribute encoder. LANE [13] learned label informed attributed network embedding under the classical matrix factorization-based network embedding models.

Heterogeneous Network Embedding. Heterogeneous networks refer to the nodes and/or edges in the network are multi-typed. Metapath2vec [7] defines meta-path based random walk to construct the heterogeneous neighborhood of nodes and then leverages a heterogeneous skip-gram model to perform network embedding. PTE [19] is a semi-supervised network embedding method for text data, which constructs large-scale heterogeneous text network from labeled information and different levels of word co-occurrence information. HERec [17] uses a meta-path based random walk strategy to generate meaningful node sequences to learn network embeddings that are first transformed by a set of fusion functions and subsequently integrated into an extended matrix factorization (MF) model [4]. However, the above methods also ignore the attribute information of nodes.

In order to integrate the network structure information and nodes attribute information in an AHIN, AEHE [8] utilizes type-aware multilayer perceptron (MLP) component to learn the attribute embedding, and adopt the autoencoder framework to learn the second-order aware embedding. GATNE [4] defines base embeddings, edge embeddings and attribute embeddings to capture both rich attribute information and multiplex topological structures from different node types. HAN [24] designs a heterogeneous graph neural network based on the hierarchical attention, including node-level and semantic-level attentions, which can learn the importance of different nodes and metapaths.

Although the existing network embedding methods have made achievements to some extent in learning network representations, they only capture part of the network information in the three views of homogeneous or heterogeneous or attributed information, resulting some useful information lost.

3   The Proposed Model

3.1   Preliminaries

Definition 1. *Attributed heterogeneous information network. An AHIN is defined as a graph $G = (V, E, \mathbf{A})$, where V is the set of all nodes, E is the set of all edges and $\mathbf{A}$ is the attribute matrix of nodes. An AHIN is also associated with a node type mapping function $\Phi : V \to O$ and an edge type mapping function $\Psi : E \to R$, where O and R denote the set of all node types and edge types respectively, and $|O| + |R| > 2$. That is, each node $v \in V$ belongs to a specified node type and each edge $e \in E$ belongs to a particular edge type.*

Definition 2. *Meta-path. Given a HIN, a meta-path is defined as a path in the form of $\rho : V_1 \xrightarrow{R_1} V_2 \xrightarrow{R_2} \cdots \xrightarrow{R_l} V_{l+1}$, where $l \geq 1$ is the length of ρ and $R = R_1 \circ R_2 \circ \ldots \circ R_l$ defines the composite relations between the node type V_1 and V_{l+1}. Different meta-paths usually have different semantics, as is shown in Fig. 1(b), the meta-path "paper-author-paper" means that two papers are written by the same author while the meta-path "author-paper-conference-paper-author" means that two papers written by two authors are published in the same conference.*

3.2   AHNE

An attributed heterogeneous information network not only contains homogeneous and heterogeneous structure information, but nodes in the network are usually associated with additional attributes. The proposed AHIN embedding algorithm in this paper can save both the homogeneous and heterogeneous topological structure information of the network and the attribute information of nodes when learning network representation. The framework of the proposed model is shown in Fig. 2. To exploit the nodes attribute information, AHNE adopts the autoencoder technology to encode and reduce the dimension of the attributes of nodes and learn nodes attribute embedding. To obtain the homogeneous structure of the network, AHNE captures the same-typed first-order and second-order neighbors of nodes and learns nodes homogeneous embedding by LINE [20]. To exploit the heterogeneous structure information of the network, AHNE captures the meta-path guided neighbors as the context sequence of nodes, and then trains the sequence with the skip-gram model to learn nodes heterogeneous embedding. Based on the attribute embedding, homogeneous embedding and heterogeneous embedding, AHNE adopts attention mechanism to learn the weight value of each embedding and fuses the three embeddings to generate the final embeddings of nodes. We illustrate these steps in detail in the following subsections.

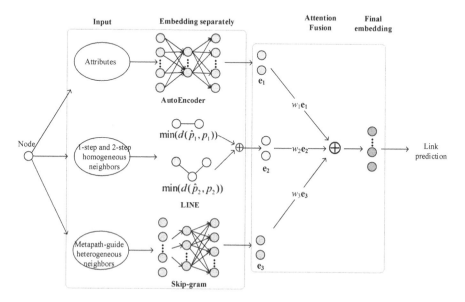

Fig. 2. The framework of the proposed method, in which $dis(\cdot, \cdot)$ is a function that measures the distance between two distributions. p_1 and $\hat{p}_1$ are the joint probability distribution and empirical probability distribution between nodes and it's same-typed first-order neighbors respectively. p_2 and $\hat{p}_2$ are the condition probability distribution and empirical probability distribution between nodes and it's same-typed second-order neighbors respectively. $\oplus$ represents connection operation.

Attribute Embedding. Many existing attributed network embedding works have proved that the attribute information of nodes plays an important role in learning the representation of the network. In order to mine the significance of nodes attribute information, an autoencoder technology is adopted to encode the attribute information into a low-dimensional space. Specifically, assuming that $\mathbf{A}^t$ is an attribute matrix for type-t ($t \in O$) nodes and i-th row of $\mathbf{A}^t$ is the attribute vector $\mathbf{a}_i^t$ of node v_i^t. Autoencoder first encodes the input attribute vector $\mathbf{a}_i^t \in \mathbb{R}^m$ into a hidden layer vector $\mathbf{h}_i^t \in \mathbb{R}^d$ ($d \ll m$) as:

$$\mathbf{h}_i^t = \sigma\left(\mathbf{W}\mathbf{a}_i^t + \mathbf{b}\right), \tag{1}$$

where σ is an activation function such as sigmoid function, $\mathbf{W}$ is the weight matrix, and $\mathbf{b}$ is the bias vector. Then, autoencoder decodes $\mathbf{h}_i^t$ to an output layer vector that is the same dimension with the input vector as follows:

$$\mathbf{a}_i^{t'} = \sigma' \left(\mathbf{W}' \mathbf{h}_i^t + \mathbf{b}' \right), \tag{2}$$

where σ' is an activation function, $\mathbf{W}'$ and $\mathbf{b}'$ are the weight matrix and the bias vector respectively that different from $\mathbf{W}$ and $\mathbf{b}$. And the dimension of $\mathbf{a}_i^{t'}$ is same as $\mathbf{a}_i^t$. Autoencoder defines the mean-square error between $\mathbf{a}_i^t$ and $\mathbf{a}_i^{t'}$ as the loss function to optimize the parameters and learn the node attribute embedding:

$$L_i^t = \left| \mathbf{a}_i^t - \mathbf{a}_i^{t'} \right|^2. \tag{3}$$

Homogeneous Embedding. The homogeneous structure of a heterogeneous information network reflects the relationship between the same-typed nodes. For example, two users are friends if they are linked in a social network and the topic of two papers are similar if one of them cites another in the citation network. In order to capture the homogeneous structure in an AHIN, AHNE extracts the first-step and second-step same-typed neighbors and trains them with LINE model to capture the first-order and second-order proximity respectively.

To model the first-order proximity, LINE defines an objective function (i.e., Kullback-Leibler divergence) to minimize the distance between the joint probability distribution and empirical probability distribution of the node v_i^t and its first-step homogeneous neighbor v_j^t:

$$D_1 = dis \left(p_1 \left(v_i^t, v_j^t \right), \hat{p}_1 \left(v_i^t, v_j^t \right) \right), \tag{4}$$

$$p_1 \left(v_i^t, v_j^t \right) = \frac{1}{1 + \exp \left(-\mathbf{u}_i^{tT} \cdot \mathbf{u}_j^t \right)}, \tag{5}$$

$$\begin{cases} \hat{p}_1 \left(v_i^t, v_j^t \right) = \frac{w_{ij}}{W} \\ W = \sum_{e_{ij} \in E^r} w_{ij} \end{cases}, \tag{6}$$

where, v_i^t and v_j^t are nodes belonging to type-t ($t \in O$), and the edge e_{ij} belongs to type-r ($r \in R$), $dis(\cdot, \cdot)$ is the distance between two distributions, $p_1 \left(v_i^t, v_j^t \right)$ and $\hat{p}_1 \left(v_i^t, v_j^t \right)$ are the joint probability and empirical probability between node v_i^t and v_j^t respectively, $\mathbf{u}_i^t \in \mathbb{R}^d$ and $\mathbf{u}_j^t \in \mathbb{R}^d$ are the low-dimensional vector representations of node v_i^t and v_j^t respectively, w_{ij} is the weight of the edge e_{ij}, and $w_{ij} = 1$ if the network is unweighted.

In order to preserve the second-order proximity, LINE minimizes the distance between the condition probability distribution and empirical probability distribution of the node v_i^t and its second-step homogeneous neighbor v_k^t:

$$D_2 = dis \left(p_2 \left(v_k^t | v_i^t \right), \hat{p}_2 \left(v_k^t | v_i^t \right) \right), \tag{7}$$

$$p_2 \left(v_k^t | v_i^t \right) = \frac{\exp \left(\mathbf{u}_k^{tT} \cdot \mathbf{u}_i^t \right)}{\sum_z^{|V^t|} \exp \left(\mathbf{u}_z^{iT} \cdot \mathbf{u}_i^t \right)}, \tag{8}$$

$$\hat{p}_2 \left(v_k^t | v_i^t \right) = \frac{w_{ik}}{d_i}, \tag{9}$$

where d_i is the number of homogeneous neighbors of node $v_i^t \in V^t$.

To preserve both the first-order and second-order proximity, LINE concatenate the node embeddings trained by the above two steps.

Heterogeneous Embedding. In order to capture the rich semantic information between different types of nodes in an AHIN, AHNE proposes a meta-path guided neighborhood as the heterogeneous context of nodes. That is, given a node v_i^t and a meta-path ρ (starting form v_i^t), the meta-path guided neighborhood is defined as node sequence of visited nodes when node v_i^t walks along the given ρ. Take the "A2" in Fig. 1 (a) as an example, given a meta-path "author-paper-conference-paper-author", node sequences such as "A2-P2-V2-P3-A3" and "A2-P3-V2-P2-A1" can be generated by meta-path guided walks. AHNE takes these seqences as the context of "A" and trains them with a skip-gram model to learn the node's heterogeneous embedding.

Attention Mechanism Based Fusion. Through the above three steps, AHNE learns the attributed heterogeneous information network embedding from three views: attribute embedding, homogeneous embedding and heterogeneous embedding. However, each embedding only reflects a part of the network features and it is important to fuse the three embeddings to learn a comprehensive AHIN embedding. In this paper, AHNE assumes that the nodes attribute information, the homogeneous and heterogeneous network structure information in an AHIN have different importance in network embedding. To address this problem, AHNE adopts the attention mechanism to learn the importance of each embedding when fusing the above three embeddings.

Let $\mathbf{AE}$, $\mathbf{HO}$ and $\mathbf{HE}$ $\in \mathbb{R}^{|V| \times d}$ denote the attribute, homogeneous and heterogeneous embedding matrix of nodes respectively, and for $\forall v \in V$, its vector representations are expressed as $\mathbf{AE}(v)$, $\mathbf{HO}(v)$, $\mathbf{HE}(v) \in \mathbb{R}^{d \times 1}$ respectively. Then, the final vector representation $f(v)$ of node v is defined as:

$$f(v) = \alpha_v^1 \mathbf{AE}(v) \oplus \alpha_v^2 \mathbf{HO}(v) \oplus \alpha_v^3 \mathbf{HE}(v), \tag{10}$$

where $\oplus$ denotes concatenation operation, α_v^1, α_v^2 and α_v^3 represent the weight values of $\mathbf{AE}(v)$, $\mathbf{HO}(v)$ and $\mathbf{HE}(v)$ when learning the final vector representation of the node v. In particular, $\alpha_v^1 + \alpha_v^2 + \alpha_v^3 = 1$, and they are defined as:

$$\alpha_v^1 = \frac{\exp \left(\sigma \left(\mathbf{x}^T \mathbf{Y} \cdot \mathbf{AE}(v) \right) \right)}{\exp \left(\sigma \left(\mathbf{x}^T \mathbf{Y} \cdot \mathbf{AE}(v) \right) \right) + \exp \left(\sigma \left(\mathbf{x}^T \mathbf{Y} \cdot \mathbf{HO}(v) \right) \right) + \exp \left(\sigma \left(\mathbf{x}^T \mathbf{Y} \cdot \mathbf{HE}(v) \right) \right)}, \tag{11}$$

$$\alpha_v^2 = \frac{\exp \left(\sigma \left(\mathbf{x}^T \mathbf{Y} \cdot \mathbf{HO}(v) \right) \right)}{\exp \left(\sigma \left(\mathbf{x}^T \mathbf{Y} \cdot \mathbf{AE}(v) \right) \right) + \exp \left(\sigma \left(\mathbf{x}^T \mathbf{Y} \cdot \mathbf{HO}(v) \right) \right) + \exp \left(\sigma \left(\mathbf{x}^T \mathbf{Y} \cdot \mathbf{HE}(v) \right) \right)}, \tag{12}$$

$$\alpha_v^3 = \frac{\exp\left(\sigma\left(\mathbf{x}^T\mathbf{Y}\cdot\mathbf{HE}(v)\right)\right)}{\exp\left(\sigma\left(\mathbf{x}^T\mathbf{Y}\cdot\mathbf{AE}(v)\right)\right) + \exp\left(\sigma\left(\mathbf{x}^T\mathbf{Y}\cdot\mathbf{HO}(v)\right)\right) + \exp\left(\sigma\left(\mathbf{x}^T\mathbf{Y}\cdot\mathbf{HE}(v)\right)\right)},$$
(13)

where, σ is a sigmoid function, $\mathbf{Y} \in \mathbb{R}^{d \times d}$ is a trainable weight matrix and $\mathbf{x} \in \mathbb{R}^d$ is the attention vector that assigns the significance to different embedding channels.

In order to optimize the parameters in attention-based fusion, we can design a loss function to train the proposed model. For example, if we aim at learning useful representations in a fully unsupervised setting for link prediction task, the loss function can be defined as follows:

$$L = -\sum_{(v_i,v_j)\in\varepsilon} \log\left(\sigma\left(f\left(v_i\right)^T \cdot f\left(v_j\right)\right)\right) - \sum_{(v_i,v_j)\in\varepsilon^-} \log\left(\sigma\left(-f\left(v_i\right)^T \cdot f\left(v_k\right)\right)\right),$$
(14)

where σ is a sigmoid function, and $\cdot$ represents the matrix product. ε and ε^- are the set of linked edges and non-linked edges sampled from the input graph respectively. Briefly, the unsupervised loss function encourages linked nodes to have similar representations, while enforcing that the representations of disparate nodes are highly distinct.

4   Experimental Evaluation

4.1   Datasets

DBLP[1] [21] is a citation network which consists of authors, papers, and venues. To construct the attributed heterogeneous network that needed in this paper, we extract two subsets of DBLP. DBLP1 consists of 2716 papers (P) that written by 4954 authors (A), and received by 8 venues[2] (V). These 8 venues are uniformly selected from four fields including Database, Artificial Intelligence, Data Mining and Computer Vision. There exist 4205 links (P2P) between the papers and 7773 links (P2A) between the papers and authors. DBLP2 contains 3928 papers written by 6999 authors, and published in 11 venues[3]. These 11 venues are uniformly selected from four domains including Information Retrieval, Data Mining, Artificial Intelligence and Database. There exist 5840 links between the papers and 10924 links between the papers and authors. In DBLP, we only extract the abstract of papers as the attribute information of papers and for authors, there is no available information that can be extracted as their attributes due to the restrict of the dataset. The bag-of-words model is used to extract attribute information from abstracts and for the two subsets of DBLP, 4737 and 6339 words are extracted as the features of papers respectively. In addition, a meta-path set

---

[1] https://www.aminer.cn/citation.
[2] The 8 venues include CVPR, ICCV, ECCV, PAKDD, ECML, NIPS, ICML and EDBT.
[3] The 11 venues include KDD, ICDM, SDM, ECIR, SIGIR, AAAI, WWW, IJCAI, VLDB, ICDE and SIGMOD.

{PAP, PVP} is employed to construct the papers' heterogeneous neighbors. Due to the lack of attribute information for authors, AHNE cannot perform attribute embedding for authors, so this work only learns the representations of papers and predicts the links between papers.

Yelp[4] is a review website that includes information of users, businesses and reviews. We also extract two subsets of the Yelp to construct the attributed heterogeneous networks. Yelp1 contains 3243 users (U) and 15904 businesses (B) that reviewed by them. There are 6148 links (U2U, friendship) between users and 41001 reviews (U2B) between users and businesses. Yelp2 contains 10822 users and 28188 businesses that reviewed by users, and there exist 26031 links between users and 112616 reviews between users and businesses. We extract the "user_id", "yelping_sincing", "review_count", "average_stars", etc. as the attribute information of users, and select the "business_id", "open", "stars", "city", "categories", etc. as the attribute information of businesses. Because of the absence of links between businesses in Yelp, AHNE cannot perform homogeneous embedding for businesses, so this work only learns the representations of users and predicts the links between users, and the meta-path {UBU} is used in this work to generate the heterogeneous neighbors for users.

4.2 Experimental Settings

In this paper, we select the DeepWalk and LINE methods of the homogeneous network embedding, the AutoEncoder and TADW methods of the attributed homogeneous network embedding, the metapath2vec and HERec methods of the heterogeneous network embedding and GATNE method of the attributed heterogeneous information network embedding as the baselines to evaluate the performance of the proposed model. In the experiments, we set $d = 16$ for DBLP datasets and $d = 8$ for Yelp datasets, which means the dimension of the final attention based fusion embeddings of papers and users are 48 and 24 respectively. In AHNE, the meta-path based walk number and walk length are set to 10 for each node. In the baselines, all algorithms are implemented by their authors and their parameters are set to default values except for the dimension of network embeddings are set to 48 and 24 for DBLP and Yelp datasets respectively.

4.3 Experimental Results

Experiments are conducted on the extracted four datasets to perform link prediction task, in which we predict the citation relationships between papers in DBLP and friendship relations between users in Yelp. Two frequently-used metrics are used to compare the link prediction performance of different methods: accuracy (ACC) and area under the ROC curve (AUC). The higher the values of ACC and AUC are, the better the prediction performance is. Table 1 shows the performance of link prediction of various methods on four datasets and the best performance is highlighted in bold. Based on this table, we have the following observations:

---

[4] https://www.yelp.com/dataset.

Table 1. The ACC and AUC of link prediction of different methods on the DBLP and Yelp datasets.

Datasets	Metrics	DeepWalk	LINE	AutoEncoder	TADW	metapath2vec	HERec	GATNE	AHNE
DBLP1	ACC	0.6293	0.6013	0.5107	0.4901	0.5754	0.5645	0.5729	**0.6846**
	AUC	0.6295	0.6019	0.5171	0.5000	0.5759	0.5653	0.5740	**0.6848**
DBLP2	ACC	0.6146	0.6328	0.5190	0.4925	0.5634	0.5503	0.5570	**0.7075**
	AUC	0.6149	0.6340	0.5224	0.5030	0.5640	0.5509	0.5610	**0.7077**
Yelp1	ACC	0.6728	0.7440	0.6967	0.6272	0.6147	0.5878	0.6797	**0.7785**
	AUC	0.6729	0.7441	0.6969	0.6292	0.6152	0.5884	0.6801	**0.7787**
Yelp2	ACC	0.7062	0.7464	0.7303	0.5994	0.6219	0.5926	0.6690	**0.7968**
	AUC	0.7063	0.7465	0.7303	0.5992	0.6222	0.5929	0.6690	**0.7967**

1. By comparing the performance of link prediction of all methods on four datasets, it can be found that the ACC and AUC values of link prediction of AHNE increases about 5%–21% in DBLP and 3%–20% in Yelp compared with baselines, which shows that the proposed method can improve the ability of network embedding by capturing the homogeneous and heterogeneous network structure information and nodes attribute information.

2. By comparing the results of homogeneous network embedding methods (DeepWalk, LINE), heterogeneous network embedding methods (metapath2vev, HERec) and attributed network embedding methods (AutoEncoder, TADW) on four datasets, it can be found that the link prediction results of homogeneous network embedding methods are better than heterogeneous network embedding methods and much better than attributed network embedding methods in DBLP dataset and the link prediction performance of homogeneous network embedding methods are better than attributed network embedding methods and much better than heterogeneous network embedding methods in Yelp dataset. This phenomenon explains the assumption that homogeneous and heterogeneous network structure information and nodes attribute information make different contributions to network embedding due to the nature of different networks.

3. By comparing the link prediction performance of LINE, AutoEncoder, metapath2vec and the proposed AHNE, it can be found that the fusion embedding learned from three views through the attention mechanism can improve the ability of embedding learned by a single view. It means that multi-views can compensate for the lack of information in a single view.

   In addition, the DBLP1 dataset is used as an example to explore the impact of embedding dimension on network representation learning in the proposed method. The dimension d is set to vary from 6 to 66 with the step is 10, which means the dimension of attention based fusion embedding varies from 18 to 198, and the link prediction results of AHNE with different d is shown in Table 2. It can be found that the results of link prediction are improved with d increases, but the results tend to be stable when d reaches a certain value, and the time and space complexity of the proposed model become higher with the increase of d.

Table 2. The link prediction result of AHNE with different d.

$3 \times d$	18	48	78	108	138	168	198
ACC	0.6246	0.6846	0.6950	0.7078	0.7048	0.7029	0.7077
AUC	0.6257	0.6848	0.6954	0.7082	0.7048	0.7033	0.7077

5   Conclusion

In this paper, we propose a novel attributed heterogeneous information network embedding algorithm named AHNE, which integrates the contributions of different views of the network in the process of network embedding. AHNE obtains the nodes attribute information, the homogeneous first-order and second-order neighborhood information and the heterogeneous neighborhood information guided by meta-paths as the three views of the AHIN. Then, it learns the embedding of these three views by different techniques. Finally, the attention mechanism is employed to fuse the embeddings learned from the three views to learn the final nodes representations. Extensive experimental results on multiple datasets show that the proposed model outperforms the start-of-the-art baselines in link prediction task. However, the proposed model has room to improve in the future. AHNE is incapable to handle the nodes that lack of partial information, such as the authors with no attribute information in DBLP and the businesses with no link information in Yelp. Therefore, our future work will focus on how to adopt the proposed model to learn nodes representations when some information is insufficient.

Acknowledgements. This research was supported by Natural Science Foundation of China (Grant no. 61672284), Natural Science Foundation of Jiangsu Province (Grant no. BK20171418), China Postdoctoral Science Foundation (Grant no. 2016M591841), Jiangsu Planned Projects for Postdoctoral Research Funds (No. 1601225C).

References

1. Bhagat, S., Cormode, G., Muthukrishnan, S.: Node classification in social networks. In: Aggarwal, C. (ed.) Social Network Data Analytics, pp. 115–148. Springer, Boston (2011). https://doi.org/10.1007/978-1-4419-8462-3_5
2. Cao, S., Lu, W., Xu, Q.: Grarep: learning graph representations with global structural information. In: Proceedings of the 24th ACM International on Conference on Information and Knowledge Management, pp. 891–900 (2015)
3. Cao, S., Lu, W., Xu, Q.: Deep neural networks for learning graph representations. In: Thirtieth AAAI Conference on Artificial Intelligence (2016)
4. Cen, Y., Zou, X., Zhang, J., Yang, H., Zhou, J., Tang, J.: Representation learning for attributed multiplex heterogeneous network. In: Proceedings of the 25th ACM SIGKDD International Conference on Knowledge Discovery & Data Mining, pp. 1358–1368 (2019)

5. Chang, S., Han, W., Tang, J., Qi, G.J., Aggarwal, C.C., Huang, T.S.: Heterogeneous network embedding via deep architectures. In: Proceedings of the 21th ACM SIGKDD International Conference on Knowledge Discovery and Data Mining, pp. 119–128 (2015)
6. Cui, P., Wang, X., Pei, J., Zhu, W.: A survey on network embedding. IEEE Trans. Knowl. Data Eng. **31**(5), 833–852 (2018)
7. Dong, Y., Chawla, N.V., Swami, A.: metapath2vec: scalable representation learning for heterogeneous networks. In: Proceedings of the 23rd ACM SIGKDD International Conference on Knowledge Discovery and Data Mining, pp. 135–144 (2017)
8. Fan, S., Shi, C., Wang, X.: Abnormal event detection via heterogeneous information network embedding. In: Proceedings of the 27th ACM International Conference on Information and Knowledge Management, pp. 1483–1486 (2018)
9. Fortunato, S.: Community detection in graphs. Phys. Rep. **486**(3–5), 75–174 (2010)
10. Goyal, P., Ferrara, E.: Graph embedding techniques, applications, and performance: a survey. Knowl.-Based Syst. **151**, 78–94 (2018)
11. Grover, A., Leskovec, J.: node2vec: scalable feature learning for networks. In: Proceedings of the 22nd ACM SIGKDD International Conference on Knowledge Discovery and Data Mining, pp. 855–864 (2016)
12. Hamilton, W.L., Ying, R., Leskovec, J.: Representation learning on graphs: methods and applications. arXiv preprint arXiv:1709.05584 (2017)
13. Huang, X., Li, J., Hu, X.: Label informed attributed network embedding. In: Proceedings of the Tenth ACM International Conference on Web Search and Data Mining, pp. 731–739 (2017)
14. Liben-Nowell, D., Kleinberg, J.: The link-prediction problem for social networks. J. Am. Soc. Inform. Sci. Technol. **58**(7), 1019–1031 (2007)
15. Liu, M., Liu, J., Chen, Y., Wang, M., Chen, H., Zheng, Q.: AHNG: representation learning on attributed heterogeneous network. Inf. Fusion **50**, 221–230 (2019)
16. Perozzi, B., Al-Rfou, R., Skiena, S.: Deepwalk: online learning of social representations. In: Proceedings of the 20th ACM SIGKDD International Conference on Knowledge Discovery and Data Mining, pp. 701–710 (2014)
17. Shi, C., Hu, B., Zhao, W.X., Philip, S.Y.: Heterogeneous information network embedding for recommendation. IEEE Trans. Knowl. Data Eng. **31**(2), 357–370 (2018)
18. Tang, J., Liu, J., Zhang, M., Mei, Q.: Visualizing large-scale and high-dimensional data. In: Proceedings of the 25th International Conference on World Wide Web, pp. 287–297 (2016)
19. Tang, J., Qu, M., Mei, Q.: PTE: predictive text embedding through large-scale heterogeneous text networks. In: Proceedings of the 21th ACM SIGKDD International Conference on Knowledge Discovery and Data Mining, pp. 1165–1174 (2015)
20. Tang, J., Qu, M., Wang, M., Zhang, M., Yan, J., Mei, Q.: Line: large-scale information network embedding. In: Proceedings of the 24th International Conference on World Wide Web, pp. 1067–1077 (2015)
21. Tang, J., Zhang, J., Yao, L., Li, J., Zhang, L., Su, Z.: Arnetminer: extraction and mining of academic social networks, pp. 990–998 (2008)
22. Tu, C., Liu, H., Liu, Z., Sun, M.: Cane: context-aware network embedding for relation modeling. In: Proceedings of the 55th Annual Meeting of the Association for Computational Linguistics (vol. 1: Long Papers), pp. 1722–1731 (2017)
23. Wang, D., Cui, P., Zhu, W.: Structural deep network embedding. In: Proceedings of the 22nd ACM SIGKDD International Conference on Knowledge Discovery and Data Mining, pp. 1225–1234 (2016)

24. Wang, X., et al.: Heterogeneous graph attention network. In: The World Wide Web Conference, pp. 2022–2032 (2019)
25. Yang, C., Liu, Z., Zhao, D., Sun, M., Chang, E.: Network representation learning with rich text information. In: Twenty-Fourth International Joint Conference on Artificial Intelligence (2015)
26. Zhang, D., Yin, J., Zhu, X., Zhang, C.: Collective classification via discriminative matrix factorization on sparsely labeled networks. In: Proceedings of the 25th ACM International on Conference on Information and Knowledge Management, pp. 1563–1572 (2016)
27. Zhang, Z., et al.: ANRL: attributed network representation learning via deep neural networks. In: IJCAI 2018, pp. 3155–3161 (2018)

Automatic Generation and Classification of Malicious FQDN

Kenichi Yoshida[1]([✉]), Kazunori Fujiwara[2], Akira Sato[1], and Shuji Sannomiya[1]

[1] University of Tsukuba, Tsukuba, Japan
yoshida.kenichi.ka@u.tsukuba.ac.jp, {akira,san}@cc.tsukuba.ac.jp
[2] Japan Registry Services Co., Ltd., Tokyo, Japan
fujiwara@jprs.co.jp

Abstract. Due to the increase in spam email and other anti-social behavior (such as the bot net command and control server) on the Internet, Domain Name System (DNS) blacklists (DNSBLs) have been created. These are "blacklists" of malicious hosts on the Internet that are reputed to send spam email and other anti-social behavior. Most email servers can be configured to reject messages that are sent from the hosts on these lists. Because it is difficult to keep up with new malicious hosts created every day, research is required to automate DNSBL generation. To address this problem, the application of machine learning is being studied thoroughly. Deep learning is considered to be a promising approach to classify the malicious host names. This study explores the risks of these approaches by showing a simple domain generation algorithm (DGA). This report shows the importance of attributes that are used rather than machine learning techniques. Researchers in machine learning and knowledge acquisition should focus on attributes that are more important in application fields than techniques when considering the practical applications.

Keywords: DNS blacklists · Malicious FQDN · LSTM

1 Introduction

Abuse of the Internet (e.g., spam mailing, phishing, and other antisocial behavior) has been a consistent issue that continues to grow every day. Blocking the abuse with blacklists is commonly used as a countermeasure. A blacklist contains malicious hosts on the Internet that are reputed to send spam email, employ phishing, and engage in other antisocial behavior. By retrieving the blacklists every time a user receives an email, the user can reject the spam email. Despite the importance of blacklists, a considerable amount of effort is required to maintain them. Keeping up with these new malicious hosts that are being created every day makes blacklist maintenance laborious.

To automate the maintenance of the list, the application of a supervised learning framework seems to be a promising approach. Deep learning is considered to be a promising approach to classify the malicious host names. For

© Springer Nature Switzerland AG 2021
H. Uehara et al. (Eds.): PKAW 2020, LNAI 12280, pp. 120–129, 2021.
https://doi.org/10.1007/978-3-030-69886-7_10

example, Spooren et al. [20] used long short-term memory (LSTM) to find the domain name strings generated by a variety of domain generation algorithms (DGAs) [19]. They compared two string-based approaches for the detection of algorithmically generated domain names, and reported the advantage of their LSTM-based approach.

This paper reports the risks of these approaches by showing a simple DGA named FakePopular. This paper describes the importance of the attributes that are used rather than machine learning techniques. In other words, the weakness of the string-based approach is stated along with the importance of better attributes. Researchers in machine learning and knowledge acquisition should focus on attributes that are more important in application fields than techniques when considering the practical applications.

The remainder of this paper is structured as follows: Sect. 2 surveys the related works in this area. Sections 3 and 4 criticize the string-based approach by explaining that a simple DGA can generate domain names that cannot be classified by the reported string-based approach. Finally, Sect. 5 summarizes the findings of this paper.

2   Related Work

RFC6471 [15] summarizes the guidelines for the use of the shared DNS-based blacklists (DNSBLs) to filter out the spam email. As suggested by the Request for Comments (RFC), the use of public blacklists to filter out spam email is a common filtering approach. Filtering spam email and discovering other antisocial activities and identifying malicious domain names are important aspects for analysis. For example, Chen et al. [10] used known malicious domains to estimate a financial loss of 346 million US$.

Given the importance of blacklists, there are dozens of blacklists in existence [1]. Because it is difficult to keep up with new malicious hosts that are being created every day, Ref. [3] offers a proxy service to gather information from multiple blacklists. Although the use of multiple blacklists can improve the recall rate to find the malicious domain names, the service rate is currently limited (up to ∼60 queries per hour for [3]).

A supervised learning framework seems to be a promising approach to classify the malicious and benign domain names. These learned models can be used as an alternative to the blacklists.

To construct classification models, string-based attributes are used for a variety of detection methods. Spooren et al. [20] used long short-term memory (LSTM) to find the domain name strings that were generated by various DGAs [19]. ExecScent [16] used Uniform Resource Locator (URL) similarities and URL specificity. Ref. [5] tried to use patterns in fully qualified domain name (FQDN) strings (e.g., count of uppercase characters, count of numerical characters, etc.) to classify suspicious DNS names.

Time-based attributes are also used in a variety of ways. FFM [9] and Flux-Buster [17] used fast flux (frequent changes in the association between the domain names and Internet Protocol (IP) addresses) as the index to find malicious domain names. Exposure [8] uses a sudden increase in the queries for the domain name as the index. DomainProfiler [11] also analyzes the changes in the frequency of the queries for the domain name.

Another attribute worth mentioning is the relationship between the domain name, the IP address, and known malicious domains. For example, Kopis [7] analyzed global DNS query resolution patterns (i.e., the relationship among the given domain name, Border Gateway Protocol(BGP) prefix, AS numbers, and the country codes of the IP address). MAM [12] assesses the dynamics of the match between the DNS names and the IP subnetworks. Segugio [18] identified malware-controlled domain names based on their relationship to a known malicious domain. Kazato et al. [14] classified the domain names based on the malicious domain names connected through the same IP addresses.

Most of these proposed methods follow a supervised learning framework and do not rely solely on a single attribute. For example, Notos [6] combines network-based, zone-based, and evidence-based features. Torabi et al. [21] combined the number of queries and the number of IP addresses changes while proposing a distributed architecture to speed up the analysis. Fukushi et al. [13] proposed a method to reduce the labeling cost to easily generate the training data.

This paper reports the risks of string-based approaches by showing a simple DGA. By showing the weakness of the method which relies solely on a single attribute, this paper discusses the importance of researching the attributes. Researchers in machine learning and knowledge acquisition should focus on attributes that are more important in application fields than techniques when considering the practical applications.

3   Criticism of String-Based Approach

To reproduce the latest research of the string-based approach and to show its risk, this investigation applied the implementation that was used in a recent study [20]. The implementation is available on the EndGame Inc. GitHub repository [2]. Figure 1 shows the structure of the LSTM that is used.

In the reproduction experiments for this investigation, the vocabulary size (number of character types) of the "Embedding" layer was set to 42, the output dimension (the input dimension of the LSTM layer) was set to 128, and the length of the input sequences (maximum length of the domain names) was set to 247. Here, the vocabulary size and the length of the input sequences were set to handle additional experiments and they are different from [20]. However, other parameters, such as the output dimension and the dropout fraction, were set to be the same. This study also used the same loss function (binary_crossentropy) and optimizer (rmsprop).

The inputs for this LSTM are marked domain names. In [20], 100,000 domain names were generated by a variety of DGAs. They were marked as "malicious". In addition, 100,000 domain names listed in the popular domain name list [4] were marked as "benign". It reported the performance of the classifier using a 5-fold cross validation.

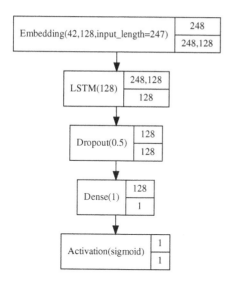

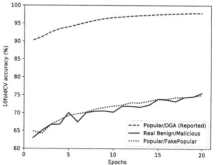

Table 1. Summary of the Experiments

Test Method	Benign/Malicious Data	Accuracy
10CV	Popular/DGA (Reported)	96.6%
	Real Benign/Malicious	70.8%
	Popular/FakePopular	71.9%
DGAmodel	Popular/DGA	99.4%
	Popular/Real Data	80.5%
	Popular/FakePopular	51.3%

Fig. 1. Structure of the LSTM to Detect Algorithmically Generated Domain Names

Fig. 2. Learning Curves of 10 cross validation

Table 1 shows the results of the reproduction experiments with additional results, and Fig. 2 shows the learning curve during the reproduction experiments. After [20], Table 1 shows the accuracy at Epoch 10.

In Table 1, the "10CV-Popular/DGA" row shows the results of the reproduction experiment (96.6%). Although this study performed a 10-fold cross validation (not a 5-fold cross validation performed in the previous work), it matched within the range of the error.

However, by applying the real benign and malicious domain names, the accuracy dropped to 70.8% ("10CV-Real Benign/Malicious" row). By implementing the DGA (named FakePopular), the accuracy dropped to 71.9% ("10CV-Popular/FakePopular" row). These are far below the accuracy that were reported in [20].

For this study, an access log of the main full-service resolver of the campus network was used to gather the real benign and malicious domain names. The DNS server is the main DNS server of the campus network. Its log contains information such as the access time, the qualified names (QNAMEs), and the replies for the QNAMEs (e.g., IP address and CNAME). This investigation gathered the QNAMEs using public DNSBLs [3]. From these gathered QNAMEs, this study randomly selected 110,000 benign QNAMEs and 110,000 malicious QNAMEs were used for the experiments.

Although the "10CV" rows show the accuracy (i.e., learning ability) of the LSTM-based method, the "DGAmodel" rows demonstrate the accuracy of the learned model from the "Popular/DGA" data. By creating the classification model from the popular domain names and the names generated by the DGAs, the learned model can classify the same data with 99.4% accuracy. However, it can classify real malicious domain names and popular domain names with 80.5% accuracy. It can classify the popular domain names and the malicious domain names generated by FakePopular with 51.3% accuracy. Almost all of the malicious domain names generated by FakePopular are classified as "benign".

These results imply the defect in the previous study. The DGAs used in the experiments were too simple to emulate real malicious domain names. It is easy to implement algorithms, such as FakePopular, to a fake classification algorithm. The next section elaborates on this point.

4   FakePopular and Its Implication

Although [20] reported the advantage of the LSTM and the string-based approach to classify the malicious domain names, its advantage suggests a new approach for the DGA. Figure 3 shows the proposed DGA, FakePopular, which is inspired by the LSTM, and the string-based classification method. It uses the LSTM to learn a typical character sequence of the popular domain names and it generates similar domain names. A simple modification (i.e., input popular domain names, and remove names registered in the popular domain name list from the output) of a Keras program example (https://github.com/keras-team/keras/blob/master/examples/lstm_text_generation.py) is sufficient to implement FakePopular.

Table 2 shows some examples of the benign domain name registered in the popular domain name list. In addition, Table 3 shows examples of the malicious domain name generated by FakePopular. As shown in Table 4, malicious domain names generated by a conventional DGA look like random strings. Meanwhile, both benign domain names registered in the popular domain name list and the domain name generated by FakePopular have many strings that are similar to English words. This difference seems to explain the difficulty to distinguish the malicious domain names generated by FakePopular from the benign domain name registered in the popular domain name list. The difference between the random sequences generated by conventional DGAs and the benign domain name registered in the popular domain name list seems to account for the high accuracy reported in the previous study.

Figure 4, 5, 6 and 7 shows the difference between the generated names by a conventional DGA and those by FakePopular quantitatively. These figures show the softmax values for the various cases. Here, the vertical axis represents the softmax values, and the softmax values for each name are arranged in an ascending order in the horizontal direction.

Figure 4 shows the softmax values for the benign names in the popular domain name list and the malicious names generated by conventional DGAs. Here, the softmax values are calculated using the model learned with the names in the popular domain name list and the names generated by conventional DGAs at epoch 10. It can be observed from this figure that the classification of the benign names in the popular domain name list and the malicious names generated by conventional DGAs is easy. Figure 5 shows the same values at epoch 1.

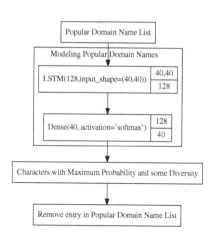

Fig. 3. FakePopular

Table 2. Real benign names in the popular domain name list

Data Set	FQDNs in Data Set
Popular:	google youtube tmall baidu facebook sohu login.com taobao yahoo wikipedia amazon sina.cn weibo pages.com live reddit xinhuanet okezone netflix office blogspot csdn yahoo.jp alipay instagram bongacams microsoft bing

Table 3. Generated Names by Fake-Popular

Data Set	FQDNs in Data Set
FakePopular	florus healmhkapees freestreet pritowosfire karaloperation causazeyillery getnation kationalingscompany iyitapelsampo andglobals dishanva alpososaceblog prissiafats careszbhar rkb rostravitudertd findound.com childingost bestcolonger kinghome bitmancherniticc mingelltbugc kunrycain afsbikra anderdoc finusinn digents birspert priceforue marketering infolitve doccizaliatraficial indias pusolinscapited ulticlint allbardlerbook

Table 4. Generated names by the DGAs that were used in a previous study

Data Set	FQDNs in Data Set
banjori	tbbbkcheverolet rufwkcheverolet ruqdkcheverolet bdufkcheverolet hzpjkcheverolet
corebot	fq25fcfo evqr5hmf3rmli mbaxyxkfofsbun1 mngrmvefm2mtkfm k8of5falofqfo cxejqlmfotovk
cryptolocker	kujtkeiammb jvppyorrlveetww slssyuywkorrd jvnppqlasqsffxgxxryd irrpbojvceeeetwlvnp
dircrypt	wcrthw bqjulgqtv jslgacuir qdtzbwlhwfnz qtedbcjkbv gdqpeasgvg qqwuhpnjaq gmjlgdwq
kraken	lvctmusxcyz psmmyuhxlt egbmbdey egbmbdey egbmbdey iuhqhbmq lvctmusxcyz smmyuhxlt
locky	wnisxbuc heuagpy jpyvnne eydusil ictjilr uirltda ipivuwsp cbtubech wwdndiqa ufbetqe wjbtpic
pykspa	wytys komeqg sysakw hiaogk dihsf rikeqs miedyw skcqqg aunib kocko mmeieg oymow ayoea
qakbot	wkuugev fcikoziviq tretxjgkvixx qxgtixqafdpttbtm qwpiffgtuchtgglb tmigagnlkyxdm qfsefmnafij
ramdo	qggsisugwskeewueseykmmmymsm skiisosmwkmeoyemmywssieaiim wssisikiksiumisgguwsmuookoy
ramnit	jajymrbihra lecyeyhn ndcfbrmorrn sjncsyhatmx swjjnlluo mhnypjoe eyyjnmrssbc ycjrmyne
simda	afybyfuvuh wybasirygazuf rynopugogetugikukyt nopowybyfetumutuwej jetorynazubutuwyt

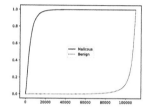

Fig. 4. Softmax values at Epoch 10

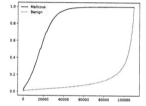

Fig. 5. Softmax values at Epoch 10

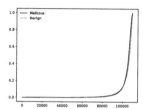

Fig. 6. Softmax values of the pre-learned model for FakePopular

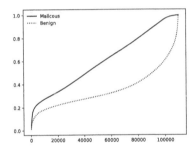
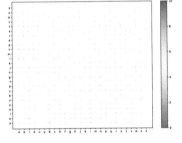

Fig. 7. Tuned Softmax values for Fake-Popular

Fig. 8. Frequency of the bigrams in the DGA data

As demonstrated in this figure, the easiness of this classification problem results in a good separation, even at epoch 1.

Figure 6 shows the softmax values for the benign names in the popular domain name list and the malicious names generated by FakePopular. The softmax values are calculated using the model learned with names in the popular domain name list and the names generated by conventional DGAs at epoch 10. As clearly shown in the Figure, most of the names generated by FakePopular are misclassified as "benign".

Figure 7 shows the softmax values for the benign names in the popular domain name list and the malicious names generated by FakePopular. Here, the softmax values are calculated using the model learned with names in the popular domain name list and the names generated by FakePopular at epoch 10. As illustrated in this figure, the classification of the benign names in the popular domain name list and the malicious names generated by FakePopular is not easy.

Figure 8, 9, 10 and 11 also shows the difference between the generated names by the conventional DGA and those by the popular domain name list and Fake-Popular quantitatively. These figures show the frequency of the bigrams in each data set. To count the frequency of each bigram, the first 40,000 bigrams were extracted from each data set and then the frequency of each bigram was counted. The horizontal axis corresponds to the first character of each bigram, and vertical axis corresponds to the second character. For these figures, color represents the frequency. To be precise, color represents the "log of (frequency of the bigram + 1)" to clearly show the difference.

Figure 8 displays the frequency of the bigrams generated by the various DGAs. As shown in the figure, their distribution has no distinct feature. However, as shown in Figure 9, the bigrams in the popular domain name list and FakePopular are biased and their distribution is similar. The similarity and the difference between the data seems to explain the difficulties of their classification tasks.

Figure 10 shows the frequency of the bigrams generated by each DGA. As shown, the names generated by each DGA are simple. Among them, corebot,

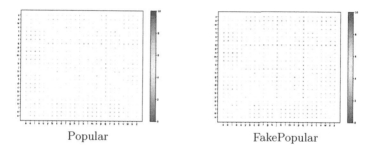

Popular   FakePopular

Fig. 9. Frequency of the bigrams in the popular domain name list and FakePopular data

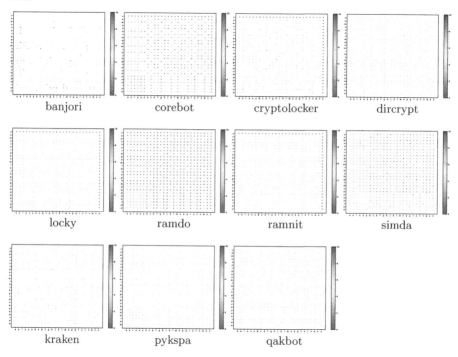

banjori   corebot   cryptolocker   dircrypt

locky   ramdo   ramnit   simda

kraken   pykspa   qakbot

Fig. 10. Frequency of the bigrams for all of the DGA data

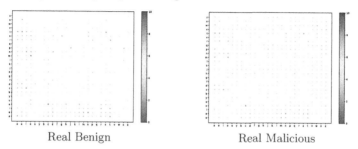

Real Benign   Real Malicious

Fig. 11. Frequency of the bigrams in real data

ramdo, and simda have some ingenuity. However, these are not enough to imitate real benign names.

Figure 11 shows the frequency of the bigrams in real data. Their distribution is similar to the popular domain name list data. Crackers seem to use a better algorithm to hide their identity.

5   Conclusion

Due to the increase in spam email and other anti-social behavior on the Internet, DNS blacklists (DNSBLs) are being created. To automate the DNSBL generation, the application of machine learning is being studied. The application of deep learning to learn typical name sequences of a malicious domain name is considered to be a promising approach.

This paper reports the risks of these approaches by showing a simple domain generation algorithm named FakePopular. FakePopular can easily pass the latest detection method. The name sequence is not adequate to be used because it is a very weak attribute. In other words, the string-based approach alone has a clear defect. A time-based approach and a combination of different attributes are appropriate.

This report shows the importance of attributes that are used rather than machine learning techniques. Researchers in machine learning and knowledge acquisition should focus on the attributes that are more important in application fields than the techniques when considering the practical applications.

References

1. DNS & RHS Blackhole Lists. https://web.archive.org/web/20130321062303/spamlinks.net/filter-dnsbl-lists.htm. Accessed 01 Jan 2020
2. Predicting Domain Generation Algorithms using LSTMs. https://github.com/endgameinc/dga_predict/. Accessed 01 Jan 2020
3. The complete IP check for sending Mailservers. http://multirbl.valli.org/. Accessed 01 Jan 2020
4. The top 500 sites on the web. https://www.alexa.com/topsites, published old version was downloaded from http://s3.amazonaws.com/alexa-static/top-1m.csv.zip Accessed 01 Jan 2020
5. Ahmed, J., Gharakheili, H.H., Raza, Q., Russell, C., Sivaraman, V.: Real-time detection of dns exfiltration and tunneling from enterprise networks. In: IFIP/IEEE Symposium on Integrated Network and Service Management (IM), pp. 649–653. IEEE (2019)
6. Antonakakis, M., Perdisci, R., Dagon, D., Lee, W., Feamster, N.: Building a dynamic reputation system for dns. In: USENIX Security Symposium, pp. 273–290 (2010)
7. Antonakakis, M., Perdisci, R., Lee, W., Vasiloglou, N., Dagon, D.: Detecting malware domains at the upper dns hierarchy. USENIX Secur. Symp. 11, 1–16 (2011)
8. Bilge, L., Sen, S., Balzarotti, D., Kirda, E., Kruegel, C.: Exposure: a passive dns analysis service to detect and report malicious domains. ACM Trans. Inf. Syst. Secur. (TISSEC) 16(4), 14 (2014)

9. Caglayan, A., Toothaker, M., Drapeau, D., Burke, D., Eaton, G.: Real-time detection of fast flux service networks. In: Cybersecurity Applications & Technology Conference for Homeland Security, pp. 285–292. IEEE (2009)

10. Chen, Y., et al.: Financial lower bounds of online advertising abuse. In: Caballero, J., Zurutuza, U., Rodríguez, R.J. (eds.) DIMVA 2016. LNCS, vol. 9721, pp. 231–254. Springer, Cham (2016). https://doi.org/10.1007/978-3-319-40667-1_12

11. Chiba, D., et al.: Domainprofiler: discovering domain names abused in future. In: 46th Annual IEEE/IFIP International Conference on Dependable Systems and Networks (DSN), pp. 491–502. IEEE (2016)

12. Dolberg, L., François, J., Engel, T.: Multi-dimensional aggregation for dns monitoring. In: 38th Annual IEEE Conference on Local Computer Networks, pp. 390–398. IEEE (2013)

13. Fukushi, N., Chiba, D., Akiyama, M., Uchida, M.: Exploration into gray area: efficient labeling for malicious domain name detection. In: IEEE 43rd Annual Computer Software and Applications Conference (COMPSAC), vol. 1, pp. 770–775. IEEE (2019)

14. Kazato, Y., Sugawara, T., Fukuda, K.: Detecting malicious domains with probabilistic threat propagation on dns graph. Comput. Softw. **33**(3), 16–28 (2016)

15. Lewis, C., Sergeant, M.: Overview of best email dns-based list (dnsbl) operational practices. Internet Request For Comments, RFC **6471** (2012)

16. Nelms, T., Perdisci, R., Ahamad, M.: Execscent: mining for new c&c domains in live networks with adaptive control protocol templates. In: Presented as part of the 22nd USENIX Security Symposium (USENIX Security 13), pp. 589–604 (2013)

17. Perdisci, R., Corona, I., Giacinto, G.: Early detection of malicious flux networks via large-scale passive dns traffic analysis. IEEE Trans. Dependable Secure Comput. **9**(5), 714–726 (2012)

18. Rahbarinia, B., Perdisci, R., Antonakakis, M.: Segugio: efficient behavior-based tracking of malware-control domains in large isp networks. In: 45th Annual IEEE/IFIP International Conference on Dependable Systems and Networks, pp. 403–414. IEEE (2015)

19. Sood, A.K., Zeadally, S.: A taxonomy of domain-generation algorithms. IEEE Secur. Priv. **14**(4), 46–53 (2016)

20. Spooren, J., Preuveneers, D., Desmet, L., Janssen, P., Joosen, W.: Detection of algorithmically generated domain names used by botnets: a dual arms race. In: Proceedings of the 34th ACM/SIGAPP Symposium on Applied Computing, pp. 1916–1923. ACM (2019)

21. Torabi, S., Boukhtouta, A., Assi, C., Debbabi, M.: Detecting internet abuse by analyzing passive dns traffic: a survey of implemented systems. IEEE Commun. Surv. Tutorials **20**(4), 3389–3415 (2018)

Analyzing Temporal Change in LoRa Communication Quality Using Massive Measurement Data

Kazuya Suzuki[1]([⊠]) and Takuya Takahashi[2]

[1] Faculty of Systems Science and Technology, Akita Prefectural University,
Yurihonjo, Akita, Japan
`kazuya-suzuki@akita-pu.ac.jp`
[2] Graduate School of Systems Science and Technology, Akita Prefectural University,
Yurihonjo, Akita, Japan

Abstract. This paper proposes a method to analyze the temporal change in the quality of LoRa communication, which is a low-power wide-area (LPWA) wireless technology for the IoT, using massive measurement data from a bus location management system. To analyze this temporal change in LoRa communication quality, many measurement data at the same position must be compared. However, buses do not always follow the same route every day. Even if buses follow the same route on different days, the measurement data are not acquired from exactly the same position. To solve these problems, we use locality-sensitive hashing (LSH) to extract comparable data from massive measurement data. Furthermore, we treat the extracted data with different distances on the same day as a series and compare regression formulas determined respectively from the plural series. As a result, it was confirmed that the received signal strength indicator (RSSI) of LoRa communication had almost no effect even in heavy rainfall of 30 mm/h. In addition, we confirmed that the radio attenuation was smaller about 2 dB than usual when there was over 7 cm of snow cover.

Keywords: LPWA · LoRa · Location data · LSH

1 Introduction

Recently, low-power wide-area (LPWA) wireless technologies, which are used for collecting small data from the IoT, have emerged and spread. However these LPWA wireless technologies, which has very small transmission rates, enable long-distance communication with low-power. LoRa [1], which is an LPWA wireless technology, can build a private network, which is called private LoRa, by using unlicensed bands. Therefore, LoRa can collect IoT data at low cost and is used in a wide range of fields [2–5].

When collecting IoT data from a wide area with LoRa, it is necessary to investigate the maximum distance for LoRa communication. There are methods

© Springer Nature Switzerland AG 2021
H. Uehara et al. (Eds.): PKAW 2020, LNAI 12280, pp. 130–137, 2021.
https://doi.org/10.1007/978-3-030-69886-7_11

for investigating the maximum communication distance of wireless technologies, such as radio propagation models and a radio wave propagation simulation. In the radio propagation model, parameters are prepared for urban areas, suburban areas and open areas; however, these parameters are not suitable for all existing environments. The radio wave propagation simulation requires information on topography and buildings in the environment; therefore, using the radio wave propagation simulation is difficult for non-experts of wireless technology.

Advances in various IoT technologies have made it easy to collect massive data. Therefore, actual measurement of the received radio signal indicator (RSSI) of LoRa communication is effective to investigate LoRa communication distance and has been reported by many researchers [1,6–9]. Although there has been many cases of collecting IoT data over a wide area over the long term, there are few reports of long-term measurement of LoRa communication quality. To continue stably collecting IoT data with LoRa communication in the long term, it is necessary to investigate how the time-varying factors such as a rainfall and fallen snow affect LoRa communication quality.

In this study, we analyzed the time-varying factors affecting LoRa communication quality by using 1.8 million measurement data points collected over 8 months by a bus location management system [2]. The system enables users to know the current location of buses in real time. In this system, the LoRa terminal attached to the bus sends current bus location information every 9 s. When the LoRa gateway receives the sending information, it measures the RSSI and sends the bus location information and RSSI to the cloud. We use the 1.8 million measurement data points stored in the cloud.

There are problems in analyzing the massive measurement data. To analyze it, the plural measurement data at the same position must be compared. However, buses do not always follow the same route every day. Even if the buses follow the same route on different days, the location data are not always sent at the same location since the LoRa terminal sends data every 9 s. To solve these problems, we use locality-sensitive hashing (LSH) [14] to extract comparable data from massive measurement data. Furthermore, we treat the extracted data with different distances on the same day as a series and compare regression formulas determined respectively from the plural series.

The paper is organized as follows. Section 2 summarizes the related work. Section 3 presents the bus location management system we developed and the measurement data used by the analysis. Section 4 proposes an analyzing method, and Sect. 5 shows the results of the analysis. Finally, Sect. 6 concludes the paper.

2   Related Works

To collect small data such as sensor data over a wide area with low power consumption, various low-power wide-area (LPWA) wireless technologies have been developed. LoRa, which is an LPWA wireless technology, enables long-distance communication by chirp modulation [10]. Since LoRa uses unlicensed bands, 920 MHz in Japan, and LoRa communication modules are commercially

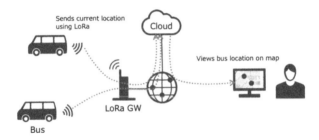

Fig. 1. Overview of bus location management system

available, anyone can easily build a private LoRa network. Therefore, many researchers are trying to realize systems for various use cases, such as a smart agriculture [4], smart grid [3], and tracking [2,5].

There have been many studies of radio propagation models, which are widely used to investigate wireless communication quality. The Okumura-Hata model [11], which is a major radio propagation model, shows the relationship between distance R and radio attenuation L as Eq. (1). A and B are parameters depending on the environment such as urban, suburban, rural, and open area. Although the model can roughly estimate the RSSI according to distance, the model frequently does not fit in many cases in actual environments.

$$L = A + B \log_{10}(R) \qquad (1)$$

Many researchers including us reported the measurement results of LoRa communication distance [1,6–9]. In our experiment, which was performed in a mountainous area where a base station was placed in a building at an altitude of 500 m, we confirmed that LoRa can communicate over 15 km with good visibility [8]. In another experiment performed on rural flat land, we confirmed that LoRa can communicate over 40 km by improving the antenna gain [9].

In this study, to extract comparable measurement data from all the measurement data, we use locality-sensitive hashing (LSH) [14]. LSH is a hash function in which data with high similarity returns the same hash value with high probability. Kami et al. [15] proposed a method for applying LSH to massive location data collected from smartphones to extract quickly places where many people gather.

3   Bus Location Management System and Its Log Data

This section gives an overview of the bus location management system [2] and the massive measurement data analyzed in this study.

Figure 1 shows an overview of the bus location management system. The LoRa terminal on the bus transmits the current location information of the bus using LoRa. The LoRa gateway receives it, measures the RSSI, and sends the location information and RSSI to the cloud. The cloud sends the latest location

Table 1. LoRa parameters

Frequency band	920 MHz
Bandwidth	250 kHz
Spreading factor	12
Bitrate	585.94 bps
RX power	13 dBm (20 mW)

information of the buses to a web browser displaying the current bus location on a map. Table 1 shows the LoRa parameters used in this system.

The LoRa gateways were placed at three locations: the city office of Yurihonjo (Fig. 3) the north and south sides of the collaboration research center (Fig. 4). This study used 1.8 million measurement data points obtained from the 3 LoRa gateways during about 8 months from June 2019 to February 2020. One measurement data item consists of a timestamp, location (latitude and longitude), and RSSI.

4 Proposed Method

To investigate the temporal change of the LoRa communication quality, it is necessary to compare plural measurement data at exactly the same location with a different date. However, buses do not always follow the same route every day. Even if the buses follow the same route on different days, the location data are not always sent at exactly the same location since the LoRa terminal sends data every 9 s. To solve these problems, we use locality-sensitive hashing (LSH) [14] to extract comparable data from massive measurement data.

Equation (2) shows a hash function calculating a hash value of measurement data x, where p_{lat}, p_{lng} are functions to extract the latitude and longitude from the measurement data, respectively. The hash function divides the value of the latitude and longitude by $tick$ and uses the floor function to truncate the number after the decimal places. This study uses 0.0001 as $tick$. This value means we get about 11.1 m and 8.6 m in the latitude and longitude direction, respectively, in Yurihonjo City.

$$hash(x) = (\lfloor p_{lat}(x)/tick \rfloor, \lfloor p_{lng}(x)/tick \rfloor) \tag{2}$$

Figure 2 shows an algorithm to extract L_1 to be compared with L_0 from L_{all}, where L_0, L_1 is the set of measurement data, and L_{all} is the set of all measurement data. The algorithm creates a set H_0 consisting of hash values calculated for all elements in L_0 (Step 2). Next, the algorithm calculates the hash values for all elements x in L_{all} and not in L_0. The algorithm creates a set L_1 by collecting values of x whose hash value is an element of H_0 (Step 3).

Although the algorithm in Fig. 2 can extract plural measurement data that are close to each other, the location of these data is not always exactly the same.

```
1: procedure input : L₀, L_all, output : L₁
2:    H₀ ⇐ { hash(x) | x ∈ L₀ }
3:    L₁ ⇐ { x | x ∈ L_all ∩ L̄₀ ∧ hash(x) ∈ H₀ }
```

Fig. 2. Extracting algorithm

Since these locations are slightly different in terms of distance from that of LoRa gateway, they cannot be simply compared. To compare measurement data with different distances from location of the LoRa gateway, this study fits the measurement data of a period to Eq. (1) and compares the regression formulas obtained by fitting.

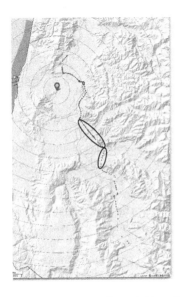

Fig. 3. Bus locations from 8:00 to 8:30 on Aug. 25, 2020 when heavy rain fell

Fig. 4. Bus locations from Feb. 5 to 10, 2020 with fallen snow

5   Analysis

5.1   Effects of Rainfall on RSSI

We investigate the effects of rainfall of over 30 mm/h on the RSSI. Figure 3 shows bus locations from 8:00 to 8:30 on August 25, 2019, when the rainfall was over 30 mm/h only in the 8-month period. From this figure, we can see that the bus passes along a straight road from about 2.8 km to 5 km and from about 5.6 km to 6.7 km from the LoRa gateway (and the measurement data on each road can treated as series data). When compared to the direction of the LoRa gateway, the

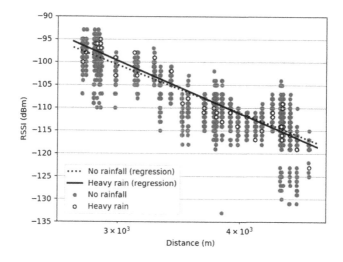

Fig. 5. Comparison of RSSI between heavy rain and no rainfall

former is a straight line extending radially from the LoRa gateway. On the other hand, the latter is slightly oblique, and the presence or absence of buildings along the road may affect the RSSI. Therefore, to investigate the effects of heavy rain on the RSSI, this study uses measurement data on the above-mentioned straight road.

Let the set of measurement data on the above-mentioned straight road during rainfall of over 30 mm/h be L_0. Given L_0, the proposed algorithm extracts L_1 from L_{all}. Figure 5 shows the relationship between the distance and the RSSI of measurement data in L_0 (Heavy rain) and L_1 (No rainfall). The two straight lines in Fig. 5 are the regression lines calculated from L_0 and L_1.

By comparing the two regression lines in Fig. 5, there is no significant difference between when there is heavy rain and no rainfall. A document [12] reports that rainfall has little effect on the 920 MHz band, which LoRa uses in Japan, and we confirmed this fact by checking actual measurement data.

5.2   Effects of Fallen Snow on RSSI

Next, we investigate the effects of fallen snow on the RSSI. Figure 4 shows bus locations from February 5 to 10, 2020, where the fallen snow was more than 7 cm in Yurihonjo City. On the north side of the collaboration research center, there are mainly paddy fields with few obstacles such as buildings and trees. Therefore, to investigate the effect of fallen snow on the RSSI, we use measurement data on a straight road from 1.5 km to 4.4 km north of the LoRa gateway, as shown in Fig. 4.

Let the set of measurement data on the above-mentioned straight road when there os fallen snow of over 7 cm be L_0. Given L_0, the proposed algorithm extracts L_1 from L_{all}. Figure 6 shows the relationship between the distance and

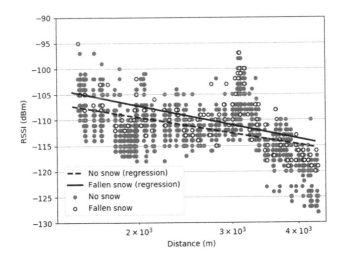

Fig. 6. Comparison of RSSI between fallen snow and no snow

the RSSI of the measurement data in L_0 (Fallen snow) and L_1 (No snow). The two straight lines in Fig. 5 are the regression lines calculated from L_0 and L_1.

By comparing the two regression lines in Fig. 6, it can be seen that the RSSI of fallen snow is about 2 dB higher than that of no snow. We consider that the reason is that the radio waves were reflected off fallen snow. In the paddy field between the straight road and the LoRa gateway, many rice ears grow in summer. However, during the period from February 5 to 10, the paddy fields were covered with fallen snow, and the obstacles on the ground were hidden. Therefore, it is considered that the radio waves were reflected off the fallen snow, so the RSSI increased.

6   Conclusion

This paper proposes a method to analyze the temporal change in the quality of LoRa communication using massive measurement data from a bus location management system. Our proposed method uses locality-sensitive hashing (LSH) to extract comparable data from massive measurement data. Furthermore, by treating the extracted data with different distances on the same day as a series and calculating regression formula from the series, the proposed method made it possible to compare the extracted data with different distances. By analyzing the measurement data using the proposed method, it was confirmed that the received signal strength indicator (RSSI) of LoRa communication had almost no effect even in heavy rainfall of 30 mm/h. In addition, we confirmed that the radio attenuation was smaller about 2 dB than usual when there was over 7 cm of snow cover.

Our future work is as follows. In this analysis, we compared the two regression lines visually with our eyes. Our first future task is to compare these two regression lines statistically instead of using our eyes. This study investigated the effects of heavy rain and fallen snow; however, there may be other factors that change over time. Therefore, our second task is to find the other factors by investigating seasonal or monthly differences.

References

1. Augustin, A., Yi, J., Clausen, T., Townsley, W.M.: A study of LoRa: long range & low power networks for the internet of things. Sensors **16**(9), 1466 (2016)
2. Suzuki, K., Takashima, H., Sato, S.: A prototype of location management system for courtesy bus of nursing home by LoRa wireless communication, IEICE Technical report, IA2019-12, pp. 11–16 (2019). (in Japanese)
3. e Silva, F.S., Barriquello, C.H., Canha, L.N., Bernardon, D.P., Hokama, W.S.: Deployment of LoRA WAN network for rural smart grid in Brazil. In: IEEE PES Transmission & Distribution Conference and Exhibition-Latin America (T&D-LA), pp. 1–5. IEEE (2018)
4. Cambra, C., Sendra, S., Lloret, J., Garcia, L.: An IoT service-oriented system for agriculture monitoring. In: 2017 IEEE International Conference on Communications (ICC), pp. 1–6. IEEE (2017)
5. Da Silva, W.R., Oliveira, L., Kumar, N., Rabêlo, R.A., Marins, C.N., Rodrigues, J.J.: An Internet of Things Tracking System Approach Based on LoRa Protocol. In: Global Communications Conference (GLOBECOM). IEEE, pp. 1–7 (2018)
6. Cattani, M., Boano, C.A., Römer, K.: An experimental evaluation of the reliability of lora long-range low-power wireless communication. J. Sens. Actuator Netw. **6**(2), 7 (2017)
7. Haxhibeqiri, J., Karaagac, A., Van den Abeele, F., Joseph, W., Moerman, I., Hoebeke, J.: LoRa indoor coverage and performance in an industrial environment: case study. In: 22nd IEEE International Conference on Emerging Technologies and Factory Automation (ETFA), pp. 1–8. IEEE (2017)
8. Takahashi, T., Suzuki, K.: Measurement of received signal strength of LoRa for agricultural IoT. In: 2019 IEICE General Conference, B-16-4 (2019). (in Japanese)
9. Sakanaka, Y., Takahashi, T., Suzuki, K.: Distance measurement of LoRa wireless communication with different antennas. In: 2020 IEICE General Conference, B-11-2 (2020). (in Japanese)
10. Vangelista, L.: Frequency shift chirp modulation: The LoRa modulation. IEEE Signal Process. Lett. **24**(12), 1818–1821 (2017)
11. Hata, M.: Empirical formula for propagation loss in land mobile radio services. IEEE Trans. Veh. Technol. **29**(3), 317–325 (1980)
12. Specific attenuation model for rain for use in prediction methods, International Telecommunication Union, Recommendation ITU-R P.838-2 (2003)
13. Geospatial Information Authority of Japan. https://maps.gsi.go.jp/
14. Pauleve, L., Jégou, H., Amsaleg, L.: Locality sensitive hashing: a comparison of hash function types and querying mechanisms Locality sensitive hashing: a comparison of hash function types and querying mechanisms. Pattern Recogn. Lett. **31**(11), 1348–1358 (2010)
15. Kami, N., Baba, T., Ikeda, S., Yoshikawa, T., Morikawa, H.: Detecting significant locations from raw GPS data using random space partitioning. Inf. Media Technol. **7**(3), 1228–1237 (2012)

Challenge Closed-Book Science Exam: A Meta-Learning Based Question Answering System

Xinyue Zheng, Peng Wang$^{(\boxtimes)}$, Qigang Wang, and Zhongchao Shi

AI Lab, Lenovo Research, Beijing 100089, China
{zhengxy10,wangpeng31,wangqg1,shizc2}@lenovo.com

Abstract. Prior work in standardized science exams requires support from large text corpus, such as targeted science corpus from Wikipedia or SimpleWikipedia. However, retrieving knowledge from the large corpus is time-consuming and questions embedded in complex semantic representation may interfere with retrieval. Inspired by the dual process theory in cognitive science, we propose a MetaQA framework, where system 1 is an intuitive meta-classifier and system 2 is a reasoning module. Specifically, our method based on meta-learning method and large language model BERT, which can efficiently solve science problems by learning from related example questions without relying on external knowledge bases. We evaluate our method on AI2 Reasoning Challenge (ARC), and the experimental results show that meta-classifier yields considerable classification performance on emerging question types. The information provided by meta-classifier significantly improves the accuracy of reasoning module from 46.6% to 64.2%, which has a competitive advantage over retrieval-based QA methods.

Keywords: Standardized science exam · Meta-learning · Question answering

1 Introduction

Standardized science exam is a challenging AI task for question answering [1], as it requires rich scientific and commonsense knowledge (see Table 1). Many researches [4, 13] solve these comprehensive science questions by retrieving from a large corpus of science-related text [14], which provide detailed supporting knowledge for the QA system [21, 23]. However, some questions are usually asked in a quite indirect way, requiring examiners to dig out the exact expected evidence of the facts. If the information of the correct viewpoint cannot be specifically extracted by the question representation, it may lead to incorrect information retrieval. Our work challenges closed-book science exams in which solvers do not rely on large amounts of supported text.

How do human learn science knowledge? When solving science problems, the first step we take to find answers is to understand what the question is about

© Springer Nature Switzerland AG 2021
H. Uehara et al. (Eds.): PKAW 2020, LNAI 12280, pp. 138–151, 2021.
https://doi.org/10.1007/978-3-030-69886-7_12

Table 1. Questions from ARC science exam, illustrating the need for rich scientific knowledge and logical reasoning ability. Bold font indicates the correct answer.

---

1. Which rapid changes are caused by heat from inside Earth? (A) landslides **(B) volcanoes** (C) avalanches (D) floods

2. What is one way to change water from a liquid to a solid? **(A) decrease the temperature** (B) increase the temperature (C) decrease the mass (D) increase the mass

3. How many basic units of information in a DNA molecule are required to encode a single amino acid? (A) 1 (B) 2 **(C)** 3 (D) 4

---

[12], so we will make a simple mapping between the questions and the knowledge points we have learned, then use a few related examples to help inference. In the process of learning new knowledge day after day, we gradually master the skills of integrating and summarizing knowledge, which will in turn promote our ability to learn new knowledge faster. Dual process theory [7,29] in cognitive science suggests that human brain need two systems of thought. Intuitive system (System 1) is mainly responsible for fast, unconscious and habitual cognition; logic analysis system (System 2) is a conscious system with logic, planning, and reasoning. Inspired by the dual process theory, our work aims to build a human-like learning system to complete science exams in a more reasonable way. As shown in Fig. 1, we propose a meta-learning based question answering framework (MetaQA), which consists of two systems. System 1 is a meta-learning module, which extracts meta-features from learning tasks to quickly classify new knowledge. System 2 adopts BERT, a large pre-trained language model with complex attention mechanisms, to conducts the reasoning procedure.

At the first stage, we use model-agnostic meta-learning method (MAML) [8] to train a meta-classifier which is able to capture the meta-information that contains similar features among different tasks, so that the meta-classifier can quickly adapt to new tasks with few samples. In this work, we regard questions with the same knowledge points k as a task. At the second stage, the BERT model learns to reason testing questions with the assistance of question labels and example questions (examine the same knowledge points) given by the meta-classifier. Experiments show that the proposed method achieves impressive performance on the closed-book exam with the help of the few-shot classification information.

This work makes the following contributions:

– We are the first to consider closed-book science exam, and propose a MetaQA system to solve this challenging task according to human cognition.
– The MetaQA system does not rely on large corpus, which is applicable for practical situations when building a targeted knowledge base requires significant human workload and time costs.

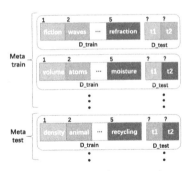 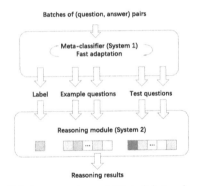

(a) Meta-learning dataset of one-shot classification.

(b) An overview of MetaQA implementation.

Fig. 1. a): An example of meta-learning dataset. The meta-train set contains multiple tasks, and each task is a few-shot knowledge points classification problem. The key goal of meta-learning is to quickly classify new categories that have not been seen before. b): Overview of MetaQA system. The input of system 1 is the batches of different tasks in meta-learning dataset, and each task is intuitively classified through fast adaptation. System 2 uses classification information (label, example questions) given by system 1 to reason the test questions.

– Experimental results show that the proposed method greatly improves the QA accuracy by +17.6%, and exceeds the performance of retrieval-based QA method.

2   Related Work

2.1   Standardized Science Exams

Various methods have been developed to tackle the science exams. Previous work [2,15] was dominated by statistical, inference methods and information extraction. With the advent of large-scale language modeling [5,17], recent researchers who take advantage of this powerful word embedding model have been shown to improve performance. Qiu et al. [26] propose NumNet+ to solve mathematical reasoning problems on DROP [6]. They use the number as graph nodes, then create directed edges based on the magnitude relationship of the numbers, and combined with RoBERTa [17] to support complex mathematical reasoning functions.

Many prior methods focus on the retrieval and analysis of problems, falling into the framework of knowledge base embedding and question answering from knowledge base. Clark et al. [3] improve question answering with external knowledge accumulated from Wikipedia or targeted corpus. However, building a comprehensive corpus for science exams is a huge workload and complex semantic representation of questions may cause interference to the retrieval process. We propose a natural solution similar to people learning concepts, who cannot record all the background knowledge, but will classify the learned knowledge points and internalize the knowledge of related example questions as a tool for answering.

2.2 Meta-Learning

Due to the huge cost involved in labeling questions, question classification datasets tend to be small [9,27], which may create methodological challenges to taxonomy. Meta-learning seeks for the ability of learning to learn, by training through a variety of similar tasks and generalizing to new tasks with a small amount of data. Meta-learning approaches fall into two main categories: (1) Memory-based methods [20,28], which try to learn from past experience by adding external memory block on neural network. Santoro et al. [28] make use of Neural Turing Machine [10], who is able to quickly encode new information, to combine information storage with retrieval functions to achieve rapid knowledge transfer and application. Simple Neural Attentive Learner (SNAIL) [19] adopts temporal convolution to collect experience, and uses soft attention to pinpoint specific pieces of details for few-shot learning. (2) Meta-learner based methods [8,22] learn highly adaptive initialized parameters by repeatedly trained on a series of tasks, so that only a small number of gradients updates are required for fast learning a new task. In the fields of image classification, natural language processing [11,20], etc., MAML has proven to be a very effective meta-learning approach.

3 Meta-Classifier System

3.1 Few-Shot Question Classification

The ARC dataset contains 7,787 genuine grad-school level, 4-choice multiple choice science questions from 12 U.S. states over the past decade. The most interesting and challenging aspects of ARC exams is the multifaceted nature, with different questions examining different types of knowledge. Xu et al. [31] classifies science questions in ARC dataset according to their knowledge points and proposes the ARC classification dataset. Their work expands the taxonomy from 9 coarse-grained *(e.g. life, forces, earth science, etc.)* to 406 fine-grained categories *(e.g. migration, friction, Atmosphere, Lithosphere, etc.)* across 6 levels of granularity.

Few-shot QC Dataset: We extract 4 levels *(L2, L3, L4, and L6)* in ARC classification hierarchy provided by Xu et al., and reconstruct the few-shot question classification dataset according to the meta-learning settings. Firstly, We remove question categories with too few instances to do 5-shot learning (less than 6 samples). For each level, Meta-training set is created by randomly sampling around half classes from ARC dataset, and the remaining classes make up a meta-test set. Table 2 presents the data statistics of the ARC few-shot question classification dataset.

Table 2. Data statistics of the ARC few-shot question classification dataset.

Measure	L1	L2	L3	L4
Meta train				
Categories	40	92	126	150
QA Pairs	4,241	4,461	4,085	3,705
Meta test				
Categories	33	77	104	124
QA Pairs	3,496	3,062	3,287	3,557
Total Categories	73	169	230	274
Total QA pairs	7,737	7,532	7,372	7,262

Few-shot QC Model: Recent question answering work benefits from large-scale language models such as ELMo [24], BERT [5], and RoBERTa [17]. These models are pre-trained by predicting missing words or next sentence from huge amounts of text, and are robust enough to be fine-tuned to new NLP tasks, such as question classification and question answering. We make use of RoBERTa-base, a 12-layer language model with bidirectional encoder representations from transformers, as meta-classifier model.

For each question, we use question text q_i and its correct answer option a_i as RoBERTa input:

$$[CLS] \; q_i \; a_i \; [SEP].$$

where [SEP] is the token for sentence segmentation, and the [CLS] is a special token for output. The [CLS] output token for each question will be fed through a softmax layer, trained by cross-entropy loss against its correct label.

3.2   Model Agnostic Meta-Learning Method

Problem Definition: For K-shot, N-way learning problem, meta-classifier learns a series of tasks from only K training sample per task ($K \leq 5$). Define the $\mathcal{Q}$ as input question space, and $\mathcal{L}$ as label space. The meta-classifier with parameters θ can be presented as $f_\theta: \mathcal{Q} \to \mathcal{L}$, and solves the following few-shot classification tasks:

$$\tau = \{ \underbrace{(q_1, l_1), ..., (q_{NK}, l_{NK})}_{\text{supporting samples * N tasks}}, \; \underbrace{(q_t, l_t)}_{\text{query samples}}, f_\theta \} \tag{1}$$

For each task, specific supporting samples and query samples are formed to train a task-specific classification model $\tilde{f}_\theta$ by minimizing the loss function $L(\tilde{f}_\theta(q_t), l_t)$.

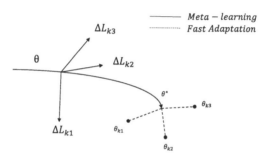

Fig. 2. Diagram of MAML algorithm, which trained through a series of tasks and set parameters at the optimal start point to adapt new tasks.

Meta-learning Method: We adopt MAML method to solve few-shot question classification. The MAML algorithm optimizes meta-learner at task level rather than data points. The meta-learner firstly learns well-initialized parameters θ in a distribution of specific tasks, and then meta-optimizes across each task's test samples by using updated parameters. The procedure can be presented in the following formula:

$$\min_{\theta} \sum_{\tau} L(D_{\tau}', \theta_{\tau}') = \sum_{\tau} L(D_{\tau}', T(D_{\tau}, \theta)). \qquad (2)$$

where D_{τ} and D_{τ}' denote the support set and query set on task τ respectively, the $T(D_{\tau}, \theta)$ is the training procedure acting on D_{τ}, and the L_{τ} is computed on updated parameters θ' with query samples D_{τ}'. When applied to few-shot question classification, question queries with the same knowledge points k are considered as task τ_k. We make use of the amount of question classes to capture meta information, which includes common characteristics among different tasks τ_k, so that the meta-information can be rapidly transferred to previously unseen classes. As shown in Fig. 2, meta-classifier can be fast adapted to new models with parameters θ_{k1}, θ_{k2} and θ_{k3} for the few-shot questions with knowledge points k_1, k_2 and k_3.

Algorithm 1 details the process of optimizing initial parameters for meta-learning. In few-shot question classification setting, the model is trained to learn questions with batches of knowledge points $K_b \sim p(K)$ sampled from support data D, and update the parameters to provide a good starting point for test samples from query data D'. Because MAML method is model-agnostic, we can easily embed MAML into RoBERTa training procedure.

4   Reasoning System

In this section, we also choose RoBERTa as reasoning model, because its powerful attention mechanism can extract key semantic information to complete inference tasks. In order to apply RoBERTa more effectively, we firstly finetune model on

---

Algorithm 1. Meta-learning for few-shot question classification

---

1: Randomly initialize θ for meta-classifier
2: **repeat**
3:     Sample batch of knowledge points $K_b \sim p(K)$
4:     **for** each knowledge point k in K_b **do**
5:         Sample support data D and query data D' for task τ_k
6:         Compute adapted parameters with j gradients step:
7:         $\theta'_k = SGD(L_{\tau_k}, \theta, j)$
8:     **end for**
9:     Update $\theta \leftarrow \theta + \alpha \frac{1}{j} \sum_{k=1}^{K} (\theta'_k - \theta)$
10: **until** Convergence

RACE [16] training set (87866 questions), a challenging set of English reading comprehension tasks in Chinese middle and high school exams. Through a single run using the same hyper-parameters in RoBERTa paper appendix, RoBERTa model gets scores of 75.9/75.1 on the validation set and test set.

Coupling meta-classifier and reasoning system is a quite complicated process, we could either construct a great number of different solvers oriented to specific question types [18], or make the meta-classifier produce incorporate information which can be directly used by reasoning model [25]. Here, we adopt the latter method – incorporating question classification information through query expansion.

We evaluate several different information expanding methods, including giving questions labels, using example questions, or combining both example questions and question labels as auxiliary information. Specifically, for a given pair, which includes test question (q_{ti}), example questions with the correct answer(q_{ei}, a_{ei}), and question label (l_i), related information will be concatenated into the beginning of the question. There are three ways to achieve information expansion:

Only label information:

$$[CLS] \; l_i \; q_{ti} \; [SEP].$$

Only example question:

$$[CLS] \; q_{ei} \; a_{ei} \; q_{ti} \; [SEP].$$

Label and example question:

$$[CLS] \; l_i \; q_{ei} \; a_{ei} \; q_{ti} \; [SEP].$$

Table 3 is an example of this process. Note that for labels under fine-grained classification, such as "LIFE_REPROD_COMPETITION" (Living Things -> Reproduction -> Competition), we only inform the reasoning model of the last level type (Competition).

Table 3. An example of query expansion for question classification labels.

Original Question Text
When air near the ground is warmed by sunlight, which of the following occurs?
Expanded Text (Label information)
Thermal Energy When air near the ground is warmed by sunlight, which of the following occurs?
Expanded Text (Example question information)
Which is most responsible for the uneven heating of the air in the atmosphere? Convection When air near the ground is warmed by sunlight, which of the following occurs?

The training process of question answering is similar to classification, where the [CLS] output token for each answer option is projected to a single logit, fed through a softmax layer, and trained through cross-entropy loss to get the correct answer.

5   Experiments

Table 2 in Sect. 4 introduced the statistics of few-shot question classification dataset. For each classification level, we specify a certain category for training data, and remaining for test data. Taking L4 as an example, the meta-train set contains 150 categories with 3,705 training samples and the meta-test set consists of 124 categories with 3,557 test questions, and there is no overlap between training and testing categories.

5.1   Few-Shot Question Classification

Few-shot question classification considers solving K-shot, N-way problem. We take 1-shot, 5-way classification as an example. For each task τ_i, we firstly sample 25 examples—1(question) x 5 (classes) to build a support set; then use MAML to optimize meta-classifier parameters on each task; and finally test our model on the query set which consists of test samples for each class. Because the question samples for each category is limited, few-shot question classification is a challenging task.

Table 4 shows that the MAML based question classification method achieves impressive performance in few-shot learning. We observe that model trained on L4 has better classification accuracy than L1. After detailed data analysis, we draw the following two inferences:

1) According to the experimental setting of meta-learning, certain tasks are randomly selected for each training time. Thus, a larger number of tasks tends to guarantee a higher generalization ability of the meta-learner. For L4 with the most tasks, it can generate a meta-classifier that is easier to quickly adapt to emerging categories.

2) Although the L4 has most categories, the questions in the same fine-grained category have a high degree of similarity. Therefore, even if the model just fits the surface features (without generalization), it may achieve high accuracy.

Table 4. Empirical evaluation results (%) of 5-shot 5-way question classification on the ARC science exam, broken down by classification granularity (L1 to L4).

Scenarios	Method	L1	L2	L3	L4
1-shot 5-way	Transfer learning	45.8	58.4	61.5	62.0
	Meta-classifier	61.8	64.9	69.8	69.9
5-shot 5-way	Transfer learning	68.7	78.1	79.0	80.7
	Meta-classifier	81.5	82.6	84.3	85.5
Number of Categories		*73*	*169*	*230*	*274*

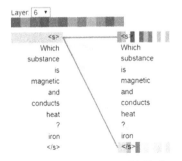 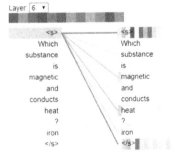

(a) Attention before MAML fast adaptation

(b) Attention after MAML fast adaptation

Fig. 3. Attention-head view for few-shot learning model, for the input text *Which substance is magnetic and conducts heat? iron.* The darker color means the higher weights. The output token <s> projects to the reasoning result of questions.

In order to verify our inference, we conduct a transfer learning experiments for in-depth analysis. We firstly train the classifier on the same training set, then finetune it on visible samples (*k*-shot each class) on test set. *Transfer learning* method in Table 4 shows that under the L1 setting, where the differences between the categories and within categories are large, the accuracy of the MAML-based method achieves 16% and 12.8% higher than the transfer method. As the level increases, the numerical difference between the results of the transfer-based method and the MAML-based method decreases, but the

MAML-based method still presents obvious advantages. The results prove that meta-classifier can effectively extract meta-features, which ensures excellent generalization performance on different tasks.

5.2 Model Visualization

In order to give an insight into the effectiveness of the MAML method on few-shot question classification, we make use of visualization tool [30] to analyze the attention weights for each word from query question, as shown in Fig. 3.

We can observe that before parameters adaptation, model only attends to the start token and the end token. After quickly fine-tuning the parameters on one supporting sample, the key information (substance, magnetic, heat, iron) of the lengthy question and answer are given higher weights. The terms with the highest attention weights (magnetic and heat) are exactly the most important clues for reasoning label *Properties of Materials*, indicating the MAML method works effectively on few-shot learning problem.

5.3 Question Answering with Few-Shot QC Information

We incorporate few-shot QC information into reasoning procedure by expanding related QC information on QA input. Figure 4 shows QA performance from L1 to L4, where the *baseline* refers to the model that does not rely on any external information; the *predicted labels and shots* represents the model using predicted information from the few-shot question classification model; the *gold labels and shots* provides the truth label and real relational example questions for test samples; the *top5 corpus* presents the performance of retrieval-based QA method, which relies on the top-5 related sentences from the ARC corpus as background knowledge. By analyzing the curve, we observe that utilizing example questions and labels produced large gains in QA performance, and the QA performance improves as the number of example questions increases.

From the results of QA performance on L1 to L4, it can be found that the finer the classification information provided by meta-classifier, the more effective information can be obtained by reasoning system. For example, the QA accuracy increases from 49.1% (L1) to 62.6% (L4) with the assistance of predicted labels and 5 example questions (Table 5). Impressively, with the information given by both gold examples and labels, the MetaQA system reaches 64.2% high accuracy, which outperforms the 63.4% accuracy of retrieval-based method.

From the comparison of *gold* curve and *predicted* curve, a certain proportion of misclassified predictions will lead to incorrect question answering decisions. With the improvement of few-shot QC accuracy from 1-shot to 5-shot, the MetaQA system obtains substantial performance gains over predicted information from meta-classifier.

5.4 Case Study

Utilizing the example questions and label information can provide an important contextual signal to the reasoning module, which would intelligently orient rea-

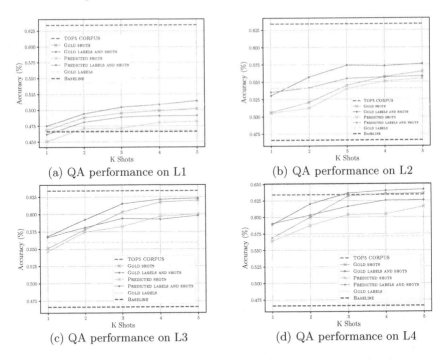

(a) QA performance on L1   (b) QA performance on L2

(c) QA performance on L3   (d) QA performance on L4

Fig. 4. Question answering performance based on question classification information from L1 to L4, compared to the baseline model and Top5 retrieval-assisted model.

Table 5. QA accuracy with the assistance of 5-shot 5-way question classification information on the ARC science exam, broken down by classification granularity (L1 to L4)

QC Info	L1	L2	L3	L4
Baseline	46.6%			
Pred Shots	48.2%	55.5%	56.0%	61.6%
Pred Labels & Shots	49.1%	55.8%	59.8%	62.6%
Gold Labels	51.3%	54.1%	55.9%	57.1%
Gold Shots	50.2%	56.5%	62.0%	63.6%
Gold Labels & Shots	51.4%	57.6%	62.3%	**64.2%**
Top5 Corpus	63.4%			

soners to determine the problem domain of the question, and ensure the MetaQA system answering with high confidence and accuracy.

The first example in Table 6 illustrates that the solver chooses the wrong answer (B) based on the question text. Given a label or an example could lead reasoner to the domain of *environmental effects on animals*, and helps to make the right decisions. The second example demonstrates that the solver still selects

Table 6. Case Study

Test Q	*Female seals usually return to the same beaches year after year to give birth. If they are repeatedly disturbed by humans at those beaches, how will the seals most likely respond?*
Ans	(B) They will give birth to more pups. ×
+Label	Environmental effects on animals
Ans	(C) They will give birth at different beaches. ✓
+e.g. Q	*A rainforest area is experiencing a severe drought. As a result, the insect population has decreased. What will the insect-eating birds most likely do? Move to a new area to find food.*
Ans	(C) They will give birth at different beaches. ✓
Test Q	*Fourth graders are planning a roller-skate race. Which surface would be the best for this race?*
Ans	(A) gravel ×
+Label	Friction
Ans	(B) sand ×
+e.g. Q	*Which material should be used on a bicycle ramp to increase friction? rough paper*
Ans	(C) blacktop. ✓

the wrong answer with the help of label information. However, if the solver is provided by related example questions, it can extract enough information to make inference and finally choose the right answer. From these two examples, we can conclude that our targeted solution - using the label information and same type questions to infer test questions, does improve the question answering performance.

6   Conclusion

This paper introduces a new framework MetaQA, which is based on a meta-classifier system and a reasoning system to challenge closed-book science exam. Inspired by cognitive science, two systems complement each other. Meta-classifier adopts meta-learning methods to enable the system to quickly classify new knowledge. The reasoning system uses strong attention mechanism to inference from information given by meta-classifier without suffering a procedure of large corpus retrieval. The experiments show the meta-classifier trained by MAML can be directly used to predict any unseen question types and achieve 85.5% high classification accuracy. With the help of meta-classifier, MetaQA system achieves gains of up to 17.6% in ARC science exam, and outperforms the corpus-based approach.

References

1. Clark, P.: Elementary school science and math tests as a driver for AI: take the aristo challenge! In: Twenty-Seventh IAAI Conference (2015)
2. Clark, P., Etzioni, O.: My computer is an honor student-but how intelligent is it? Standardized tests as a measure of AI. AI Mag. **37**(1), 5–12 (2016)
3. Clark, P., et al.: From'F' to 'A' on the ny regents science exams: an overview of the aristo project. arXiv preprint arXiv:1909.01958 (2019)
4. Clark, P., Harrison, P., Balasubramanian, N.: A study of the knowledge base requirements for passing an elementary science test. In: Proceedings of the 2013 workshop on Automated knowledge base construction, pp. 37–42. ACM (2013)
5. Devlin, J., Chang, M.W., Lee, K., Toutanova, K.: Bert: pre-training of deep bidirectional transformers for language understanding. arXiv preprint arXiv:1810.04805 (2018)
6. Dua, D., Wang, Y., Dasigi, P., Stanovsky, G., Singh, S., Gardner, M.: Drop: a reading comprehension benchmark requiring discrete reasoning over paragraphs. arXiv preprint arXiv:1903.00161 (2019)
7. Evans, J.S.B.T.: Dual-processing accounts of reasoning, judgment, and social cognition. Annu. Rev. Psychol. **59**, 255–278 (2008)
8. Finn, C., Abbeel, P., Levine, S.: Model-agnostic meta-learning for fast adaptation of deep networks. In: Proceedings of the 34th International Conference on Machine Learning-Volume 70, pp. 1126–1135. JMLR. org (2017)
9. Godea, A., Nielsen, R.: Annotating educational questions for student response analysis. In: Proceedings of the Eleventh International Conference on Language Resources and Evaluation (LREC 2018) (2018)
10. Graves, A., Wayne, G., Danihelka, I.: Neural turing machines. arXiv preprint arXiv:1410.5401 (2014)
11. Gu, J., Wang, Y., Chen, Y., Cho, K., Li, V.O.: Meta-learning for low-resource neural machine translation. arXiv preprint arXiv:1808.08437 (2018)
12. Hovy, E., Gerber, L., Hermjakob, U., Lin, C.Y., Ravichandran, D.: Toward semantics-based answer pinpointing. In: Proceedings of the First International Conference on Human Language Technology Research (2001)
13. Jansen, P., Sharp, R., Surdeanu, M., Clark, P.: Framing qa as building and ranking intersentence answer justifications. Comput. Linguist. **43**(2), 407–449 (2017)
14. Jansen, P.A., Wainwright, E., Marmorstein, S., Morrison, C.T.: Worldtree: a corpus of explanation graphs for elementary science questions supporting multi-hop inference. arXiv preprint arXiv:1802.03052 (2018)
15. Khashabi, D., Khot, T., Sabharwal, A., Roth, D.: Question answering as global reasoning over semantic abstractions. In: Thirty-Second AAAI Conference on Artificial Intelligence (2018)
16. Lai, G., Xie, Q., Liu, H., Yang, Y., Hovy, E.: Race: large-scale reading comprehension dataset from examinations. arXiv preprint arXiv:1704.04683 (2017)
17. Liu, Y., et al.: Roberta: a robustly optimized bert pretraining approach. arXiv preprint arXiv:1907.11692 (2019)
18. Minsky, M.: Society of Mind. Simon and Schuster, New York (1988)
19. Mishra, N., Rohaninejad, M., Chen, X., Abbeel, P.: A simple neural attentive meta-learner (2017)
20. Munkhdalai, T., Yu, H.: Meta networks. In: Proceedings of the 34th International Conference on Machine Learning-Volume 70, pp. 2554–2563. JMLR. org (2017)

21. Musa, R., et al.: Answering science exam questions using query reformulation with background knowledge (2018)
22. Nichol, A., Schulman, J.: Reptile: a scalable metalearning algorithm, vol. 2. arXiv preprint arXiv:1803.02999 (2018)
23. Pan, X., Sun, K., Yu, D., Ji, H., Yu, D.: Improving question answering with external knowledge. arXiv preprint arXiv:1902.00993 (2019)
24. Peters, M.E., et al.: Deep contextualized word representations. arXiv preprint arXiv:1802.05365 (2018)
25. Qiu, Y., Frei, H.P.: Concept based query expansion. In: Proceedings of the 16th annual international ACM SIGIR Conference on Research and Development in Information Retrieval, pp. 160–169. ACM (1993)
26. Ran, Q., Lin, Y., Li, P., Zhou, J., Liu, Z.: Numnet: machine reading comprehension with numerical reasoning. arXiv preprint arXiv:1910.06701 (2019)
27. Roberts, K., et al., K.: Automatically classifying question types for consumer health questions. In: AMIA Annual Symposium Proceedings, vol. 2014, p. 1018. American Medical Informatics Association (2014)
28. Santoro, A., Bartunov, S., Botvinick, M., Wierstra, D., Lillicrap, T.: One-shot learning with memory-augmented neural networks. arXiv preprint arXiv:1605.06065 (2016)
29. Sloman, S.A.: The empirical case for two systems of reasoning. Psychol. Bull. **119**, 3 (1996)
30. Vig, J.: A multiscale visualization of attention in the transformer model. arXiv preprint arXiv:1906.05714 (2019)
31. Xu, D., et al., J.: Multi-class hierarchical question classification for multiple choice science exams. arXiv preprint arXiv:1908.05441 (2019)

Identification of B2B Brand Components and Their Performance's Relevance Using a Business Card Exchange Network

Tomonori Manabe[1]([✉])[iD], Kei Nakagawa[2][iD], and Keigo Hidawa[1]

[1] Sansan, Inc., Aoyama Oval Building 13F, 5-52-2 Jingumae,
Shibuya-ku, Tokyo 150-0001, Japan
tom.manabe@gmail.com
[2] Nomura Asset Management Co., Ltd., 2-2-1, Toyosu,
Koto-ku, Tokyo 135-0061, Japan
kei.nak.0315@gmail.com
https://en.sansan-dsoc.com/, https://global.nomura-am.co.jp/

Abstract. Recently, the business-to-business (B2B) corporate brands have garnered attention. Studies using large-scale B2B company brand surveys across companies and industries have not been conducted because it is generally difficult to identify people who possess some familiarity with B2B companies externally. In this study, we use a B2B corporate brand survey data using a large business card exchange network in Japan as a proxy variable for brand power. We use the survey data to investigate the relationship between stakeholders' impressions of B2B corporate brands and corporate performance. The results show that firms with high brand have high performance. We also identified the B2B brand components using supervised topic models, and we clarified the relationship with performance. These results are not only new findings for B2B brand research but also useful for brand strategies of B2B companies.

Keywords: B2B brand · B2B marketing · Natural language processing

1 Introduction

Corporate brand is a critical element of a company's intangible assets [13]. Historically, branding has been a concept related to consumer goods, and its theory has been developed mainly as added value to products in the business-to-customer (B2C) market [8,9,14]. In recent years, however, it has been revealed that corporate brands influence purchase decisions even in the business-to-business (B2B) market. Notably, the importance of fostering emotional ties and trust with stakeholders has been clarified [12,21], and the importance of B2B corporate brands has garnered attention [24].

Unlike mass communication-based branding of consumer goods, B2B corporate branding is characterized by the forming of impressions on people who come into contact with sales activities, neighboring companies in the business

© Springer Nature Switzerland AG 2021
H. Uehara et al. (Eds.): PKAW 2020, LNAI 12280, pp. 152–167, 2021.
https://doi.org/10.1007/978-3-030-69886-7_13

network, and stakeholders [9]. Therefore, to investigate B2B corporate brands and empirically study the relationship between B2B corporate brand power and performance, brand recognition and reputation need to be quantified from people around the company, as noted above. However, it is generally difficult to externally identify people who possess some familiarity with such B2B companies. Studies using large-scale B2B company brand surveys across companies and industries have, therefore, not been conducted. Few studies [17,18] using large-scale B2B company brand surveys across companies and industries have been conducted.

In this study, we use the B2B corporate brand index (Eight Company Score [ECS][1]) measured by Sansan, Inc.[22] as a proxy variable for the B2B corporate brand. The ECS is compiled from survey data based on the business card exchange network of the business card management application Eight, which is mainly used in Japan and has 2.5 million registered users. In the survey, those who hold cards acquired from certain companies are randomly selected from among all Eight users and asked to rate their impressions of that company's brand and give free comments (detailed in Sect. 3). Being business cardholders, they are certain to have had a business-related encounter with the company at least once, and they are expected to have knowledge about the company and to work in a related industry. The ECS also benefits from its surveying more than 1,600 Japanese firms of various sizes and industries by using a large business card exchange network. The survey population is, thus, well-suited for B2B company brand research.

The research questions (RQs) we aim to address with the ECS are:

RQ1. Is B2B company brand related to corporate performance?
RQ2. What are the components of a B2B company's brand impression?

To answer these, we analyze the ECS using natural language processing and statistical methods.

The remainder of this paper is as follows. Section 2 summarizes related work and clarifies our contributions. Section 3 provides a brief description of the dataset and definitions of corporate brand and performance. Sections 4 and 5 show the empirical results of addressing our research questions. Section 6 concludes the paper.

2   Related Work

Corporate value is the sum of tangible and intangible assets. Intangible assets are nonphysical resources that are not readily apparent in public financial information [10]. In recent years, the amount of investment in intangible assets has

---

[1] Eight Company Score is a brand power index of B2B companies released by Sansan, Inc., in 2018. Sansan, Inc. conducts an arbitrary large-scale survey questionnaire to users through the business card management app Eight and builds the ECS based on the results.

continued to grow owing to investment in environmental, social, and governance (ESG) factors and achieving the Sustainable Development Goals (SDGs) [6].

Brand equity is one of the most crucial elements of a company's intangible assets [13]. Historically, brands have undergone theoretical development and empirical analysis in the B2C market [8]. As branding is mostly related to consumers' emotions, it has been considered to play a small role in the B2B market, where more rational decision-making is supposedly present than in the B2C market [16].

However, even in the B2B market, corporate brands influence purchase decision making, and emotional ties with stakeholders and fostering of trust are especially important [12,21]. The number of studies on B2B branding continues to increase [24].

Brand awareness in B2B companies is often derived from direct contact with salespeople [9]. And recognition and reputation in the surrounding of the B2B company are important for branding [2]. The importance of stakeholder engagement for corporate sustainability has also been argued [1], and the impression of the whole company, rather than the individual products, is more important concerning a brand in the B2B market [9].

These characteristics of B2B branding give rise to the need to accumulate corporate brand evaluations and measures of reputation from people surrounding the company, including stakeholders, to measure the branding. In general, however, such surveys are difficult to conduct because of the more opaque identity of corporate stakeholders from the outside. The lack of such survey data leaves many aspects of B2B corporate brands unclear. Leek et al. [16] listed several research directions of B2B branding that should be warranting future studies.

In the present study, we attempt to clarify the benefits (**RQ1**) and components (**RQ2**) of B2B branding.

Several studies have used this ECS in their analysis to show the association with performance (market capitalization [17], ROA [18]). However, these studies did not verify using data from multiple time points. Our study provides a more comprehensive analysis, including the change in brand scores over time.

3   Description of Dataset

This section provides an overview of the ECS and how to create a brand score as a proxy variable and defines corporate performance.

3.1   Eight Company Score

Sansan's ECS is an index for evaluating Japanese corporate brand impressions among the company's stakeholders. The index is created by randomly sending a survey questionnaire to selected users from 2.5 million users of the business card management app Eight, and compiling the response results. These users have acquired business cards of the company being examined. The survey is based on voluntary responses, and all personal information of the respondents is

Table 1. Eight Company Score; The number of surveyed firms and the respondents. SD: standard deviation

	2018		2019	
	May	Nov	May	Nov
Surveyed firms	1403	1633	1402	1408
Surveyed listed firms	582	591	823	824
Surveyed listed and B2B firms	312	315	426	426
Average respondents per company (SD)	190 (29)	142 (21)	155 (25)	173 (36)
Average respondents's free comments per company (SD)	55 (12)	94 (16)	103 (19)	121 (27)

anonymized. The survey is conducted biannually in May and November. Table 1 shows the number of surveyed firms and respondents at each point in time.

The questionnaire requests rating of three items – brand, service, and people – in addition to free comments about the subject company. Respondents are asked to rank responses on the following three questions on an 11-point scale, scoring from 0 to 10. Q1, brand: "Do you think this firm's brand image is attractive?" Q2, service: "Do you think that this firm's products or services are useful to your company or society?" Q3, people: "Do you think people at this firm give a good impression?" The November 2019 survey added a question about the level of perception (also from 0 to 10) about the company. Q4, recognition: "How much do you know about this firm?". Respondents then give their impressions about the subject firms in the form of free comments. Three firms selected by the survey company comprise the number of surveyed firms per respondent.

Of respondents in the subject period, 43% did not fill in the free comment field. The total number of free comments for the entire period was 545,599 (mean per company, 326; standard deviation [SD], 86), with a mean of 21.3 Japanese characters per comment (minimum: 1, maximum: 255). We used the Mecab-ipadic-NEologd dictionary [23] to create the Bag-of-Words from the free texts, limiting the parts of speech to nouns, adjectives, verbs, adverbs, and conjunctions.

3.2 Definition of Corporate Brand Score

We define the brand score of a company as the weighted average of the brand ratings (Q1) with the cognitive level of respondents as the weight as follows.

From the tabulation of cognitive ratings in the fourth survey, we found 4.4% of respondents with cognitive = 0 (Fig. 1A). Free comments also included statements such as "don't know" and "I've never heard of the company." These results indicate that a certain number of respondents lacked knowledge of companies even if they had acquired a business card of someone from that company.

When calculating the average of a company's brand rating as a company's brand strength, including the scores of such non-cognitive respondents would reduce reliability. We, therefore, considered respondents with a cognitive rating of 0 should be excluded from the average. However, surveys other than November 2019 did not include a survey item for cognitive ratings. We, therefore, created a model to predict whether the cognitive rating is 0 or not from the Bag-of-Words of free comments using the fourth survey's data. Then, using the model, we calculated the probability of non-cognition based on the free comments for each respondent given in the past three surveys.

We predicted that such a model is feasible because the comments of respondents with cognition =0 are mainly blank or statements indicating they do not know or remember.

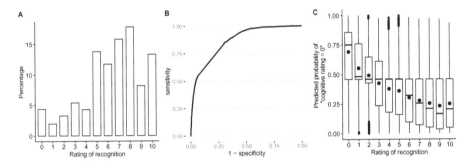

Fig. 1. Binary prediction model for non-cognitive. A: Distribution of cognitive ratings. The share of 0 is 4.4%. B: ROC curve for the binary classification. C: Distribution of predicted probability of cognitive rating =0 by actual cognitive rating

We constructed a binary classification model using the comment set of respondents with a cognitive rating of 0 (n = 7,699) and with a cognitive rating of 1 or higher (n = 170,872) as training data. The input data are the term-document matrix created from the Bag-of-Words of the comments, adding the number of characters in the comments and the flags indicating whether the comments are blank as elements of the input variables. We used weighted logistic regression with L1 regularization for the imbalanced dataset (4:96). The complexity parameter is set to the value that minimizes the prediction error of the model by 10 times cross-validation. The estimators are calculated using the glmnet package in R [11]. Datasets were randomly divided into training and test data at a 3:1 ratio. In Fig. 1B, the receiver operating characteristic (ROC) curve is reported. The area under the curve (AUC) is 0.86.

Using this classification model, we assigned prediction probabilities of cognition $= 0$ to the test data. The distribution of these probabilities for each cognitive rating is shown in Fig. 1C. The distribution of the prediction probability is downward as the recognition rating increases. The smaller the value of this prediction probability is, the less likely the respondents are to be unaware of the firm, and the more reliable their brand evaluation is. Using this non-cognitive prediction model, we calculated the non-cognitive prediction probability $p(cognitive = 0)$ from the free comments for all the remaining survey time data. We excluded responses with a predictive probability of non-cognition greater than 0.5 as unreliable responses. We then define the firm's brand score (Eq. 1) as the weighted average of the brand ratings (Q1) with $AwarenessRate = (1 - p(cognitive = 0))$.

$$AwarenessRate = \begin{cases} 1 - p(cognitive = 0), & \text{if } p(cognitive = 0) < 0.5 \\ 0, & \text{otherwise} \end{cases}$$

$$BrandScore_i = \frac{\sum_{j=1}^{n_i} AwarenessRate_{ij} \cdot BrandRating_{ij}}{\sum_{j=1}^{n_i} AwarenessRate_{ij}} \tag{1}$$

where, $BrandScore_i$ denotes firm i's $BrandScore$. $AwarenessRate_{ij}$ and $BrandRating_{ij}$ denotes $AwarenessRate$ and $BrandRating$ of respondent j in firm i, n_i denotes the number of respondents regarding firm i.

3.3   Definition of Corporate Performance

We use price book-value ratio (PBR) and return on sales (ROS) as proxies in investigating **RQ1** and **RQ2**.

PBR is the ratio of market capitalization to net assets. PBR can be used as a simple proxy to measure the value of intangible assets. PBR has also long been known as an important investment index [7]. We use PBR as of the month of the biannual ECS survey. ROS is the ratio of net income to sales. ROS has also been known as an important investment index [26]. For ROS, we use the latest data revealed at the time of the biannual ECS survey.

Table 2 summarizes statistics of the variables we used in the following analysis. Table 3 shows the correlation matrix among them.

Table 2. Summary statistics as of may 2018

	n	Mean	SD	Median	Min	Max	Skew	Kurtosis
Brand score	582	6.70	0.73	6.72	4.00	8.48	−0.09	−0.23
Sales (million units)	540	834, 694	2, 099, 187	191, 242	944	29, 379, 510	7	72
PBR	559	2.96	4.71	1.55	0.31	48.44	5.00	32.43
ROS	532	0.08	0.08	0.07	−0.17	0.49	2.00	7.39

Table 3. Correlation matrix

	Brand score	Sales	PBR	ROS
Brand score	1		0.31	−0.14	0.03

Brand score	1		0.31	−0.14	0.03
Sales	0.31	1	−0.12	−0.06
PBR	−0.14	−0.12	1	0.25
ROS	0.03	−0.06	0.25	1

4   RQ1: Is B2B Company Brand Related to Corporate Performance?

Here, we analyze the relationship between brand score and performance defined in the previous section. Table 4 shows the estimates of the coefficients of the linear regressions where the dependent variable is PBR and ROS. The regression model uses sales revenue as a control variable for firm size, the dummy variables for the industry sector, and time fixed effects. Sales revenue, PBR, and ROS are all logarithmically transformed. We excluded data with negative values from the regression. The brand score is the average across the years because ROS is annual data.

Columns (1) and (3) of Table 4 show the results for all listed companies, while columns (2) and (4) show the results when the data are limited to B2B companies. In all cases, the brand score is statistically significantly positive (at the 1% level) for firm performance. An increase of one standard deviation in brand score leads to approximately a 26% (56% for B2B) increase in ROS and a 18% (41% for B2B) increase in PBR. For both ROS and B2B, the partial coefficients of the brand score are higher when the data set is limited to B2B companies.

Furthermore, to show the relationship changes over time, we analyzed the relationship between the change in PBR and ROS, and the change in the brand score (Eq. 2).

$$
(\frac{\Delta y}{y})_{it} = \Delta BrandScore_{it} + BrandScore_{it-1} + y_{it-1} + ln(Sales_{it})
$$
$$
+ (\frac{\Delta Sales}{Sales})_{it} + TimeFixedEffects + \epsilon_{it}
\tag{2}
$$

where y_{it} is the ROS or PBR at time t of firm i, Δy_{it} represents the difference $y_{it} - y_{it-1}$, $(\frac{\Delta y}{y})_{it}$ represents the rate of change $(\frac{\Delta y_{it}}{y_{it}})$ at time t, and $\Delta BrandScore_{it}$ denotes the time difference of the brand score between t and $t-1$ for the firm i. We add y_{it-1}, $BrandScore_{it-1}$, sales revenue, sales growth rate, and fixed time effects (but only PBR) as control variables. This model also controls for unobserved company-specific variables because it uses the temporal change of corporate performance and brand score.

Columns (1)-(4) of Table 5 show the estimated partial regression coefficients for this model. The time difference of the brand score is statistically significantly

Table 4. Relationship between brand score and performance

	Dependent variable:			
	ln(ROS)		ln(PBR)	
	(1)	(2)	(3)	(4)
Brand score	0.234***	0.444***	0.168***	0.343***
	(0.050)	(0.081)	(0.029)	(0.046)
ln(Sales)	−0.101***	−0.253***	−0.226***	−0.288***
	(0.037)	(0.056)	(0.022)	(0.033)
Industry dummy	Yes	Yes	Yes	Yes
Time fixed effects	Yes	Yes	Yes	Yes
Type of business	All	B2B	All	B2B
Time unit	Year (2018, 2019)		Half-year (May and Nov 2018 and 2019)	
Observations	1,028	575	2,129	1,175
R^2	0.206	0.257	0.351	0.417

Notes: *p<0.1; **p<0.05; ***p<0.01

positive for the rate of change of ROS and PBR. A one-unit increase in brand score from 2018 to 2019 leads to an approximately 64% (90% for B2B) increase in ROS. A one-unit increase in brand score in 6 months leads to a 4.5% (5.6% for B2B) increase in PBR. Furthermore, we find that $BrandScore_{t-1}$ has statistically significant positive coefficients on the rate of change in PBR for B2B firms. This result indicates that firms with a high brand score 6 months prior tend to have a subsequent increase in PBR; i.e., the brand score is a leading indicator of PBR.

To confirm this, we add the lagged $t-1$ term of $\Delta BrandScore$ to the model and obtain the relationship between the rate of change of PBR at t (Table 5 columns 5, 6). We add $BrandScore_{t-2}$, lagged PBR change rate at $t-1$, and PBR_{t-2} as control variables.

The partial regression coefficients of $\Delta BrandScore_{t-1}$ for the B2B firm data are statistically significant and positive. A one-unit increase in brand score from 6 months prior leads to an approximate 12.4% increase in PBR after 6 months. The partial regression coefficient of $BrandScore_{t-2}$ is also positive, indicating firms with a high $BrandScore$ 1 year prior tend to have increased PBR. While these coefficients are significant in the analysis in which only B2B data were used, they are not statistically significant in the analysis in which all data were used.

4.1   Discussion

Brand score was significantly positively associated with corporate performance, ROS, and PBR. The positive association with PBR indicates that brand value is shared between stakeholders and shareholders. The positive association with ROS indicates that companies with higher brands could add price premiums.

Table 5. Relationship between rate of change in performance and brand score difference

	Dependent variable:					
	$(\frac{\Delta ROS}{ROS})_t$		$(\frac{\Delta PBR}{PBR})_t$			
	(1)	(2)	(3)	(4)	(5)	(6)
$\Delta BrandScore_t$	0.643**	0.902*	0.045**	0.056*	0.051**	0.124***
	(0.263)	(0.510)	(0.019)	(0.031)	(0.026)	(0.043)
$BrandScore_{t-1}$	−0.031	−0.021	0.015	0.048***		
	(0.105)	(0.218)	(0.009)	(0.017)		
ROS_{t-1}	0.127	0.199				
	(0.803)	(1.487)				
PBR_{t-1}			−0.004***	−0.001		
			(0.001)	(0.002)		
$\Delta BrandScore_{t-1}$					0.030	0.146***
					(0.029)	(0.050)
$BrandScore_{t-2}$					0.009	0.042*
					(0.013)	(0.023)
$(\frac{\Delta PBR}{PBR})_{t-1}$					0.061	0.183***
					(0.038)	(0.057)
PBR_{t-2}					−0.003	−0.004
					(0.002)	(0.003)
$ln(Sales_t)$	0.018	0.020	−0.006	−0.020***	−0.007	−0.017*
	(0.042)	(0.080)	(0.004)	(0.007)	(0.005)	(0.009)
$(\frac{\Delta Sales}{Sales})_t$	0.805*	0.852	0.112	0.187*	0.094	0.197
	(0.439)	(0.771)	(0.070)	(0.110)	(0.078)	(0.121)
Time fixed effects	No	No	Yes	Yes	Yes	Yes
Type of business	All	B2B	All	B2B	All	B2B
Time	t = 2019		t = Nov 2018, May and Nov 2019		t = May and Nov of 2019	
Observations	536	296	1,610	881	1,067	585
R^2	0.018	0.016	0.173	0.145	0.193	0.181

Note: *p<0.1; **p<0.05; ***p<0.01

The results show the same tendency when the data set is limited to B2B companies. This result is consistent with previous findings [9] that a company's brand impression plays an important role in the B2B market as well as in the B2C market. Furthermore, the time difference of brand score is statistically significantly positive for the rate of change of ROS and PBR. Especially for PBR, there is a significant positive correlation only in B2B companies. Therefore, this result suggests the firm's reputation, which is a factor for the PBR increase, may be shared with stakeholders before investors, especially for B2B firms.

5 RQ2: What Are the Components of a B2B Company's Brand Impression?

We approached RQ2 using the company's brand score and free comments on them in the ECS.

5.1 Supervised Topic Models

Here, we use supervised latent Dirichlet allocation (sLDA [3]) to extract latent topics associated with corporate brands from ECS free comments and corresponding brand scores. Although most topic models, such as latent Dirichlet allocation (LDA [4]), are unsupervised: only the words in the documents are modeled; sLDA infers latent topics predictive of the labels. We estimate the latent topics for predicting brand rating from 0 to 10 with sLDA.

We exclude the dataset of free comments with blank spaces and only one character. We also exclude non-cognitive prediction probabilities below 0.5. The total number of sentences used in this analysis is 423,973. We exclude words with a frequency of less than 20 and from the top five.

We use the lda package in R [5] to estimate the sLDA model. The parameters for sLDA estimation are set as follows: alpha = 1.0, eta = 0.1, variance = 5.2, num.e.iterations = 10, num.m.iterations = 4.

Regarding the number of topics K, we change K from 2 to 20 and calculate the R-squared and perplexity of the predicted and actual labels for each number of topics using five-fold cross-validation. We plot the perplexity and R-squared for each topic number. K is determined as 10, as the perplexity reaches the lower limit around 10, and the R-squared is almost saturated around 10.

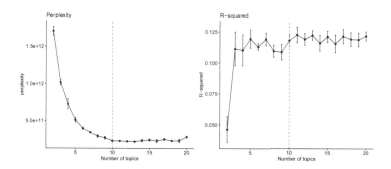

Fig. 2. Perplexity and R-squared variation with the number of topics, where the error bar is the standard error. The vertical line indicates the number of topics = 10.

Table 6 shows the 10 most likely words and the coefficient for the brand ratings for the 10 extracted topics. Additionally, we interpret each topic by referring to most likely words and the contents of free comments with high topic probability. Column 3 in Table 6 shows the interpretation of each topic. Two third-party raters confirmed the validity of the labeling. The raters were asked to score the labeling on a scale of 1 to 5 (1: not applicable at all, 5: very applicable) for each comment whose topic affiliation probability exceeded 0.5. The overall mean scores of the two raters were 3.9 (SD = 1.3) and 4.0 (SD = 1.3), and except for certain topics, the labeling's suitability was judged to be "roughly applicable" on average (Table 6 columns 5, 6).

The coefficient in Table 6 represents the expected brand rating of the respondents who describe each topic. The topic with the highest coefficient to brand rating is "Polite, Sincere, Kind, Cheerful," and that with the lowest is "Behind, Outdated."

Table 6. Latent topics related to brand ratings

#	Most likely words	Label	Coef	Validity	
				A	B
1	Strong, company, major, industry, maker, equipment, long-established, local, regional, products	Long-established, Community-based, Leading Company	7.3	3.0	3.4
2	Not..., support, thing, work, sales, deal, impression, charge, person in charge, before	Impressions of the Sales Staff	5.8	3.6	4.0
3	Be, help, from now on, always, make..., awful, asked to..., expectation, use	Partnership	8.2	4.2	4.6
4	Not..., like..., come, be, recently, thing, really, now, where, feel	Comparison with the Competition, Critique	5.4	3.4	4.2
5	Person, very, response, good, employee, many, polite, impression, easy, be given	Polite, Sincere, Kind, Cheerful	8.4	4.6	4.5
6	Like..., new, power, enterprise, business, advanced, attraction, society, development, proceed firmly	Advanced, Challenging, Developmental, Technical	8.1	4.0	3.7
7	Not..., not much, know, realize, impression, thing, do, what, nothing, hard to	No Impression	4.8	3.9	3.8
8	High, trust, large company, enterprise, security, can, technique, firmly, solid, quality	Reliability, Security, Solidity, Quality	7.6	4.6	4.1
9	Person, many, not..., like..., feeling, outdated, bad, employee, too much, compare	Behind, Outdated	4.6	3.8	3.8
10	Manufacturer, Japan, enterprise, brand, representative, world, top, the industry, domestic, lumber	Top Brands, Industry-leading	7.7	4.0	4.0

5.2   Relationship Between Each Latent Topic and Corporate Performance

These topics related to brand rating can be considered as the components of a company's brand impression because these have explanatory power for the difference of brand rating. Additionally, the difference in the frequency of topics in a set of free comments for a certain company is considered to represent the characteristics of the corporate brand impression. Specifically, in all free comments on company j, the ratio of words assigned to topic k is calculated as

$$\bar{z}_{j,k} = \frac{\sum_{d_j} \sum_{i=1}^{N_{d_j}} I(z_{d_j,i} = k)}{\sum_{d_j} N_{d_j}}, \tag{3}$$

and this is defined as the topic k frequency ratio of the company. Here, d_j is the free comments on company j, N_{d_j} is the number of words in the comments d_j, and $z_{d_j,i}$ represents the topic of the i-th word in d_j.

Figure 3 shows the relationship between topic k frequency ratio $\bar{z}_{j,k}$ and company size (sales log). There is a clear relationship between the two. For example, "Top Brands, Industry-leading," and "Reliability, Security, Solidity, Quality" are high in large companies. However, the appearance ratios of "Polite, Sincere, Kind, Cheerful" and "Impressions of the Sales Staff" are relatively small.

Furthermore, we investigated the relationship between the topic ratio $\bar{z}_{j,k}$, brand score, and corporate performance using multiple regression analysis. We add company size (logarithm of sales), survey month dummy, and industry dummy as control variables. Moreover, as the total value of the topic ratio is 1, we estimated each partial regression coefficient by excluding the regression intercept [25]. Partial regression coefficients estimated are shown in Fig. 4.

This result indicates what kind of topic ratio characteristics high brand score and high-performance companies have. Companies with a high frequency of "Advanced, Challenging, Developmental, Technical" topics tend to have a high brand score, PBR, and ROS. However, topics such as "Polite, Sincere, Kind, Cheerful" and "Partnership" that show good quality of human relations and social capital are strongly related to brand score but weakly related to performance.

5.3   Discussion

We identified the component of brand impression using sLDA with the brand score as the label for the free comments in the ECS.

We also found an association between the topic ratio and the performance of the firm. The topic of "No Impression" shows the negative association with the brand score. This is consistent with previous findings that brand recognition is foundation for B2B brand building [12,15]. The topic of "Advanced, Challenging, Developmental, Technical" shows a significant positive association not only with brand score but also with both PBR and ROS. Companies with the high topic

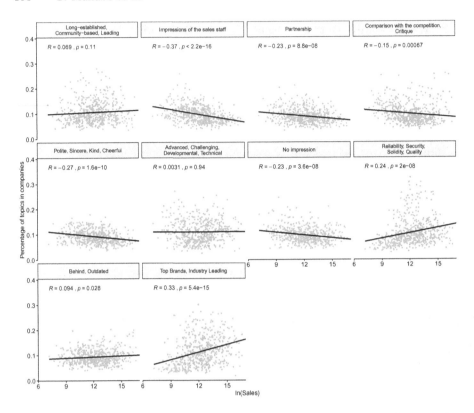

Fig. 3. Scatter plots of the firm size and each topic ratio. R represents the regression coefficient and p represents the regression coefficient $p-value$. Data from the November 2019 survey are used.

rate can add premiums and are regarded by investors; therefore, this is one of the most important topic of all.

In previous studies, risk-reduction has been emphasized as an important function of B2B brands [15,20]. Our results show that B2B brands include not only risk-reduction components but also positive components such as innovation and the potential for innovation and development. For a company to survive and grow, it not only needs to avoid risk but also needs to keep up with the changes of the times. Transactions with technologically advanced companies can incorporate advanced technology into products and production processes, and expect not only functional advantages but also halo effects, such as image development of external innovation. Against this backdrop, innovativeness can function as a brand factor.

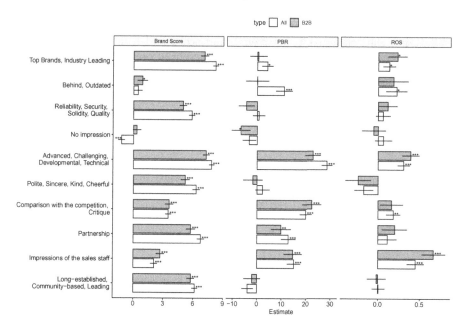

Fig. 4. Partial regression coefficients of the topic ratio $\bar{z}_{j,k}$ for brand score, PBR, and ROS. The error bar is the standard error of the coefficients. $^{*}p<0.1$; $^{**}p<0.05$; $^{***}p<0.01$

6   Conclusion

In this study, we examined the relationship between stakeholders' impressions of B2B corporate brands and corporate performance using the ECS, a corporate brand evaluation index formed on business card owners, and using a large-scale business card exchange network in Japan.

The results show that firms with high brand scores have higher PBR and ROS. The results for PBR indicate that a part of the firm's valuation is shared between stakeholders and investors. The ROS results suggest that brands are associated with higher profit margins, and brand equity could be a price premium, even in B2B. Additionally, we showed that the change in brand score precedes the change of PBR in B2B firms. This result suggests that stakeholders hold the valuation and reputation of B2B firms before investors.

We then investigated the components of the brand impressions of B2B companies. The free-description data of the ECS were analyzed using the sLDA [19] method, and 10 topics related to the brand rating were extracted. Moreover, we analyzed the relationship between the percentage of topics appearing in each firm, the firm's brand score, and the performance indicators. We found that the topic ratio of "Advanced, Challenging, Developmental, Technical" was significantly and positively related to all indicators of the corporate brand and performance. These results are not only new findings for B2B brand research but also useful for brand strategies of B2B companies.

Limitations of this study are that the ECS survey's time period is still short. In analyzing the relationship between brand score and firm performance, the temporal precedence of the brand score is an essential point of discussion; however, more time-series data are required to more strongly confirm the relationship between the time lag of brand score and firm performance.

References

1. Bal, M., Bryde, D., Fearon, D., Ochieng, E.: Stakeholder engagement: achieving sustainability in the construction sector. Sustainability **5**(2), 695–710 (2013)
2. Bendixen, M., Bukasa, K.A., Abratt, R.: Brand equity in the business-to-business market. Ind. Market. Manag. **33**(5), 371–380 (2004)
3. Blei, D.M., McAuliffe, J.D.: Supervised topic models (2010)
4. Blei, D.M., Ng, A.Y., Jordan, M.I.: Latent dirichlet allocation. J. Mach. Learn. Res **3**, 993–1022 (2003)
5. Chang, J.: lda: Collapsed Gibbs Sampling Methods for Topic Models (2015). https://CRAN.R-project.org/package=lda, r package version 1.4.2
6. Elsten, C., Hill, N.: Intangible asset market value study? les Nouvelles-J. Licensing Exec. Soc. 52(4) (2017)
7. Fama, E.F., French, K.R.: The cross-section of expected stock returns. J. Financ. **47**(2), 427–465 (1992)
8. Farquhar, P.H.: Managing brand equity. Market. Res. **1**, 24–33 (1989)
9. Gordon, G.L., Calantone, R.J., di Benedetto, C.A.: Brand equity in the business-to-business sector: an exploratory study. J. Product and Brand Manag. **2**(3), 4 (1993)
10. Hall, R.: The strategic analysis of intangible resources. Strat. Manag. J. **13**, 135–144 (1992)
11. Hastie, T., Qian, J.: Glmnet vignette (2016). https://web.stanford.edu/~hastie/glmnet/glmnet_alpha.html
12. Homburg, C., Klarmann, M., Schmitt, J.: Brand awareness in business markets: when is it related to firm performance. Intern. J. Res. Market. **27**, 201–212 (2010)
13. Itami, H., Roehl, T.W.: Mobilizing Invisible Assets. Harvard University Press (1991)
14. Kevin, L.K., Lehmann, D.R.: Brands and branding: research findings and future priorities. Market. Sci. **25**(6), 740–759 (2006)
15. Kuhn, K.A.L., Alpert, F., Pope, N.K.: An application of Keller's brand equity model in a B2B context. Qual. Market Res. **11**(1), 40–58 (2008)
16. Leek, S., Christodoulides, G.: A literature review and future agenda for B2B branding: challenges of branding in a B2B context. Ind. Market. Manag. **40**, 830–837 (2011)
17. Manabe, T., Nakagawa, K.: Empirical research on B2B corporate brand evaluation and stock price value relevance (in press). J. Japan Soc. Manag. Inf. (in Japanese) **29**(2) (2020)
18. Manabe, T., Nakagawa, K.: Relationship between corporate brand and ROA in industrial markets (in press). J. Secur. Anal. Assoc. Japan (in Japanese) **60**(6) (2020)
19. Mcauliffe, J.D., Blei, D.M.: Supervised topic models. In: Advances in Neural Information Processing Systems. pp. 121–128 (2008)

20. Mudambi, S.: Branding importance in business-to-business markets. Ind. Market. Manag. **31**(6), 525–533 (2002)
21. Roberts, P.W., Dowling, G.R.: Corporate reputation and sustained superior financial performance. J. Bus. Res. **69**, 2664–2677 (2002)
22. Sansan Inc.: Eight Compnay Score HP. https://bbes.sansan.com/. Accessed 1 March 2020
23. Sato, T.: Mecab-ipadic-neologd: neologism dictionary for MeCab (2016). https://github.com/neologd/mecab-ipadic-neologd/blob/master/README.ja. md Accessed 1 March 2020
24. Seyedghorban, Z., Matanda, M.J., LaPlaca, P.: Advancing theory and knowledge in the business-to-business branding literature. J. Bus. Res. (69) (2016)
25. Snee, R.: Design and analysis of mixture experiments. J. Quality Technol. 3 (1971)
26. Soliman, M.T.: The use of DuPont analysis by market participants. Account. Rev. **83**(3), 823–853 (2008)

Semi-automatic Construction of Sight Words Dictionary for Filipino Text Readability

Joseph Marvin Imperial[1,2(✉)] and Ethel Ong[1]

[1] De La Salle University, Manila, Philippines
{joseph_imperial,ethel.ong}@dlsu.edu.ph
[2] National University, Manila, Philippines

Abstract. Readability formulas consider word familiarity as one of the factors for predicting the readability of children's books. Word familiarity is dependent on the frequency in which the words are encountered in daily reading. Often referred to as "sight words", developing effective recognition of these high-frequency words can assist young readers to develop their reading fluency and comprehension. In this paper, we describe our work in building a dictionary of sight words for Filipino with the use of a corpus of Filipino literary materials written for children. We expanded the dictionary to a total of 664 words with the use of pre-trained word embedding model. The availability of such dictionary can facilitate the development of a readability formula for Filipino text, especially in the context of its lexical complexity.

Keywords: Text readability · High-frequency words · Filipino text

1 Introduction

Reading is an important life skill that children acquire during their early years. In many schools, students are expected to be able to read simple materials by second grade. However, when a prescribed reading material exceeds the reading ability of students, they become discouraged and disinterested and lose confidence in completing the task [4,16]. Several studies have investigated reading instruction programs to develop the necessary reading skills among students, which include the readability of text. Readability refers to features of the written text that can help increase the readers' understanding and comprehension. The readability of a text can be quantified using readability formulas that look at these varying text features to predict the reading difficulty of a given material and to help authors write texts that are accessible to their target audience [9].

Sight words or high-frequency words are commonly encountered in any text or daily reading. Mastering a vocabulary of sight words can assist young readers to read words they are familiar with or have encountered in previous text by memory or sight [22]. Reading instructions place emphasis on phonics and

© Springer Nature Switzerland AG 2021
H. Uehara et al. (Eds.): PKAW 2020, LNAI 12280, pp. 168–177, 2021.
https://doi.org/10.1007/978-3-030-69886-7_14

phonemic awareness, as well as learning high-frequency sight words to lay the foundation for children to become adequate readers [17,22]. Sight words recognition leads to effortless reading [23] by doing away with the need for readers to pause and attempt to figure out an unfamiliar word which can disrupt their comprehension [22].

In the Philippines, the Department of Education uses the Philippine Informal Reading Inventory (Phil-IRI) as an assessment tool to determine whether children at certain grade levels can read age-appropriate materials [26] and to aid in identifying the interventions needed by learners. However, the Phil-IRI manual [29] did not elaborate on the specific process or formula that they used for selecting graded text materials for the assessments. Readability metrics and technology tools can support the proper identification of grade levels of reading materials. However, there is limited work done on the development of a readability formula for Filipino text, especially in the context of its lexical complexity [15,21,32].

In this paper, we describe our work in building a dictionary of sight words or high-frequency words from a corpus of Filipino literary materials written for children in Grades 1 to 3. We discuss the step-by-step process of extracting sight words from storybooks followed by strategies to expand the dictionary using word embedding. We end our paper with a summary of our findings and recommendations for further work in readability assessment of Filipino text.

2   Related Works

Readability assessment refers to identifying the level of ease or difficulty of materials for readers to understand and comprehend the text [15,34]. The task can be done with the use of readability formulas that consider a wide range of linguistic features, such as the average sentence length in words, the percentage of easy words and the number of words known to the reader [6,9,20,24]. One of the most popular readability formulas for the English text, the Flesch-Kincaid Reading Ease [20], assigns a grade level to a given text based on the average sentence length and average number of syllables. Other readability formulas like Dale and Chall [5] and McLaughlin [24] used surface-based feature such as word count and syllable count to leverage text difficulty.

According to Chall and Dale [5], "vocabulary is also a strong predictor of text difficulty". Studies have reported the role that sight words play in reading acquisition [17] and building reading fluency [18]. Sight words refer to words encountered frequently in text that a reader can immediately recognize without the need to adhere to traditional letter-sound decoding strategies [22]. Thorndike's Teacher's Word Book [31] was the first extensive listing of English words by frequency that gave educators a means for measuring the difficulty of text [9].

The development of sight words leveraged on the idea that the first words we learn are the simplest and shortest. However, such is not the case for Filipino where it is considered as a morphologically-rich language. In Filipino, phonemes are easy to learn and words are directly read according to how they are spelled

[1]. Thus, a Filipino word may contain more than six letters and still be readable by first grade learners due the fact that the spelling of the word and how it is read are direct and straightforward. On the other hand, a common verb may render itself difficult for children to decode when varying inflections have been applied to its base form. Given these, Filipino sight words may not necessarily be the shortest words found in the language nor the common words found in the Dolch list [8] and Fry's Instant Words [11].

3   Extracting Seed Words from Storybooks

We collected 89 expert-labelled storybooks written in Filipino from a university library. These books are the prescribed reading materials for first graders up to third graders (referred as L1, L2, and L3, respectively) in the context of the Philippine basic education. Three corpora are generated, each containing the aggregate files of stories for each of the grade levels. Information about the contents of the corpora such as the total book count, total word count and total sentence count are shown in Table 1.

Table 1. Distribution of words and sentences for each of the grade level corpus.

Corpus	# of Books	Word count	Sentence count
L1	29	6,561	1,059
L2	30	13,603	1,610
L3	30	36,022	3,330
Total	89	52,186	5,999

Figure 1 shows the process for building the sight words dictionary from Filipino text, which was adapted from the combined works of [3,8,10,28]. The process commences with the automatic aggregation of all unique words present in the storybook files for each corpus. Each unique word is then associated with a frequency count based on the number of times it appeared in the corpus. This frequency-based analysis of extracting high-frequency words from each of the grade level storybooks is considered as the backbone for building the popular sight words lists that are still in use today – the Dolch's list [8] and Fry's Instant Words [11] for English, and the Arabic sight words list [28].

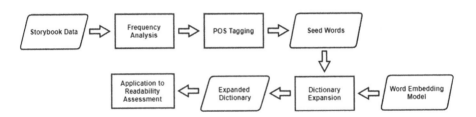

Fig. 1. The process of building the sight words dictionary.

We aggregated the first 100 top-occurring words per corpus, totaling **300 words** for all grade levels combined. Each list is composed of content words and function words. Content words are the nouns, pronouns, verbs, adjectives and adverbs that carry meaning or information to provide context to a sentence [12]. On the other hand, function words, such as *the, a, and*, show the relationships of the content words in a sentence.

A Filipino part-of-speech (POS) tagger developed by [13] is then used to identify the grammatical categories of each word to expand the knowledge contained in the word list. Table 2 shows the resulting top five frequently occurring words and their corresponding POS tag and frequency count for L1. The English translation of each word is provided in parenthesis.

Table 2. Top high-frequency content words for L1.

Word	POS	Count
nanay (mother)	noun	69
isang (one)	adjective (numeric)	47
bahay (house)	noun	29
maya (later)	adverb (frequency)	29
limang (five)	adjective (numeric)	25

We note that words from story books of higher grade levels tend to be more specific and have more variances than words in lower grade levels which tend to be more general. This observation can be seen in Table 3; for a given conceptual category such as *Persons*, the increasing variations of words associated with the theme is prominent. For example, L1 stories use familiar family members as characters, such as *nanay* and *mama* (*mother*), *papa* and *tatay* (*father*), *bata* (*child*), *lola* (*grandmother*) and *kuya* (*brother*); and general terms such as *kaibigan* (*friend*) and *lalaki* (*man*).

Table 3. Increasing granularity of words for a given theme (*Persons*).

Level	Persons
L1	*nanay, mama, papa, kapatid, tatay, kaibigan, lola, kuya, bata, lalaki, bisita*
L2	*nanay, ina, mama, tao, bata, ama, dyisus, tito, bathala, kuya, tatay, ninong, ate, kalaro, kaibigan, bruha, ginang*
L3	*nanay, anak, ama, tatay, prinsipe, hari, kuya, magulang, kapatid, prinsesa, lola, donya, datu, reyna, ermitanyo, engkanto, asawa*

4   Expanding the Dictionary

The current sight words dictionary contains 100 words for each grade level or a total of 300 unique seed words. Going over each list, we noted that there are missing words which are semantically related to the seed words. An example of this is the word *lola* which translates to *grandmother*. *Lola* is found in the L1 list but its counterpart term for male, which is *lolo* for *grandfather*, is not present. **Should these semantically related words be included in the list of sight words that L1 learners must be familiar with?** Thus, there is a need to expand the current 300-word list to include common words that are semantically related to the seed words. These include words expressing gender (*lola* and *lolo* for *grandmother* and *grandfather*) as well as common co-occuring words in the same semantic categories, e.g.., parts of the body. For the purpose of our study, we define the semantic relation between two words to include antonyms, meronyms, hyponyms and hypernyms. We turn to word embeddings to perform the task of expanding our sight words dictionary.

4.1   Word Embeddings

Word embeddings or word vectors are representations of words in a vector space. Each unique word is mapped and given its own vector value of real numbers. Words commonly appearing in a sentence or share the same context tend to have their vectors close to each other. With this, word embeddings can be used to capture the semantic and syntactic relationships of words. Using word embeddings, arithmetic operations can be performed to extract co-occurring context words such as vector(*king*) - vector(*man*) + vector(*woman*) = vector(*queen*) [25]. However, word embedding models tend to be more accurate in identifying relationships of words in the vector space when they are trained with extremely large corpus of text from a specific language.

For this task, we made use of an open-sourced, pre-trained word embedding model for Filipino from FastText [14]. The Filipino word embedding model has been pre-trained from the articles of Wikipedia and the publicly-available web-scraped data of the Common Crawl project using the Continuous Bag-of-Words (CBOW) model [2]. Word embeddings using the CBOW architecture provides a continuous distributed representation of words based on context. This means that it can be used to predict semantically and contextually related words for the dictionary. The model can be defined formally as follows:

$$\hat{r} = \sum_{i-c \leq j \leq i+ci \neq j} r_j \tag{1}$$

where $\hat{r}$ is the word vector for the center word w_i from the vocabulary V. Output words are obtained by summing all context word vectors r_j at index j. The objective function of the model maximizes the averaged log probability:

$$\frac{1}{T} \sum_{t=1}^{T} = \log P(w_i | w_{i-c}^{i+c}) \tag{2}$$

Furthermore, we note that word embeddings such as the one integrated in this study are often used for various multilingual natural language processing tasks with outstanding results [33].

4.2   Dictionary Entries

For each grade level, the word embedding model is queried using the content or information-carrying seed words to extract context-related words. Each content word can only be expanded with a maximum of three related words with cosine similarity scores of at least **0.90** which signifies strong relationship in meaning and context between two words [25]. Since semantically similar words are grouped in the vector space of a word embedding model, lowering the threshold value would retrieve words that are possibly not in the same context as the queried seed word. We used this criteria to preserve the contextual similarity of words in the dictionary. Given this, we were not able to obtain additional related words for all seed words in each grade level. A total of **364** additional context-related content words were obtained through word embeddings as shown in Table 4.

Table 4. Tally of additional words per grade level.

Corpus	Seed words	Additional words	Total
L1	100	96	196
L2	100	120	220
L3	100	148	248
Total	300	364	664

Table 5 shows some examples of content words obtained for three seed words from each grade level. The capability of the word embedding model as a resource for providing semantically similar words is seen in all grade levels. We note the presence of several lexical semantic relations between the seed words and the related words from the word embedding model such as *antonyms, meronyms, hyponyms* and *hypernyms*.

In L1, we see the inclusion of gender-based words such as *father* for the seed word *mother*. Antonyms are also present in the samples for higher grade levels such as *night* and *day* for L2 and *fast* and *slow* for L3. The word pairs in L1 such as *house-room, time-minute, water-droplet* are examples of meronyms – words that signify the constituent part or the component member of a whole. In L2, the expanded words *forehead* and *cheek* are meronyms of the seed word *face*. The results from our experiments strengthen the basis of using a word embedding model as an approach to expanding the sight words dictionary.

Table 5. Sample seed words and with related words from word embeddings.

Level	Seed word	Related words
L1	*nanay (mother)*	*tatay (father), tita (aunt)*
	aso (dog)	*pusa (cat), oso (bear), manok (chicken)*
	bahay (house)	*silid (room), tahanan (home)*
	oras (time)	*minuto (minute), orasan (clock)*
	tubig (water)	*hangin (air), patak (droplet)*
L2	*gabi (night)*	*hating gabi (midnight), araw (day)*
	mukha (face)	*noo (forehead), pisngi (cheek), ulo (head)*
	pula (red)	*pulang (red), dilaw (yellow)*
	damit (dress)	*kasuotan (outfit), suot (wear)*
	puno (tree)	*damo (grass), tangkay (twig)*
L3	*mabilis (fast)*	*mabagal (slow), mabilisan (quick)*
	kaibigan (friends)	*pagkakaibigan (friendship)*
	ginto (gold)	*gintong (gold), pilak (silver), tanso (copper)*
	bag (bag)	*katad (leather), sapatos (shoes)*
	utos (command)	*kautusan (commandment)*

5   Discussion

The establishment of a sight words dictionary for the Filipino language opens numerous opportunities where it can be used in readability assessment, reading intervention programs and oral reading fluency.

5.1   Readability Assessment

Readability formulas consider word difficulty as one of the factors for predicting the readability of children's books by grade levels [9]. Similar to the purpose of constructing the English sight words such as the Dolch and the Fry lists, our sight words dictionary for Filipino can be used by publishers, writers and educators to assess the readability of Filipino text materials prescribed for Grades 1 to 3 learners. Because the sight words were derived from books that children may be assigned to read, teaching these sight words as part of the reading and language curriculum can help children to decode these words effortlessly, allowing them to enjoy reading and to construct meaning from what they read [22].

Reading programs aim to find meaningful fictional and non-fictional text at each learner's reading level to support the use of reading strategies and comprehension skills. Currently, the words comprising our sight words dictionary were derived from fictional children's storybooks. This list can be used as part of the basic education subject that teaches the Filipino language to Grades 1 to 3 learners. Future work should consider validating the contents of the dictionary by deriving sight words from different types of text, in particular, narrative and expository social studies, otherwise known as *Araling Panlipunan*. This is the other subject in the Philippine basic education curriculum where the prescribed textbook is written in Filipino.

5.2 Oral Reading Fluency

Reading also entails the ability to orally pronounce words correctly. This can be achieved by building fluency in sight words. Fluency is "the ability to read accurately, quickly, effortlessly and with appropriate expression and meaning" [30]. When students are proficient at sight words recognition, they can devote less attention to decoding a word and more attention towards comprehension to make meaning while reading. To achieve fluency, young learners should be able to recognize 50% to 75% of the words present in story books in various grade levels [8,10]. Thus, it is important to give due consideration on the words that comprise the sight words dictionary to help students enhance their fluency [22].

Hinzman and Reed [18] classified sight words into two types: decodable sight words that frequently occur in printed English and can be read by sounding them out which, e.g., *"and"*,*"like"* and *"get"*; and irregular sight words which do not follow the letter-sound convention and should be recognized automatically to achieve reading fluency. Some of the words in the Dolch list cannot be sounded out based according to how they are spelled. Instead, learners are usually told to memorize sections of the list according to their grade level [7]. This is further expounded on the report of National Institute of Child Health and Human Development [27] in 2000 on the use of sight words as reading aid where findings suggested that readers learn more by using phonic instruction to help them in decoding each word. However, this problem is not exhibited with our Filipino sight words list due to the fact that Filipino words are directly pronounced based on spelling. While sight words in the English language are typically high-frequency and shortest words that do not follow the phoneme convention (or spelling convention), such is not the case for Filipino. Instead, sight words are high frequency words that can contain single or multiple syllabus and that children at a certain age should be knowledgeable or familiar with.

6 Conclusion and Future Work

Educators have used readability formulas to grade passages in order to prescribe reading materials that are appropriate to the abilities and grade level of children. This is necessary to develop the essential reading and comprehension skills needed to survive in schools and social settings, as well as the future job market. Readability formulas consider the linguistic features of text which include the difficulty of a given word. This gave rise to numerous research-based sight words list mostly for the English language. Reading experts have suggested that the sight words should also include words children will encounter in books that will be prescribed as part of the reading program.

In this paper, we describe our approach in building a sight words dictionary for Filipino by extracting these from children's books intended for Grades 1 – 3 learners. We generated a dictionary containing 664 words: 196 for L1, 220 for L2 and 248 for L3 using frequency analysis, POS tagging and word embedding strategies. The resulting sight words list can be used as part of a readability formula that is currently being developed for Filipino text [19].

Future work would entail the validation of the entries through expert review, comparison with sight words derived from other types of text (e.g., narrative and expository social studies), and oral fluency assessment with the target learners. A word familiarity test can be conducted following the approach of [9] to determine the percentage of readers in the specified grade who are familiar with the word. The process used in deriving our dictionary can also be applied to derive similar high-frequency words list for higher grade levels.

References

1. Gabay Tungkol sa Ispeling, Bokabularyo at Balarilang Pilipino. https://padepa. ndfp.org/gabayispeling.htm
2. Bojanowski, P., Grave, E., Joulin, A., Mikolov, T.: Enriching word vectors with subword information. Trans. Assoc. Comput. Ling. **5**, 135–146 (2017)
3. Bracewell, D.: Semi-automatic creation of an emotion dictionary using Wordnet and its evaluation. In: Proceedings of the 2008 IEEE Conference on Cybernetics and Intelligent Systems, pp. 1385–1389. IEEE (2008). https://doi.org/10.1109/ ICCIS.2008.4670735
4. Cambria, J.: Motivating and engaging students in reading. New England Read. Assoc. J. **46**, 16–29 (2010)
5. Chall, J., Dale, E.: Readability Revisited. The New Dale-Chall Readability Formula. Brookline Books, Cambridge, MA (1995)
6. Dale, E., Chall, J.: The concept of readability. Elementary English **26**, 23 (1949)
7. Dolch, E.W.: Problems in reading. Garrard Press (1948)
8. Dolch, E.: A basic sight vocabulary. The Elementary School J. **36**(6), 456–460 (1936)
9. DuBay, W.H.: The Principles of Readability. Impact Information (2004)
10. Fry, E.: The new instant word list. The Reading Teacher **34**(3), 284–289 (1980)
11. Fry, E.B., Kress, J.E.: The Reading Teacher's Book of Lists. Jossey-Bass, San Francisco (2012)
12. Ginzburg, R.S., Khidekel, S.S., Knyazeva, G.Y., Sankin, A.A.: A course in modern English lexicology. Higher School Publishing House (1966)
13. Go, M.P., Nocon, N.: Using Stanford part-of-speech tagger for the morphologically-rich Filipino language. In: Proceedings of the 31st Pacific Asia Conference on Language, Information and Computation, pp. 81–88 (2017)
14. Grave, E., Bojanowski, P., Gupta, P., Joulin, A., Mikolov, T.: Learning word vectors for 157 languages. In: Proceedings of the International Conference on Language Resources and Evaluation (LREC 2018) (2018)
15. Guevarra, R.C.: Development of a Filipino text readability index. University of the Philippines, Tech. rep. (2011)
16. Hasyim, F.: The effects of self-efficacy on motivation of reading English academic text. Ahmad Dahlan J. English Stud. **5**(1), 25–34 (2018)

17. Hayes, C.: The Effects of Sight Word Instruction on Students' Reading Abilities. Master's thesis, Goucher College (2016)

18. Hinzman, M., Reed, D.: Teaching sight words as a part of comprehensive reading instruction (2018) https://iowareadingresearch.org/blog/teaching-sight-words

19. Imperial, J.M.R., Ong, E.C.: Application of lexical features towards improvement of filipino readability identification of children's literature. Philippine Computing Science Congress (2020)

20. Kincaid, J.P., Jr., R.P.F., Rogers, R.L., Chissom, B.S.: Derivation of new readability formulas (Automated Readability Index, Fog Count and Flesch Reading Ease Formula) for Navy enlisted personnel. Technical Report, Institute for Simulation and Training, University of Central Florida (1975)

21. Macahilig, H.: A content-based readability formula for filipino texts. The Normal Lights **8**(1), (2015)

22. Marzouk, N.: Building Fluency of Sight Words. Master's thesis, College at Brockport, State University of New York (2008)

23. McArthur, G., et al.: Sight word and phonics training in children with dyslexia. J. Learn. Disabilities **48**(4), 391–407 (2015). https://doi.org/10.1177/0022219413504996

24. McLaughlin, G.: SMOG grading: A new readability formula. J. Reading **12**(8), 639–646 (1969)

25. Mikolov, T., Sutskever, I., Chen, K., Corrado, G.S., Dean, J.: Distributed representations of words and phrases and their compositionality. In: Advances in Neural Information Processing Systems. pp. 3111–3119 (2013)

26. Mocon-Ciriaco, C.: Deped explains context of news report on 70k Bicol kids being non-readers (2020). https://businessmirror.com.ph/2020/02/17/deped-explains-context-of-news-report-on-70k-bicol-kids-being-non-readers/

27. National Reading Panel (US): Report of the national reading panel: Teaching children to read: An evidence-based assessment of the scientific research literature on reading and its implications for reading instruction. National Institute of Child Health and Human Development (2000)

28. Oweini, A., Hazoury, K.: Towards a sight word list in Arabic. Int. Rev. Educ. **56**, 457–478 (2010). https://doi.org/10.1007/s11159-010-9170-z

29. Phil-IRI: 2018 Updated Phil-IRI Manual (2018). https://www.teacherph.com/phil-iri-manual-2018/

30. Rasinski, T.: The Fluent Reader: Oral and Silent Reading Strategies for Building Word Recognition, Fluency and Comprehension, 2nd edn. Scholastic, New York (2010)

31. Thorndike, E.: The Teacher's Workbook. Columbia University, NY, Teacher's College (1921)

32. Villamin, A., de Guzman, E.: Pilipino readability formula: The derivation of a readability formula and a Pilipino word list (1979)

33. Wu, F., Weld, D.S.: Open information extraction using wikipedia. In: Proceedings of the 48th Annual Meeting of the Association For Computational Linguistics, pp. 118–127. Association for Computational Linguistics (2010)

34. Zamanian, M., Heydari, P.: Readability of texts: State of the art. Theory and Pract. Lang. Stud. **2**(1), 43–53 (2012). https://doi.org/10.4304/tpls.2.1.43-53

Automated Concern Exploration in Pandemic Situations - COVID-19 as a Use Case

Jingli Shi[1]([✉]), Weihua Li[1]([✉]), Yi Yang[1]([✉]), Naimeng Yao[2]([✉]), Quan Bai[2]([✉]), Sira Yongchareon[1]([✉]), and Jian Yu[1]([✉])

[1] Auckland University of Technology, Auckland, New Zealand
{jingli.shi,weihua.li,yi.yang,sira.yongchareon,jian.yu}@aut.ac.nz
[2] University of Tasmania, Hobart, Australia
{naimengy,quan.bai}@utas.edu.au

Abstract. The recent outbreak of the coronavirus disease (COVID-19) rapidly spreads across most of the countries. To alleviate the panics and prevent any potential social crisis, it is essential to effectively detect public concerns through social media. Twitter, a popular online social network, allows people to share their thoughts, views and opinions towards the latest events and news. In this study, we propose a deep learning-based framework to explore public concerns for COVID-19 automatically, where Twitter has been utilised as the key source of information. We extract and analyse public concerns towards the pandemic. Furthermore, as part of the proposed framework, a knowledge graph of the extracted public concern has been constructed to investigate the interconnections.

Keywords: COVID-19 · Concern exploration · Opinion mining

1 Introduction

The outbreak of COVID-19 has been recognised as a severe global threat by the World Health Organisation (WHO), and it has been impacting the world in various aspects [13]. A striking particularity of this pandemic is the spread of both physical disease and mental panic [4]. People tend to express their opinions and concerns about this crisis through one of the most prevalent communicational channels, i.e., online social networks [7,12]. Such information provides strong evidence on what public concerns to be addressed urgently. This also explicitly reveals where to intervene with key communication campaigns, how to determine the measure for alleviating public fear [3]. Therefore, it is essential to automatically capture and detect public concerns in this pandemic situation.

Concern reveals negative beliefs about worry. Thus, it is essential to extract people's opinions, sentiments, emotions from their generated texts for concern detection. Sentiment analysis and opinion mining, the sub-field of Natural Language Processing (NLP), have been recognised as an important role in making sense of the textual data, e.g., Tweets from Twitter[1] [14]. In the context of

---

[1] https://twitter.com/.

© Springer Nature Switzerland AG 2021
H. Uehara et al. (Eds.): PKAW 2020, LNAI 12280, pp. 178–185, 2021.
https://doi.org/10.1007/978-3-030-69886-7_15

COVID-19, it turns out to be an essential technique to analyse public opinions and detect corresponding concerns.

In this paper, we formally define public concern and propose an automated framework to detect representative concerns from social media data by facilitating deep-learning models using the COVID-19 as typical case. Furthermore, the proposed approach can interpret the meanings of the extracted concerns and unravel their interconnections through KG. Analytical experiments were conducted in this research to demonstrate the validity of our approach.

2 Related Works

A number of researchers collected and published COVID-19 datasets, which greatly contribute to the studies of online conversation dynamics in the context of epidemic outbreak [2,10]. Boberg et al. analyse the factual basis of public fears based on the alternative news media's output on Facebook[2] during the early Corona crisis [1]. Jahanbin et al. analyse the corpus of COVID-19 tweets and identify common responses to the pandemic over time [8]. Li et al. attempt to identify situational information of COVID-19 and explore how it is being disseminated on social media [11]. Most of the researchers conduct statical analysis in regards to the keywords and trending topics.

Nowadays, Deep learning has been widely applied to NLP and social media data filtering, which yields remarkable performance [9]. Jelodar et al. utilise NLP and Recurrent Neural Network (RNN) for COVID-19 related discussion extraction and topic modelling from social media, where a supervised method is developed to analyse people opinion of COVID-19-related comments from Reddit forums[3] [9]. Fan et al. propose a hybrid machine learning pipeline for automated mapping of events and locations from social media posts during disasters, where a fine-tuned Bidirectional Encoder Representations from Transformers (BERT) has been adopted to classify the posts [6].

Knowledge Graph (KG) has been acknowledged as an effective technique for collating all the facts and presenting interconnected results in many AI and NLP tasks. Yoo et al. develop a novel method, i.e., PolarisX, to automatically expand a KG by utilising a fine-tuned pre-trained multilingual BERT model, where the data is constantly collected from news sites and social media platforms in real-time [15]. However, very few research works have been dedicated to mining the fine-grained opinions for exploring and monitoring the social concerns.

3 Automated Public Concern Detection

Figure 1 demonstrates the proposed automated concern detection framework, a hierarchical multi-stage process with four main components, including data pre-processing, deep learning models, typical concern extraction and clustering, and concern knowledge graph construction.

---

[2] https://www.facebook.com/.
[3] https://www.reddit.com/.

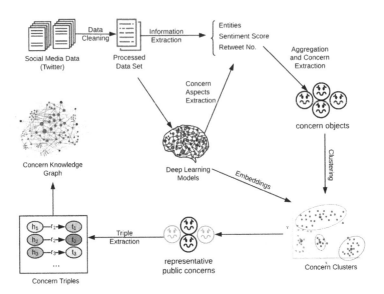

Fig. 1. Automated concern detection framework

3.1 Data Pre-processing and Information Extraction

The initial module of the framework tends to improve the quality the social media data through pre-processing by removing meaningless data fractions, such as URL, hash-tag and punctuation. As for the information extraction, three elements, i.e., concern entities, sentiment score and re-tweet number, are supposed to be captured.

3.2 Deep Learning Models

Deep learning models function as a semantic analyser in the automated concern detection framework. BERT appears to be a pre-trained language model released by Google, which is capable of taking up a number of classic NLP tasks [5,15]. We fine-tune the pre-trained BERT model for two purposes, i.e., extracting potential public concern entities and create embeddings for the detected concerns.

In the latter, we obtain the embeddings of public concern entities through fine-tuning the BERT model, where 12 transformer encoder layers are utilised, and each output per token from each layer can be used as a word embedding.

$$H_i = \frac{\sum_{k=n}^{m} \sum_{l=L_{12-x}}^{L11} h_k^{(l)}}{(m-n+1) \cdot x}, x < 12, \tag{1}$$

where H_i represents the embedding of ith concern entity and $h_k^{(l)}$ refers to the embedding of $k^{(th)}$ token at Layer k.

3.3   Concern Extraction and Clustering

By utilising the power of BERT fine-tuned model, we conduct typical concern identification through extracting and clustering potential public concern entities.

Each concern comes with four dimensions, i.e., entity e_i, re-tweet count r_i, frequency number f_i and sentiment polarity p_i. There are numerous concerns incorporated in the social media data, but only those attracting most people's attention are supposed to be identified. Thus, we measure concern c_i's degree $d(c_i)$ using Eq. (2).

$$d(c_i^t) = \alpha \cdot r_i + \beta \cdot f_i + (1 - \alpha - \beta) \cdot p_i, \tag{2}$$

where α and β balance the trade-off among three parties. A higher value of $d(c_i^t)$ corresponds to greater significant attention from the public, and vice versa. Concerns whose degree is above a certain threshold will be selected.

Next, we attempt to further narrow down the range of important concerns by picking the representative ones. In this paper, we adopt K-means, an unsupervised learning algorithm, for clustering the concerns. Given the embeddings of the concern entities produced by the fine-tuned BERT model, we formulate the objective function for concern clustering as follows:

$$\underset{o_k \in O}{\mathrm{argmin}}\ dist(o_k, H_i)^2, \tag{3}$$

where o_k denotes the kth cluster centroids in set O with $k \in K$ and O is the collection of o_k. H_i refers to the concern vector obtained through the summation of last few layers' outputs of BERT for i^{th} concern entity, which has been formulated in Eq. (1). $dist(.)$ represents a function calculating the standard(L_2) Euclidean distance. Therefore, by considering both concern degree and the distance to the centroid in the corresponding cluster, the selected set of concerns is denoted as $\{c_i^t | d(c_i^t) > \theta_a \wedge dist(o_j, H_i)^2 < \theta_j\}$, where θ_j describes the distance threshold for concern cluster j.

3.4   Concern Knowledge Graph

A concern knowledge graph is a collection of relational facts that are represented in the form of concern triples $(subject, relationship, object)$. The existence of a particular concern triple indicates a pair of existing concern facts and their semantic relationship extracted from the social media data. For example, in tweet *"Prince Charles has tested positive for Corona."*, *"Prince Charles"* has been extracted as a subject of a concern triple, then determine predicate *"tested"* as relationship and *"positive Corona"* as the object.

4   Experiments

4.1   Dataset

The Twitter COVID-19 dataset[4] used in the experiments is recognised as a public dataset, collected by Lamsal [10]. Real-time Twitter feed related to corona virus-related tweets have been incorporated by applying the keyword filters, such as "corona", "coronavirus", "COVID", "COVID19" and variants of "sarscov2".

4.2   Results Analysis

In this subsection, we provide the analysis results by analysing the COVID-19 data using the automated concern detection approach. First, public concerns are detected by ranking concern degrees based on Eq. (2). Next, pre-trained BERT language model has been applied to generate context-aware embeddings of public concerns. The concern embeddings produced by BERT are more suitable to feed into K-Means clustering to find the semantic similarity among concerns.

To determine the optimal cluster value of K-Means clustering, Silhouette analysis has been conducted to determine the separation distance of concern cluster. It can be seen from Fig. 2 that $K = 5$ is selected as it reaches the second peak value of Silhouette score. For concerns clustering, the value is largest with $K = 2$, but we select $K = 5$ to make concerns cluster more diverse.

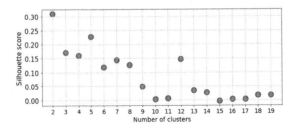

Fig. 2. Silhouette coefficient analysis for K-Means Clustering

All concern features $(x_1, ..., x_n), n = 768$ from BERT are fed into K-Means clustering. Next, we employ the Principle Component Analysis (PCA) algorithm to reduce embedding dimensions and project to a two-dimensional space in Fig. 3. Given $K = 5$, the concerns can be divided into five clusters, where the circle size indicates the concern degree. Concerns within one cluster demonstrate semantic associations. For instance, in Cluster 2, both "dr. usama riaz" and "qambar shahdadkot" are related to Pakistan.

With the assistance of automated concern detection approach, we conduct further experiments to investigate the variation of public concern, where a consecutive 3-day Twitter dataset, ranges from 25 Mar 2020 to 27 March 2020, has

---

[4] https://ieee-dataport.org/open-access/corona-virus-COVID-19-tweets-dataset.

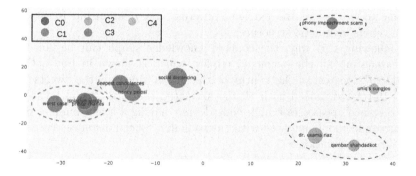

Fig. 3. Concern cluster of twitter dataset on 25th march 2020

been analysed. The extracted top concerns using our proposed approach have been demonstrated in Fig. 4, where circle size refers to the concern score and different colours show different concerns.

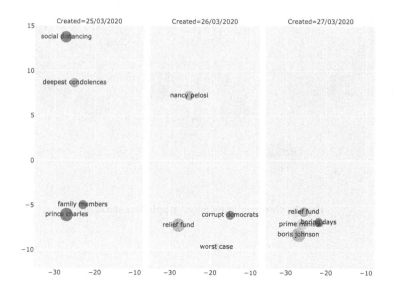

Fig. 4. Public concern from 25th to 27th march 2020

4.3   Result Visualisation

It is difficult to acquire the semantic meaning of public concerns by using independent terms. Thus, data structure triples with subject-relationship-object statement are used to build concern knowledge graph and interpret public concerns in a more meaningful way. In a triple structure, either subject or object turns out to be one of the extract concerns, and relationship is established through tweets' syntactic structure.

By following this way, the concern knowledge graph can be constructed by concatenating all the extracted triples, which is shown in Fig. 5. Concern "COVID-19" locates at the centre of the graph since all the tweets appear COVID-19-related, linked with all the extracted concerns. It can be seen that "social distance" possesses a high node degree, having a larger number of other concerns connected. Compared with "inshaallah", "social distance" turns out to be a priori consideration.

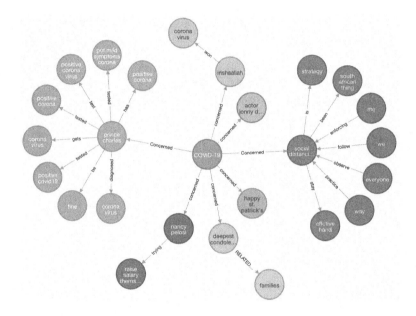

Fig. 5. Concern knowledge graph visualization

5   Conclusion and Future Work

In this paper, we proposed a novel deep-learning-based framework to automatically detect the concern. By taking in the social media data, e.g., Twitter tweets, our approach has proven capabilities in producing insights of public concerns naturally, and the proposed approach effectively identified and explained the public concerns on COVID-19 pandemics. Furthermore, we generated triples based on the extracted public concerns and constructed a concern knowledge graph, which greatly assists in understanding the interconnections among public concerns. Another shining point of the approach is its manual-annotation free. Our study also illustrates the feasibility and potential of using social media, i.e.,

Twitter, to investigate people's concerns in the period of epidemic. Experiments have been conducted to demonstrate and test the validity of our automated concern detection framework.

In the future, we plan to consider the temporal features and explore the evolutionary pattern of public concerns during the COVID-19 period along with the number of confirmed infections. Meanwhile, we will also leverage knowledge graph databases like Wikidata, DBPedia and Yago to optimise triple extraction, and apply our approach to other tasks, e.g., disaster mitigation and fake news detection.

References

1. Boberg, S., Quandt, T., Schatto-Eckrodt, T., Frischlich, L.: Pandemic populism: Facebook pages of alternative news media and the corona crisis-a computational content analysis. arXiv preprint arXiv:2004.02566 (2020)
2. Chen, E., Lerman, K., Ferrara, E.: Covid-19: The first public coronavirus twitter dataset. arXiv preprint arXiv:2003.07372 (2020)
3. Cinelli, M., et al.: The covid-19 social media infodemic. arXiv preprint arXiv:2003.05004 (2020)
4. Depoux, A., Martin, S., Karafillakis, E., Preet, R., Wilder-Smith, A., Larson, H.: The pandemic of social media panic travels faster than the covid-19 outbreak. J. Travel Med. (2020)
5. Devlin, J., Chang, M.W., Lee, K., Toutanova, K.: Bert: Pre-training of deep bidirectional transformers for language understanding. arXiv preprint arXiv:1810.04805 (2018)
6. Fan, C., Wu, F., Mostafavi, A.: A hybrid machine learning pipeline for automated mapping of events and locations from social media in disasters. IEEE Access **8**, 10478–10490 (2020)
7. Hu, Y., Bai, Q., Li, W.: Context-aware influence diffusion in online social networks. In: Ohara, K., Bai, Q. (eds.) PKAW 2019. LNCS (LNAI), vol. 11669, pp. 153–162. Springer, Cham (2019). https://doi.org/10.1007/978-3-030-30639-7_13
8. Jahanbin, K., Rahmanian, V.: Using twitter and web news mining to predict covid-19 outbreak (2020)
9. Jelodar, H., Wang, Y., Orji, R., Huang, H.: Deep sentiment classification and topic discovery on novel coronavirus or covid-19 online discussions: Nlp using lstm recurrent neural network approach. arXiv preprint arXiv:2004.11695 (2020)
10. Lamsal, R.: Corona virus (covid-19) tweets dataset (2020). https://doi.org/10.21227/781w-ef42
11. Li, L., et al.: Characterizing the propagation of situational information in social media during covid-19 epidemic: a case study on weibo. IEEE Trans. Comput. Social Syst. **7**(2), 556–562 (2020)
12. Li, W., Bai, Q., Zhang, M., Nguyen, T.D.: Automated influence maintenance in social networks: an agent-based approach. IEEE Trans. Knowl. Data Eng. **31**(10), 1884–1897 (2018)
13. Sohrabi, C., et al.: World health organization declares global emergency: a review of the 2019 novel coronavirus (covid-19). Int. J. Surg. **76**, 71–76 (2020)
14. Wang, R., Zhou, D., Jiang, M., Si, J., Yang, Y.: A survey on opinion mining: from stance to product aspect. IEEE Access **7**, 41101–41124 (2019)
15. Yoo, S., Jeong, O.: Automating the expansion of a knowledge graph. Expert Syst. Appl. **141**, 112965 (2020)

Author Index

Printed in the United States
By Bookmasters